Right and Wrong

Right and Wrong

Charles Fried

Harvard University Press
Cambridge, Massachusetts
London, England
1978

Copyright © 1978 by the President and Fellows of Harvard College

All rights reserved

Second Printing 1978

Printed in the United States of America

Library of Congress Cataloging in Publication Data
Fried, Charles, 1935–
  Right and wrong.

  Includes index.
  1. Ethics. 2. Right and wrong. I. Title.
BJ1012.F74   170   77–16479
ISBN 0-674-76905-8

For Anne

Preface

I began work on this book in 1971 during a sabbatical leave supported in part by a grant from the John Simon Guggenheim Memorial Foundation. My focus at the time was rights, and my inquiries grew out of dissatisfaction with the account of legal rights becoming increasingly popular in the field of economics and the law. I never published the manuscript I produced in that year, but versions of it have found their way into Part II of the present work. I presented one excerpt from that original manuscript at a conference on "Markets and Morals" held at the Batelle Memorial Institute in May 1973, and that paper has been published under the title "Difficulties in the Economic Analysis of Rights," in G. Dworkin, G. Bermant, and P. Brown, eds., *Markets and Morals* (Washington, D.C.: Hemisphere Publishing Co., 1977). I consider some of the same arguments in Chapter 4 of this book, in the section entitled "Bargaining and Moral Foundations."

Feeling checked in my attempts to integrate rights, personal obligations, and institutional obligations into a coherent system, I turned to a concrete problem exhibiting these various elements. The result was my *Medical Experimentation: Personal Integrity and Social Policy* (Amsterdam and New York: Elsevier Publishing Co., 1974). That exercise encouraged me to attempt the general problem once again.

The National Science Foundation* and the Harvard Law School provided the leisure and material conditions which al-

* National Science Foundation Grant No. soc. 75–13506. Any opinions, finding, conclusions, or recommendations expressed in this work are my own and do not necessarily reflect the views of the National Science Foundation.

lowed me to concentrate on this work and to bring it to completion. Many friends and colleagues read portions of the manuscript in early drafts. I received particular encouragement and assistance from Sissela Bok, Stephen Breyer, Frank Michelman, Thomas Nagel, Robert Nozick, Mitchell Polinsky, William Puka, and Richard Stewart. Sissela Bok also provided me with a wealth of references for Chapter 3. Lena G. Goldberg, Bernard Russell, and Jerrold Tannenbaum provided research assistance and criticism. My mother, Marta Fried, checked the typescript for errors. Gayle McKeen assisted me in preparing the index.

An earlier version of the argument in Chapter 1, with much more attention to legal examples and applications, appeared in *The Journal of Legal Studies* 5 (1976) : 165. The argument of Chapter 7, as it applies to lawyers, was presented in "The Lawyer as Friend: Moral Foundations of the Lawyer-Client Relation," *Yale Law Journal* 85 (1976) : 1060.

Contents

III
Roles

I have other affairs to attend to. I came into this world, not chiefly to make this a good place to live in, but to live in it, be it good or bad. A man has not everything to do, but something; and because he cannot do *everything*, it is not necessary that he should do *something* wrong.

HENRY DAVID THOREAU, "On Civil Disobedience"

Introduction

THIS IS a book about how a moral man lives his life: how he approaches choices between his own interests and those of others, what he should do if helping one person means hurting another, how far he must take on himself the burdens of the world's suffering. My central concern is to discern structure and limits in the demands morality makes upon us. The demands of morality are inexorable, and our vocation for morality is the basis of our worth as persons. Yet these demands are not all-consuming—they leave room for discretion, for creativity. We are constrained but not smothered by morality once we acknowledge that there are limits to our responsibility for the world's good and ill, that we are responsible for some things but not everything.

The idea that there are limits to a moral agent's responsibility for the state of the world may seem arbitrary, if not callous and immoral. And yet it is an idea with deep roots. For instance, traditional theology teaches that even God, who is all-powerful and all-good, is not responsible for the wickedness of His creatures: whatever evil man brings into the world is *man's* evil and does not detract from God's perfect goodness. I do not know whether the doctrines of religion are true or false, but I do believe that the concept of personal responsibility, which lies at the heart of the problem of evil, lies at the heart of moral philosophy as well. The moral vision which I shall be investigating distinguishes between the evil which a moral agent does and the evils which he allows to occur.

Though the conception I shall elaborate surely recognizes that a world without pain or grief or loss would be a good world, yet I believe we err if we conclude that the avoidance of suffering and

1

the institution of a regime of universal contentment is either our sole or even our first moral duty. Our first moral duty is to do right and to avoid wrong. We must do no wrong—even if by doing wrong, suffering would be reduced and the sum of happiness increased. Indeed, we must not do wrong even in order to prevent more, greater wrongs by others. If those others do wrong it is their wrong, for which they are responsible. This concept of personal responsibility leads to an account of moral choice and of substantive moral values that is rich, complex, and true to the facts. Central to this account is the individual's capacity to choose freely and effectively, to choose between right and wrong.

Standing behind this emphasis on right and wrong and on personal efficacy is a commitment to the moral situation of the individual. Individualism is often seen as a selfish doctrine allowing individuals to ignore the interests of others. Right and wrong, however, emphasize not the individual's selfish concerns but his moral integrity, and in this we come closer to the historic heart of individualism. If deontology, the theory of right and wrong, is solicitous of the individual, it is primarily solicitous of his claim to preserve his moral integrity, to refrain from being the agent of wrong, even if such fastidiousness means forgoing the opportunity to promote great good or to prevent great harm. In this respect the primacy of right and wrong is a doctrine that shows its traditional religious origins in contrast to the secular, melioristic foundations of those theories which hold that it is consequences alone which count. Consequentialism is often suffused with the hope that the harshness, compromise, and sacrifice of the present will be offset by the gains of the future. Marx and his followers are the best examples of this attitude. Religious views, on the other hand, certainly traditional Christianity with its doctrine of original sin, expect the secular future to share the imperfections and suffering of the present and the past. With such expectations it follows that the focus must be on personal moral perfection. Thus Christianity rejects consequentialism on the (consequentialist) ground that man is unlikely to gain the whole world (or its betterment) even if he were prepared to lose his soul. And of course one need believe neither in original sin nor in any theology at all to share this sense of our situation.

The moral vision I examine is complex, because it recognizes the good and the bad but does not embrace (in Blake's phrase) the single vision which reduces all judgment and choice to a calculus of more or less in the realm of consequences. Working out all the consequences of our choices is indeed difficult, but the task of morality consists at least as much in determining what things are good or bad, right or wrong, and in making these judgments fit together.

In this essay at that task, I consider first the inexorable demands of right and wrong—those things which we must not do, however much good we might bring about. And yet it is obvious we do pursue the good, our own and the good of others. The forms and conditions of that pursuit must be put together with the constraining categories of right and wrong. The first part of this book considers the concepts of right and wrong, using two examples of wrong—physical harm and lying. This examination of right and wrong grounds the consideration in Part II of rights. Rights are a second-order concept. It is our right to pursue our good so long as we meet our obligations and do no wrong, while others wrong us if they violate our rights. And so, though we exercise our rights in the pursuit of our good, yet rights themselves are categorical, drawing their force from the domain of right and wrong. Finally, Part III deals with the ways in which the exercise of our rights and the pursuit of our goods are themselves susceptible to judgment and arrangement. Though many things are within our rights, some exercises are better than others. As we organize our efforts in terms of the goods we seek, the exercise of our rights falls into patterns; these patterns are the roles we assume, the engagements we make, the structures of goods we pursue. As friends and kin we pursue the good of others; as healers and counselors we pursue that good in more restricted and conventional ways; as thinkers and artists we pursue truth and beauty.

These, then, are the principal elements of my inquiry: personal efficacy and the integrity of the individual, right and wrong related to the goods we pursue, the system of rights built on the foundation of right and wrong, and the system of roles arising out of the systematic ways we exercise our rights and pursue the good. I shall explore not only the way these elements fit together to compel conclusions and actions, but also the contents of these concepts: what are the wrongs we must not commit, what are our rights as individuals and as members of organized communities, and what roles do good men take up, what are the goals and constraints of those roles, and how do moral men come to understand their lives lived within them.

I

Wrongs

1

Elements

RIGHT AND WRONG

THIS IS the central concept of my work. Ordinary moral understanding, as well as many major traditions of Western moral theory, recognize that there are some things which a moral man will not do, no matter what. The harming of innocent people, lying, enslavement, and degradation—these are all things decent people shrink from, though great good might seem to come in particular cases from resorting to them. Consequentialists acknowledge this deep thrust, and the arguments they offer to account for it come down to this: The category of the good is the single overriding moral category, identifying those states of affairs which we should wish to obtain. All other moral concepts are secondary and derivative. Right and wrong are the derivative categories directing choice, but they do so under the sovereign mandate of the category of the good. Thus, if there is any apparent divergence between the right and the good, this is only because sometimes the greatest good is attained if individuals do not pursue it directly. An example is the economic theory of Adam Smith, which holds that it is right for individuals to pursue their own advantage because by doing so they are more likely to contribute to the greatest good of the greatest number, more likely than if they were enjoined to pursue the greatest good directly. So also consequentialism may promulgate the view that certain traditional wrongs—for instance, lying, killing innocent people—are "absolutely" wrong, not because they are indeed always wrong or because their avoidance is to be elevated above the pursuit of the greatest good, but because if the prohibition is given in this forceful way, imperfect human agents are on the whole more likely to avoid doing unjustified harm.

On what basis, the consequentialist asks, can one admit the independence of moral categories competing with the category of the good? It is states of the world, including states of mind, which we care about, choose, and therefore value. And so it is states of the world which must determine utterly the contents of morality. Surely we must be able to say whether one state of the world is better than another and which one is best of all. Whatever the conception of that end state, the consequentialist asserts that it cannot be rational to be concerned with how the end state comes about, except as that concern bears upon the very production of that end state. In short, it is ends not means which determine morality. Moreover, consequentialism is driven to hold that there is some one single end state, or type of end state, or characteristic of end states which is morally significant, for then this characteristic provides a criterion for choosing between end states, a criterion which is itself consequentialist.

The opposing conception of right and wrong, the conception that there are some things we must not do no matter what good we hope to accomplish, has always stood as a provocation and a scandal to consequentialism. If a state of the world is the best possible state and we bring it about at the least possible cost, what else can matter? Yet the opposing conception (the deontological) holds that how one achieves one's goals has a moral significance which is not subsumed in the importance and magnitude of the goals. Whether we get to the desired end state by deliberately hurting innocent people, by violating their rights, by lies and violence, is intensely important. And yet the deontologist does not deny that states of the world are sources of value and even agrees that the good inherent in states of the world (including our own states of mind) is the only *good*. If a happy state of the world existed that had been brought about through wrong and violation of right, and if those wrongs could no longer be righted, there is nothing that says that this happiness would not count as real happiness and should not be enjoyed; still, if this happiness had been ours to choose only by wrongful means, we would have had to wave it away. We would have to wave it away because right and wrong are the foundations of our moral personality. We choose our goods, but if what we choose is to have value as a good, then the entity doing the choosing must have value, and the process of choice must be such that what comes out of it has value. In the view I shall elaborate, right and wrong have an independent and overriding status because they establish our basic position as freely choosing entities. That is why nothing we choose can be more important than the ground—right and wrong—for our choosing. Right and wrong are the expressions of respect for persons—respect for others and self-respect.

For both views, then, right and wrong are directive concepts, addressed in the second person, as it were, to an agent choosing a course of action. Good and bad, on the other hand, evaluate states of the world in general, however produced, whether as a product of choice or not. The difference between the views is that consequentialism subordinates the right to the good, while for deontology the two realms, while related, are distinct. The goodness of the ultimate consequences does not guarantee the rightness of the actions which produced them. The two realms are not only distinct for the deontologist, but the right is prior to the good. How this priority works out, and particularly how it works out in light of the obvious fact that action is, after all, directed at producing results, are questions which will be considered preliminarily in this chapter and in detail through this book.*

RIGHT AND WRONG AS ABSOLUTE

It is part of the idea that lying or murder are wrong, not just bad, that these are things you must not do—no matter what. They are not mere negatives that enter into a calculus to be outweighed by the good you might do or the greater harm you might avoid. Thus the norms which express deontological judgments—for example, Do not commit murder—may be said to be absolute. They do not say: "Avoid lying, other things being equal" but "Do not lie, period." This absoluteness is an expression of how deontological norms or judgments differ from those

---

* My attention will be directed particularly to wrongs, those things which we must not do. The concept of right is more general. In its general significance it is used in philosophical terminology to refer to the whole domain of the obligatory, the domain of duty, the domain of deontology as opposed to the domain of the good. But it can mean a variety of other things as well. Often it is used in the negative as an equivalent of wrong: "Lying is not right." When something is said to be right, this does not mean invariably that it must be done, but perhaps only that it may be done, that is, that it is not wrong. Finally, one may speak of *a right*, as in the right to vote. This last use, the sense in which one speaks of *rights*, is theoretically related to the first, but grammatically distinct. In this work I shall consider the right in general and rights, but not the concept of right contained in usages such as "the right thing to do."

of consequentialism. But absoluteness is only a suggestive first approximation of a much more complex characteristic. This characteristic can only be fully appreciated as a number of such norms are considered in detail and contrasted with their consequentialist versions. In every case the norm has boundaries and what lies outside those boundaries is not forbidden at all. Thus lying is wrong, while withholding a truth which another needs may be perfectly permissible—but that is because withholding truth is not lying. Murder is wrong but killing in self-defense is not. The absoluteness of the norm is preserved in these cases, but only by virtue of a process which defines its boundaries. That process is different from the process by which good and bad are weighed in consequentialism, and so the distinctiveness of judgments of right and wrong is preserved.*

Even within such boundaries we can imagine extreme cases where killing an innocent person may save a whole nation. In such cases it seems fanatical to maintain the absoluteness of the judgment, to do right even if the heavens will in fact fall. And so the catastrophic may cause the absoluteness of right and wrong to yield, but even then it would be a non sequitur to argue (as consequentialists are fond of doing) that this proves that judgments of right and wrong are always a matter of degree, depending on the relative goods to be attained and harms to be avoided. I believe, on the contrary, that the concept of the catastrophic is a distinct concept just because it identifies the extreme situations in which the usual categories of judgment (including the category of right and wrong) no longer apply. At the other end of the spectrum, there is the concept of the trivial, the *de minimis* where the absolute categories do not yet apply. And the trivial also does not prove that right and wrong are really only a matter of degree. It is because of these complexities and because the term absolute is really only suggestive of a more complex structure, that I also refer to the norms of right and wrong not as absolute but as categorical.†

---

* Consider this case: Is it wrong to take another's property? Well, what of emergencies, as when I need your car to get to the hospital and you won't consent? Perhaps what is wrong in that case is not taking the car but taking it without compensating you for its use. What if I do not have the money? Perhaps what is wrong is not compensating you when I can. Though qualified in various ways, the judgment still seems to be absolute.

† It is ironic that it is the dominant form of consequentialism—hedonistic utilitarianism—which is really absolutist. Hedonistic utilitarianism offers a single criterion, the sovereign standard of pleasure and pain, in terms of

When we say that one must not grievously harm an innocent person, that one must not lie, these are categorical prohibitions in the sense that (within limits) no amount of good can justify them. But they are not absolute in the sense that we may never be justified in doing acts which have these very results—the death of an innocent person, the propagation of false beliefs—as a consequence. They are absolute in the sense that they point out certain *acts* we must not perform. They are not absolute in the consequentialist's sense; they do not state that a certain state of the world is of such supreme importance that the value of everything else must be judged by its tendency to produce that state. So here we see a complex relation between deontological judgments on what we *do* and evaluative (axiological) judgments on states of the world—with which we are also concerned. We must indeed be concerned with producing good in the world, but without violating the absolute norms of right and wrong.

It is a crucial thesis of this work, then, that there are categorical norms, and that judgments of right and wrong take the form of categorical norms. Given the centrality of this concept, I offer this specification. First, a *norm* is a judgment addressed to an agent, directing choice. Thus a norm differs from value judgments in general in that value judgments do not necessarily direct choice, although choices may be made by reference to them. If I say that the August moon is particularly beautiful or that Hadrian was a wise emperor, consistency requires that I take the opportunity to gaze upon the moon in August when nothing stands in the way or emulate Hadrian should I find myself in his situation, but it is obviously not the point of these judgments to prescribe such conduct. To say, however, that lying is wrong is just to direct all potential auditors to avoid lies. Second, a norm is *categorical* when its application is not contingent upon the

---

which all choice is absolutely determined. Consequences and only consequences count because pleasure and pain are themselves consequences, and the consequences of consequences. Utilitarianism is supremely pragmatic about the worth of all the particular things people do, seek, and avoid—beauty, knowledge, food, friendship, mutual aid, truth-telling and lying, revenge, punishment, death—for all these things are good and bad only and insofar as they do or do not conduce to the one sovereign good. And other forms of consequentialism—for instance religious ethics, which substitue beatitude for Bentham's pleasure, or ethics that view survival of the species as the sovereign good—display exactly the same logical structure. It is this logical structure that makes consequentialism peculiarly susceptible to mathematicization. Moral choice can be modeled as a mathematical exercise, the point of which is to find the maximum of a function, given the initial conditions of choice.

agent's adopting some other independent end, which the norm will lead him to attain; it is not like the norm "If you wish to live to be ninety, don't smoke." This is Kant's distinction between categorical and hypothetical imperatives. But third, my conception contains a further element, which is captured (though with more rigor than I ultimately intend) by the term absoluteness. A categorical norm does more than direct that a particular value be given weight in making choices. It is not like the directive that the suffering of animals be taken into account in one's choices, and that if the cost is not too great that their suffering be minimized. Rather, a categorical norm displaces other judgments in its domain, so that other values and ends may not be urged as reasons for violating the norm. It is preemptive. This latter characteristic of categorical norms is the most distinctive and the most troublesome. In fact, I have already indicated that in a sense it is an approximation of a more complex notion. A categorical norm may be overwhelmed by extreme circumstances. So also it may be underwhelmed, as it were, by the triviality of the instance of its application. But so long as the consequences fall within a very broad range, the categorical norm holds, no matter what those consequences. To propound a categorical norm, to argue that an action is wrong, is to invite inquiry into the kinds of action intended to be covered, but not an inquiry into the costs of compliance.

Finally, there is the question whether all deontological norms are absolute or categorical. There are judgments of right and wrong which in their very statement invite the weighing of consequences and of competing considerations. Individuals have a right to a fair share of scarce resources and a duty to contribute to a regime of fair shares, but what share is fair will vary with the circumstances and is in part a matter of the consequences of what each person does. Similarly, it is wrong to expose the person or property of another to undue risk of harm, but what risk is undue is a function of the good to be attained and the likelihood and magnitude of the harm. Yet these judgments too are categorical, though in a complex way which I will elaborate only after I have developed the analysis of intentional harms. Briefly the idea is that, even where the specification of the wrong (taking more than one's fair share, subjecting others to undue risk) includes a weighing of consequences, once the weighing has been done then it is also absolutely wrong to go against the conclusion of that process. Where, as in the case of fairness, consequences are weighed in a special way (for example, in order to equalize rather than maximize net benefits) then the absoluteness of the obligation is one that forbids sacrificing equality for any amount of greater net benefits. Finally, there are many cases where the only right thing to do is to maximize net good consequences— usually subject to certain constraints. And in those cases it is wrong to do anything else.

THE COMPLEXITY OF DEONTOLOGICAL SYSTEMS

Although the inexorable nature of the norms of right and wrong makes the moral system based on them seem harsh and rigid, the opposite is in fact the case. Deontologic systems are typically complex, consisting of a number of specific norms. Though there are connections between these norms and they are all generated by a common general conception of moral personality, still they reduce neither to each other nor to some single overriding moral precept. The domain of right can no more be exhausted by some one all-inclusive norm than the concept of human happiness can be boiled down to some particular enjoyment. Moreover, even as a system, categorical norms do not take up the totality of moral space. One cannot live one's life by the demands of the domain of right. After having avoided wrong and done one's duty, an infinity of choices is left to be made. Indeed, it is consequentialist systems like utilitarianism which are oppressive in the totality of the claim they make on moral agents. For utilitarians there is always only one right thing to do, and that is to promote in all possible ways at every moment the greatest happiness of the greatest number.* To stop even for a moment or

* Utility theory, a modern version of utilitarianism, seems to escape this criticism by standing ready to recognize any number of distinct values related in whatever complex ways one wishes. The mediating, homogenizing entity of utility is posited as a theoretical entity only. In utility theory no one aims at utility as such or even cares about it. Utility is postulated as the mathematical expression of the relative strengths of the material ends people do pursue. So long as the relation between material ends can take any logical form at all, including the logical forms of deontology, there is no harm in this view, and very little bite. It does no more than report the structure of ends that a person may or does have. It may be, however, that this presentation of the system of ends as formally equivalent to the maximization of some very complexly related set of preferences is much less illuminating than a presentation in terms of right and wrong, good and bad. It may miss, for instance, the reason *why* the ends are related as they are. Also, there is the danger that certain complex relations of ends, such as obtain in a deontological system, will be distorted in the name of a more convenient mathematical

to rest content with a second best is a failure of duty. And if we seek to excuse ourselves by saying that everyone needs a rest from time to time, or as Bernard Williams put it, everyone needs to knock off doing good works occasionally, the utilitarian will allow that too, *if* this is how we best maintain our efficiency in the pursuit of overall utility. In contrast to this oppressive, obsessive regime the limited absolutism of deontology is a positive relief.

That the system of right and wrong is both limited and multifarious is a large part of what makes it appealing and true to the complex facts of our moral life. Now, the term absolute certainly has a nasty, pervasive ring to it, and it is important to see exactly how it is that right and wrong, absolute though they are, keep from spreading out and taking over the whole of our moral lives. They do not, but in speculating how they might and why they do not, we shall come to a better understanding of the domain of right and wrong in general. We shall see how the very *form* of categorical norms (norms of right and wrong) expresses the same conception of human personality as do the *contents* of the norms. Consider the norms "Do not lie" or "Kill no innocent person." It is intuitively obvious that these are distinct norms which do not boil down to versions of each other or of some third norm—this is the multiplicity of categorical norms. Also, it is obvious that in most situations there is a great deal of choice left over, even after we have complied in scrupulous detail with these norms—this is the limited nature of the norms. But it might be otherwise. If, for instance, we looked at the norm about killing as a consequentialist might, we would see it as describing a bad state of affairs: the death of an innocent person. How would the consequentialist go on to give it absolute or categorical force? He might say that the death was bad in itself, which means that its badness is not just a function of some further states (fear, grief, lost opportunities) to which it tended to conduce, but that standing alone it was bad. This, however, would hardly capture the force of the judgment that the killing was categorically wrong. For to say that the death of an innocent person is bad in itself commits you to no more than concluding that, other things

---

presentation, which will then be asserted to be more rational. Or perhaps the reader or theorist will forget that utility is no more than an ex post, explanatory, theoretical entity, which is no part of anyone's actual system of ends.

equal, it should be avoided, that as a moral negative it must be outweighed to be permissible. But this says nothing at all about how easily it may be outweighed, what good can justify this bad. It may be, for instance, that almost any good at all might justify killing an innocent person, and still we can say the death is bad in itself. Nor is anything much changed if we say that what is bad in itself is not the death but the actual act of killing—for we must know what negative weight the killing has and not just that it has a negative weight. Can this killing be justified, for instance, as a way of preventing two killings by someone else?

Would the consequentialist express this absoluteness of the norm by saying that the result of the killing, the death, is not only bad in itself but somehow absolutely bad, where this must mean that it is so bad a consequence that nothing can outweigh it? That would certainly be very categorical, but it obviously goes too far. For if the death of an innocent person really were that bad, then the norm would be no longer a limited, but a pervasive one. What, for instance, if some action of mine carried a very slight risk of causing the death of an innocent person? If the absoluteness of the norm is to be interpreted as making the fact of death so overwhelmingly bad, it seems clear that I must not take even the slightest risk of killing an innocent person. But really everything I do carries some risk that it will contribute to the death of an innocent person. Indeed, we cannot even save the situation by limiting our calculations to foreseeable consequences, for the limits of the foreseeable are set by what we are obliged to look out for. If the consequence is as bad as all that, then we must also hunt about to see if there is any conceivable way that we might inadvertently be facilitating it. Of course there will always be some conceivable way, and that will be enough to stop us.

This line of analysis is enough to show that some quite plausible interpretations of absolute norms lead to impossibly stringent conclusions, lead in fact to total paralysis. But the case is in fact even worse. For if the absoluteness of the norm is interpreted to mean that the consequence—such as the death of an innocent person—is overwhelmingly bad, then not only are we forbidden to do anything, for anything carries with it a risk of death, we are indeed required to do nothing but seek out ways to minimize the deaths of innocent persons. For if such a death is so bad that no good can outweigh it, we are surely not justified in pursuing some good, even if that good does not present this risk, when we might instead be *preventing* this most undesirable of all consequences. So this interpretation is not actually a prescription for paralysis, it is more like an obsession. The norm, by virtue of this view of its absoluteness, takes over the whole of our moral life. Finally, since every action will endanger the life of some innocent, even an action intended to rescue some *other* innocent, we cannot escape the further corollary of this interpretation that we must choose that course and only that course of action expected to produce the greatest net saving of life—including, if need be, the deliberate, cold-blooded killing of an innocent person.

The situation is worse still, for this interpretation is not only obsessive, it also opens the possibility of insoluble contradictions within any system containing more than one absolute norm. The judgment that it is categorically wrong to lie would be interpreted in an analogous way to mean that a false belief is absolutely bad—that is, so bad that nothing can justify producing or even not eradicating it. But obviously, telling the truth will very often increase to some small extent the chances that an innocent person will die, and in any event the time spent in eradicating false belief will *not* be spent in warding off the danger of death from innocent persons.

Now, deontological systems avoid the paralysis, obsession, and contradiction of this interpretation. They are at once less and more stringent. They would not allow killing an innocent even to save several innocents from death; but the consequentialist interpretation would require the killing. Obviously, the interpretation of categorical norms in terms of consequences is profoundly inappropriate (it is a consequentialist interpretation of absolute norms), but how are the norms of right and wrong to be interpreted so as to avoid these results? How are they to be contained and specified? These questions bring us back to the notion of personal and limited responsibility with which this work began. They bring us back to the vision of the proper domain of human choice, which generates both the form and contents of the system of right and wrong.

A first approximation of the domain of categorical norms is the domain of actions. It is a good start to see that what is condemned as wrong is not some consequence, some state of affairs (a man dead, a false belief—these things are bad, not wrong) but the *action* which produces these states of affairs. Now, this is all right for any action which includes all its morally relevant features within the description of the action itself. Thus, for example, a norm condemning a certain sexual practice as wrong could be taken to condemn only the proscribed action without reference to any of its possible consequences. And of course such a categorical norm easily escapes the problems of paralysis, obsession, and contradiction. There are many things one can do other than engage in the forbidden action. If lying is defined as the act of asserting as true what is believed to be false, this provides another example. There is no problem in principle about forbidding that act absolutely. Since it is not consequences or states of the world as such that are proscribed, it is irrelevant that we might be causing, risking causing, or failing to avoid the same consequences (such as false beliefs) as tend to be caused by the forbidden action. Since we are not enjoined to minimize false beliefs at all costs but only not to lie at all costs, we can honor the prohibition and still have ample room left over for other things.

Thus there is no problem about prohibitions of actions which are defined by a close description of the gestures involved in accomplishing them, but most significant actions in our lives are defined in terms of their consequences. As to these, categorical prohibitions threaten to land us once more in obsession, paralysis, and contradiction. Killing an innocent person, for instance, or violating another's rights is a perfectly general description of any action at all that produces that particular result. We do not say that it is wrong to stab, strangle, club, or shoot an innocent person, but just to kill. So also consider humiliating another. There are no narrowly specified ways of doing this; yet it is wrong. And in general, right and wrong are concerned with the most important aspects of our lives, not just with a few ritual observances, and the consequences we produce or suffer are intensely important. Accordingly, most important norms, whether categorical or not, are concerned with the production of particular consequences and not with the gestures that bring them about. They have the form "Do not do *that*" where "that" is not a gesture, like picking your nose, but the production of a result. The trouble is that once judgments of right and wrong take this form, how are we to maintain their categorical force without falling into the traps and absurdities I have sketched?

CAUSATION AND NEGATIVE DUTIES

It has recently been proposed that we avoid these difficulties and focus our moral vision by considering not the undefined, unlimited range of all possible consequences of our actions but rather just those harmful consequences of which we are the *cause.** But the concept of cause is at once too wide and too narrow a focusing criterion of what it is wrong to do. It is too wide, since when we are still considering what to do, the causal criterion scarcely narrows the range of our concerns at all. If, for instance, it is wrong to *cause* the death of an innocent person, then we are still faced with the fact that any act might be the cause of death, and if all such acts are absolutely wrong, no act is permitted.† And the causal criterion is too narrow if it excludes

* Particularly, it is claimed that this causal criterion would exclude responsibility in three classes of situations: (1) where we might have prevented the bad state of affairs from happening but did not ourselves set in motion the train of events which led to the unfortunate outcome; (2) where some act of ours did set the fatal train in motion, but the course of events by which it arrived at that destination was so unpredictable and bizarre that the result could not reasonably be laid at our doorstep; and (3) where the result came about through the deliberate choice of another responsible agent, for whom our action at most provided the occasion or opportunity to accomplish his own purposes. See, generally, H. L. A. Hart and A. M. Honoré, *Causation in the Law* (Oxford: Oxford University Press, 1959) .

† Consider this variant of the causal thesis: An act is absolutely wrong only if the actor believes that the act is substantially certain to cause a forbidden result.

Does this not allow the causal criterion to specify an absolute norm without what I call the danger of obsession? Perhaps, but there are grave difficulties encountered in following this route. How "substantial" must the certainty be? If the answer is that substantiality is a matter of moral judgment, then it is clear that the norm is not absolute after all, since how certain the result must be will be a function of *normative* issues such as the magnitude of the harm, its probability, and the importance of the other ends being pursued. But that is precisely the judgment which the consequentialist demands every time. If substantiality is a non-normative approximation, such as 99 per cent, this objection is avoided, but at a great price in plausibility. For now what is to be a difference in moral kinds—between absolute and consequentialist types of norms—will depend on a highly arbitrary non-moral difference of degree. We shall have to say that acting where the result is believed to be 99 per cent certain is absolutely forbidden, but where the result is believed to be only 98 per cent certain, then consequentialist balancing is in order. The intentionality test I shall propose avoids this anomaly: between an intended and a foreseen consequence is a difference in kind which mirrors the difference in kind between categorical and consequentialist judgments. Finally, the causal criterion will have to reimport intention after all. For it would be absurd to say that one who intends the forbidden result but knows his chances of success are slim does not violate an absolute prohibition while one who does not intend that result but knows his chances are great acts absolutely wrongly. To avoid this anomaly, the causal criterion would have every case where a forbidden result occurs by way of the deliberate act of another—for instance, if we bribe or persuade another to act as our agent. Finally, the concept of cause is itself highly controversial and problematic. Why exactly is it that when I fail to perform some act, knowing that I could have prevented a bad result, I am not said—in the absence of some preexisting duty—to have caused that result? And if I did act, but the result would have happened irrespective of my act, can I be said to have caused it? In any event, the causal criterion turns out to be proposed primarily to limit the range of consequences for which a person may be held responsible *after* he has acted, and particularly the range of harmful consequences for which an agent should be made to pay compensation. Now, this is not necessarily the same question as what it is right or wrong to do. For instance, a person may have acted quite properly in engaging in some useful but hazardous activity, but still he should be responsible to the innocent victims of the accidental harm he causes. Norms of right and wrong, however, are addressed first of all to choice, to an agent before he acts.

Another suggestion to account for the stringency of what I call the norms of right and wrong is the distinction offered by Philippa Foot between positive and negative duties. The proposal is that positive duties—duties to confer benefits or to prevent harm from occurring—are more easily outweighed (for instance by our wish to pursue our own interests) than are negative duties. Negative duties, duties *not* to harm others, Foot asserts, are far more insistent. This distinction would explain why it may be forbidden to ward off evil from one person by inflicting even a lesser evil on another. This distinction between positive and negative duties is obviously related to the distinction, familiar in both legal and moral contexts, between acts and omissions. It is generally true that a person is neither civilly nor criminally liable for harm unless the harm came about through his action. The mere fact that he failed to prevent the harm will not generally ground liability unless there was some special duty—a duty which the mere opportunity to be of service does not of itself create. Indeed the positive/negative duty distinction

---

to be amended by adding the clause "or intends to cause that result," but then, of course, whatever difficulties about intention were sought to have been avoided reappear and one might just as well speak of intention straightaway.

might be seen as the forward-looking, directive version of the act/omission distinction.

Both Foot's distinction and the distinction between acts and omissions suffer from the same defects as the more general causal criterion. Indeed, they depend on the concept of cause. Foot's negative duties, after all, must include negative duties not to *cause* certain results. This does leave us prey to the difficulties in the concept of cause. That alone is not disastrous: in moral philosophy we may often be forced to swallow some quite unchewed metaphysical morsels, and we should be prepared to do so, provided only that the morsels appear to have a strong intuitive grounding. But we have the further problem that as soon as the negative duty is specified in terms of results (for example, the duty not to cause the death of an innocent person) it is obviously far too demanding—considered beforehand, anything at all might cause that result. So without some further attenuation, the danger of paralysis, obsession, or contradiction looms once again. Foot is able to avoid these difficulties only because for her, even negative duties are not absolute or categorical; they are simply more stringent than, they tend to override, positive duties. But for my argument, if the force of categorical norms is to be maintained and yet absurdity avoided, some other or further way must be found to limit the range of consequences to which the norms apply.

INTENTION: THE PERSON AS AGENT AND OBJECT

Intention   Categorical norms are morally possible because they are concerned with what we do, rather than with what we allow to happen. To be sure, morality is concerned in some way or another with all the consequences to which we might contribute or which we might avoid. The categorical norms, however, designate what it would be wrong to *do* (in this way the concept resembles that of negative duties), but their absolute force attaches only to what we intend, and not to the whole range of things which come about as a result of what we do intentionally. This link of intentionality between a moral agent and what he accomplishes, a link which is crucial in the application of these norms, is simply another aspect, the procedural aspect, of the substantive contents of the norms. Both aspects express an underlying moral conception of the person. It is respect for persons as the ultimate moral particulars which is expressed by the contents of categorical norms. The mode of application, the procedural aspect, expresses this same centrality of the individual's personal efficacy as a moral agent.

This procedural aspect of categorical norms, by distinguishing what we do from what we merely allow to happen, allows the norms to retain their categorical force while avoiding the hazards of paralysis, obsession, and contradiction. This procedural aspect allows us to move beyond descriptions of acts as gestures to bring consequences within the ambit of absolute norms, without, however, forcing us to an obsessive or paralyzing concern with those effects. For so long as the bad effect just happens, then we have not violated an absolute norm by allowing that effect to happen, even if we could have prevented it, even if it came about as a side effect of something we were doing. But, of course, the notion of doing as opposed to allowing to happen, suggestive though it may be, is vague and requires further specification. This specification is provided by the concept of intention.

The norms of right and wrong proscribe *intentionally* bringing about the forbidden result. If that result occurs inadvertently or as a mere concomitant of one's conduct or because one failed to seize an opportunity to prevent that result, then whatever else may be said of the conduct—it may be careless or callous, and may be condemned for that reason—it does not violate the categorical prohibition. This distinction between intended and unintended but possibly foreseen consequences necessarily occurs whenever bringing about a particular result is condemned as categorically wrong. Thus, for instance, David Daube writes of the Talmudic injunction against handing over a hostage to be killed or a woman to be molested, noting that the injunction holds even if the refusal results in a similar fate for a greater number of equally innocent persons. The handing over is an intentional act of betrayal, for the consequences of which the betrayer is responsible, while the still more dire consequences of not betraying are not his responsibility. Similarly, some legal doctrines condemn, or judge more severely, or permit a more limited range of excuses for intentionally bringing about certain harmful results. The international law of war condemns intentional infliction of civilian casualties, while permitting the causing of such casualties as a side effect, even a certain one, of military action against military targets. Finally, this distinction is formalized in the so-called law of double effect, by which certain bad results—for example, the death of an innocent person, the sinful act of another—may not be "directly" willed, that is, chosen either as one's ultimate goal or as the means to one goal, though they may be tolerated in appropriate circumstances as the foreseen concomitants of one's chosen means or ends.

This emphasis on intention has the virtues both of the causal proposal and of the distinctions between act and omission, between positive and negative duties. It has their virtues, but without their defects.* Now, one intends a result if that result is chosen either as one's ultimate end or as one's means to that end. One intends a result just in case one can say that one acted (or failed to act) in order to produce that result, just in case one would have to include that result in answer to the question "Why did you do that?" or "Why did you fail to do that?" Moreover, there are consequences of one's acting which, though foreseen with ever so much likelihood, are not intended at all. These results are mere side effects and one does not violate a categorical norm just by causing mere side effects to occur. The concept of intention comes into every categorical norm which is couched in terms of results. "Do not do X" (where X is an effect of one's actions) becomes "Do not intend X" or "Do not choose X either as your end or as the means to your end." Of course, there are categorical norms which speak in terms of actions *tout court*. For instance, the norm forbidding lying or perhaps some explicitly described sexual practice does not speak in terms of results at all, and so the need to confine an absolute norm of this kind to intended results does not arise. But even in such cases the act itself is in its very conception intentional: One who says something false believing it to be true does not lie.

* Thus the intention criterion would absolve the legislator who passes a beneficial law, knowing it will provide occasions for corruption, though we would condemn a legislator who corrupted voters or officials for the purpose of obtaining this legislation. This is because the incidental corruption is not part of his intention. The causal criterion would reach the same conclusion —that the legislator is not responsible for the corruption—because he did not cause it; that is, because it was a result of the choice of responsible agents. But, as we have seen, this is not quite sound—if the legislator had persuaded his cronies to use bribery and corruption, we would want to condemn him in that case too, and we could do so on the intention criterion although the bribery ran through the choices of independent moral agents. Similarly, if we fail to do something with the intention, for the purpose, of harming an innocent person, the intention criterion condemns us as severely as if we wielded the instrument of harm in our hands, but the act/omission or positive/negative duty distinction may not. Finally, intention provides a needed limitation of any supposed negative duty not to harm others—with that limitation the duty can sensibly be claimed to be categorical.

Problems about Intention There are serious difficulties in any systematic use of the concept of intention, and the literature is replete with criticisms and refutations. The two major forms of criticism relate (1) to the coherence of the distinction between what we intend and what we merely allow to happen—the extent to which we can state the principle of distinction so as to determine in all cases whether a particular result is intended as the agent's end or means to his end or whether it is a mere concomitant of his plans—and (2) to its moral relevance—even if we could discover a principle of application or if we had sufficient confidence in our intuitive ability to distinguish what is intended from mere concomitants of what is intended, the question would still remain why we should make such a distinction, what morally relevant feature such a distinction picks out.

The principal objection to the coherence of the intention concept acknowledges the importance of *ultimate ends* but denies the possibility of distinguishing *means* from side effects, where neither are desired for their own sake. Here are two cases which have been adduced to point out this difficulty:

I. A, seeking to free his friend from prison, explodes a charge under the wall, knowing that a guard stationed on top of the wall will be killed in the explosion, though this death is immaterial to his plan. May we say that he did not intend the death of the guard, but that if he had shot the guard to obtain his keys he did so intend? Putting aside the point of making such a distinction, on what criterion is the distinction made?

II. A party of explorers is trapped in a cave, in whose narrow opening a rather fat member of the party is lodged, and the waters are rising. If a member of the party explodes a charge next to the fat man, should we say that he intended the fat man's death as a means or that it is a mere side effect of (a) freeing the party, (b) removing the fat man's body from the opening, or most implausibly, (c) blowing him to atoms? How can we tell; why should we care?

There is a traditional criterion for distinguishing an intended means from an unintended but foreseen concomitant, the counterfactual test: if the morally relevant result at issue (in Case I, the death of the guard) could somehow miraculously be prevented and events thereafter allowed to take their natural course, would the actor still have chosen to act as he did? The gruesome case of the fat man in the cave is supposed to show that this means of discrimination can prove anything and everything. Since it is not by virtue of the fat man's *death* that the plan fails but only by virtue of the continued presence of his body in the mouth of the cave, then if the fat man did *not* die, the blaster would still have lit the fuse on the dynamite. Unfortunately, one may always be able to designate some aspect of the result as the chosen means and another aspect as an undesired side-effect. And the gambit can be blocked only if we find some way of saying that certain consequences come in such tightly bound units that they may not be disaggregated—blowing the fat man to atoms cannot be severed in analysis from killing him.*

I do not have a foolproof criterion for identifying the results we intend and distinguishing them from those we merely allow to happen, for distinguishing—in Thomas Nagel's phrase—between "what one does to people and what merely happens to them as a result of what one does." The counterfactual test, for instance, is not incorrect but is defective in that in the hardest cases it appears to depend on the very concepts—intention, purpose—it is meant to explicate. Crucial as intention is, I must be content to leave it unanalyzed, a primitive term. This is a less unsatisfactory state in which to leave the argument than might first appear. The argument I shall be developing will explicate this formally unanalyzed concept of intention to a considerable extent. And after all, I am not interested in the concept of intention in the abstract, but as it serves to specify the absolute norms of right and wrong. There may very well not be a satisfactory analysis of intention for every domain of human activity— from literary criticism to the behavior of large groups—or at any rate not *one* single analysis. Indeed, I suggest that the concept of intended as opposed to foreseen consequences has its clearest application just in respect to actions and results which invoke the stringent norms of right and wrong.

Intention as Efficacious Desire   There is a connection between intention and the contents of categorical norms. The two illuminate each other. The central concept in each case is that of respect for persons. It is wrong to do those things which violate the integrity of other persons, but whether we have indeed done wrong will depend on whether as agents we have engaged our persons in causing harm to another. It is striking that the state

---

* This argument is developed in Chapter 2.

of the world ends up being the same whether that state was produced as a means or as a mere concomitant. (The guard is just as dead in either version of case I.) Since the resulting states of the world themselves offer no clue as to why the production of one as a means and the other as a side effect should invoke different moral judgments, can we find the difference in the heart of the agent? But what do we look for there? Not his intention, surely: that would make the circle of argument so close as to be ludicrous. Is it his desire, then? Is it what he appears to value or take pleasure in? But this also will not do. We have no more reason in the case of a means than in the case of a side effect to believe that the agent desired the result for its own sake, while we can be sure in both cases that the agent at least was willing that the relevant result occur as a price of achieving his ultimate goal.*

The concept of intention closes this gap between states of the world and the agent's state of mind. Right and wrong are clearly not determined solely by states of the world. The badness of bad states of the world does not account for the whole force of categorical norms. If we add the agent's state of heart to our state descriptions, we still have a gap to close. And even if we relate the two states, so that we speak of the special superstate which consists of an evil state of mind followed by the bad state of affairs, we still have not closed the gap. The gap is closed only if we realize (1) that judgments of right and wrong are judgments speaking *to* individuals and guiding their actions—they do not evaluate states (or even superstates) of the world and (2) that in guiding actions these judgments speak neither just about the outcomes of actions nor just about states of mind regarding those outcomes, but about a unity of mind and efficacy which is represented by the concept of intention. Absolute norms relate to the efficacious *choice* of good and evil. The absolute norms are not even primarily concerned with desires. To desire evil may be morally bad, but it is not murder, theft, rape. It is the special

---

* An argument has been offered to explain why the law may distinguish intended from merely foreseen results. An agent who chooses an evil as his means has shown himself disposed to persist in seeking to produce the harmful result if he fails at first, while in the case of a mere concomitant it is at least conceivable for the agent to be relieved if the harm does not eventuate. This argument has no application to the case where the unintended but foreseen result was sure to happen. And at any rate it is inapposite to moral norms designed to tell agents what they may or may not do.

union of results and desire in intentional action which calls forth the types of moral rules I have called absolute.

Now, here is an apparent paradox: the result is not wrong, and the desire for the result is not wrong, and even being the causal agency of the result is not *necessarily* wrong (as in the case of unintended side effects) ; yet bringing the result about intentionally is wrong. How can this be? Is not intention the compound of causal efficacy and desire? And if so, why is the whole here more (evil) than the sum of its parts? The answer is that the "whole" is not simply a compound of those two parts—causal efficacy plus desire; at any rate, the moral quality of the whole is not simply the sum of the moral qualities of the two parts. Intentional action is the primary unit, and notions like desire and wish are incomplete notions when abstracted from this unit. They are like aiming without the target; they need action to complete them.*

---

* Gilbert Harman has recently sketched an account of practical reasoning and intention which seems to me to complement the conception of intention and its relation to ethics I offer here. ("Practical Reasoning," *Review of Metaphysics* 29 [1976]: 431.) Harman distinguishes, as I do, between intended consequences and foreseen but unintended consequences. His example is that of a sniper who in firing his gun knowingly heats the barrel and alerts the enemy, neither of which he intends to do. Harman adds the following refinement: One who attempts something which is not reasonably in his power to bring about—such as hitting a target at a great distance—also does not intend that result, even if he succeeds. (Harman does say that in both instances—the foreseen but unintended result and the attempted but unlikely result—the actor acts intentionally, though he does not intend the result.) Now, the argument Harman offers for this set of distinctions seems very close to mine: "Intentions are primitive in the sense that they are not to be analyzed away in terms of reasons, beliefs, desires, and behavior" (p. 436). Intending or forming an intention is a way of bringing about the intended result, thus distinguishing intentions from predictions, desires, or hopes. This special efficacy of intentions also explains why an actor has not done what she intended if the desired result comes about in some unexpected way. "Mabel intends to drive to Ted's house, to find him, and to kill him. By chance, Ted happens to walk by as Mabel backs out of her driveway and she runs him down without seeing him . . . She does not kill him intentionally . . . Her intention is not simply 'to kill Ted' . . . It also includes a plan specifying how that intention will lead her to do what she intends" (p. 444).

Finally, it is this special efficacy of intention which explains the means/side-effect distinction, on which I insist as well. "An intention is a conclusion of practical reasoning that says that the very conclusion guarantees [the result]" (p. 483). This distinguishes intention from belief or prediction, which is the conclusion of theoretical reasoning. The sniper intends to kill his victim and his intention brings about that result. That his shot will alert the enemy and heat the barrel of his gun are, by contrast, at most predictions,

Intentional action is the primitive concept of human efficacy. Desire and consequences are different aspects (at opposite ends, as it were) of that concept. Counterfactual and dispositional tests tease out, clarify these aspects—"Would you have acted anyway, even if . . ." But these tests too are not the *meaning* of intention. We view our own agency differently from the agency of natural objects in the world. We have purposes and we know these purposes. We know these purposes in a special way, as we know ourselves. We do not need to observe or infer them. It is part of our faith in ourselves that our purposes do issue in changes in the world, but it is not as if we wielded our bodies as tools when we acted. Our bodies, actions, motions are not themselves the result of our actions, they are our actions. There is no more basic action which sits behind these.

Morality is about the good and the right way of our being in the world *as human beings*. We relate to the world as human beings as we pursue our purposes in the world, as we act intentionally. Thus, just as it is a mistake to separate more than provisionally desire from action, so it is a mistake to separate more than provisionally moral judgment on our desires from moral judgment on the results we produce in the world. The paradigmatic moral judgment is on intentional action as such. That is why the most stringent, the absolute, judgments are on acts which are defined by a unity of intentionality and result. This primacy of intention explains why in law and morals a sharp line is drawn between the results (intended either for their own sake or as means) and the concomitants (even foreseen and certain concomitants) of our action. We see a paradox in this distinction only if we assume that because the consequences in the world are the same in the two cases, the judgment on them must be the same. Intention gives prominence to the central conception of human efficacy, which is efficacy according to purpose; at the same time, intention contrasts to that kind of efficacy the causality of which merely runs through my person or my movements but is not invested with the personal involvement of purpose.*

conclusions of theoretical reasoning. Further, we can see why, in this view of intention as plan, means as well as ultimate goals are contrasted to mere concomitants.

* There is a sentimental correlate of consequentialism which holds that just as we really should be accountable equally for all the consequences of our actions, still if we should enter into questions of the heart then it should be only by our ultimate ends—and not also by our chosen means—that we

This argument does not prove too much. It does not lead to the conclusion that there may never be grounds for condemning an agent who knowingly causes harm he does not intend. Indeed, as I have suggested already, to expose others to undue risks of harm is wrong, as it may be wrong on occasion to stand by indifferently while another person suffers a preventable injury. Nevertheless, in such cases, where one does not do injury but the injury comes about as a result of what one does (or does not do), the condemnation depends on a different and more complex argument. In such cases we must inquire not only into the degree of the risk but also into the agent's reason for creating that risk. And the conclusion of that inquiry will depend not just on the relative discounted magnitudes of the good pursued weighed against the concomitant risks. It will be a question, too, of whether the agent had a right to be pursuing a particular end and whether the potential victim had some particular claim to the special care or benevolence of the agent. A crude utilitarian balancing of benefits and burdens is no more appropriate in the domain of unintentional than intentional harm. But the determination of the structures of judgment depends on our having in hand a theory of rights and particularly positive rights, the positive claims we may have to each other's care or effort. Part II presents such a theory, but as I shall argue, the theory of rights must use as one of its points of departure the notion that there are some things we may not do to each other, no matter what, some things that are categorically wrong. Once that conception is in hand we may proceed to consider more complex and balanced wrongs—from unduly risky conduct to failing to make a sufficient effort to cure the defects of an unjust form of government.

RESPECT FOR PERSONS

Just as the concepts of right and wrong imply a special conception of efficacy which is personal efficacy, so also the substantive

---

are to be judged. This notion of ultimate ends, however, is not really clear—it is said to refer to those things which we pursue for their own sake and for no other reason. But what is it that is pursued for its own sake, really? It turns out that ultimate ends have a way of receding into some unifying abstraction like pleasure, utility, or the good. The view I propose, on the other hand, makes not ultimate ends—whatever they may be—central, but rather the more concrete, particular conception of a plan, project, or purpose. So where a man acts, intending a result though only as a means, it is as important that he intended that result as that he intended it while intending something beyond it.

contents of the norms of right and wrong express the value of persons, of respect for personality. What we may not do to each other, the things which are wrong, are precisely those forms of personal interaction which deny to our victim the status of a freely choosing, rationally valuing, specially efficacious person, the special status of moral personality. To lie or to do intentional, grievous harm to the body of another represents a denial of the personal status of that other, a denial not necessarily implicit in allowing that harm to come about as a mere concomitant of our actions. If we use harming another as the means to our end, then we assert that another person may indeed *be* our means, while if we merely accept the risk that others will be harmed as we pursue our ends, and do not make that harm a part of our projects, then it is still possible to assert that those others are not reduced to the status of means in our system. (Whether we may not sometimes act wrongly by imposing certain risks of harm on others is a further question, which I shall also answer in the affirmative, but as part of the detailed analysis of rights in Part II.) When we accomplish our purposes through lies, it is not so much that among the consequences of our action must be counted the fact that another person entertains a false belief—after all, that may be trivial enough—but rather that we have asserted that the mind, the rationality of another, is available to us as the track on which the train of our purposes may run.

Thus, what constitutes doing wrong to another may also be regarded as a denial of the respect owed another's moral personality. And it is a principal hypothesis of this work that the absolute quality of categorical norms (what one might call their logic), the concepts of action and intention necessary to the application of those norms (the psychology of the system), and the substantive moral basis of the norms, the respect for persons, all fit together in a system. Though I have identified respect for persons as a value, the connection between that respect and the concept of right and wrong shows that this value is wholly different from all other values. All other values gather their moral force as they determine choice. By contrast, the value of personhood—as I will argue in detail throughout this book—far from being chosen, is the presupposition and substrate of the very concept of choice. And that is why the norms surrounding respect for person may not be compromised, why these norms are absolute in respect to the various ends we choose to pursue.

2

Harm

I N THIS chapter I examine one crucial categorical norm:
that it is wrong to do physical harm to an innocent person.
Now, physical harm is not the only or necessarily the worst
kind of injury. A man's liberty to speak his mind or travel
freely may be more important to him than security against some
sorts of harm, as may be his property or his reputation. Certain
violations of these other interests may also be wrong, just as
wrong as doing physical harm. I shall not offer accounts of all
such wrongs. I suppose that arguments analogous to those I
give regarding harm and lying are available in other cases. I
claim only that the norm forbidding physical harm has priority,
at least in the exposition of a theory of right and wrong.

By physical harm I mean an impingement upon the body
which either causes pain or impairs functioning. Thus a sharp,
painful blow which, however, neither cuts nor bruises would constitute harm. So also would a laceration of the skin, since any
break in the skin impairs the functioning of that tissue. On the
other hand, to cut hair or a fingernail or to paint the skin with
some nontoxic substance might constitute an offense to dignity
but would not stand as a physical harm. This definition covers a
wide range of consequences. It covers everything from killing to
pinching and thus raises an important theoretical question. Can
it be that pinching has the same moral quality as killing? I shall
offer very little in the way of enlightenment regarding the
morality of pinching, although if one takes physical harms further along the line of seriousness—maiming, blinding, or even
temporary infliction of severe pain—I have no difficulty concluding that, in all of these cases, the formal nature of the moral
judgment, the categorical prohibition, is the same. These are

30

harms we must not intend to inflict, and consideration of consequences as such cannot outweigh that judgment. As we shall see, there are excuses and justifications for killing, and so there must be also for maiming and the infliction of pain. Nor is there any reason to insist that just because all instances along this gamut have the same formal structure (being the subjects of categorical prohibitions), the excusing and justifying conditions must therefore also be the same. There may, after all, also be an absolute prohibition against engaging in sex for pay, but that would not mean that the excuses and justifications for so doing would be the same as those offered for killing.

It is interesting, however, that the judgment may well run out at the lower end of the scale, that even absolute notions recognize a concept of triviality. There does indeed seem to be something absurd about wheeling out the heavy moral artillery to deal with pinching. A prohibition may be categorical, but the boundaries of that concept may be susceptible of judgments of degree, at least to the extent that one must recognize the trivial and the absurd. But it does not follow from the proposition that there is no absolute prohibition against pinching, in view of the triviality of the harm, that therefore the prohibition against intentionally killing an innocent person is also a matter of degree, also is not absolute. And even as to killing, I do not know how to answer the person who asks me whether I would be willing to kill an innocent person to save the whole of humanity from excruciating suffering and death. There are boundaries to each of these concepts, and the concepts themselves often become blurred, indeterminate, subject to judgments of prudence at those boundaries. We can accept this without at all concluding that therefore the concepts have no central core, or that they are subject throughout to judgments of degree.

In explicating this norm, I shall show how the concept of intention introduced in the previous chapter is appropriate to specify and make practicable the judgments that a particular kind of act, harming an innocent person, is wrong. Whatever may be the problems about intention in other contexts, intention as the mode of application clearly complements the substantive content of the norm. That intentional physical harm (choosing the harm of another as one's end or as the means to one's end) should be the subject of this norm also works to explain the logic of the norm, its categorical force. The two elements, intention and doing harm, may be seen as picturing a relation between a moral agent and the object of his agency, a relation which is inconsistent with the basic notion of respect for persons. And that inconsistency explains why the prohibition is categorical. The absolute norm is grounded in the importance to us of our physical integrity and in the special evil of a relation established between people in which one person exercises his peculiarly human efficacy to attack another's physical integrity. It is just because the person of the victim is threatened by the person of the actor that the relation has a special moral significance. From the victim's perspective, to be hurt by a natural force or by accident is different from being the object of an intentional attack, even though the actual injury may be identical. The intention makes for the offense.

DIRECTNESS AND PARTICULARITY

Consider these two cases:

III. Plunging a dagger into someone's heart.

IV. Revaluing your currency with the foreseeable result that your country's wheat crop will be more expensive and less readily available for famine relief and the further foreseeable result that some persons weakened by hunger in distant lands will die.

It is our intuitive response that without some very special and narrowly drawn justification, the conduct in case III is wrong, while the moral quality of the conduct in case IV depends on a wide variety of considerations: the purpose of the revaluation, the likely response of other countries, the history behind the move, the background of international practice, and so on. In short, it seems natural to bring the first of these cases within the ambit of the categorical norm "Do no harm." The conduct in the second case, however, must inevitably be subjected to some form of consequentialist analysis. Now, the consequentialist would argue that so must case III, that no plausible ground can exist for determining the moral quality of the act in case IV by weighing the good accomplished against the concomitant harm while refusing to have the judgment in case III depend on exactly the same kind of weighing. If that is what we must do in case IV, then—it is claimed—this is all we can *ever* do.

The Person and Disintegrating Universality   If we could not distinguish between cases III and IV, if we could not say that directly harming was wrong in some special way, if we had to weigh and balance all the consequences to see if stabbing an innocent person to death was wrong, then our whole position as free moral agents, our status as persons, would be grievously undermined. (I shall specify what I mean by directness in due course.) The connection between the concept of personality and the special moral quality of directly caused harm is based on the (metaphysical) fact that persons, the ultimate object of moral judgments, are particular entities, and more precisely particular *bodies*. This is not a necessary truth, and fanciful suppositions may be adduced to show how the concept of the person might cut across physical boundaries in some other way. But these notions are only possible in a world where choice and reflection emanate from entities other than the kinds of physical entities that actually exist.*

Now, if the person is to remain at the center of moral judgment, this link to the concrete must be maintained by the very form of our moral norms. We must avoid what I shall call disintegrating universality. The concept of personality, of individuality, is after all, a precarious one. Why is the particular embodied unit of the individual the primitive, the primary unit? Why are not larger or smaller units the significant ones? Why not the species, for instance? Why not some abstract idea, some conception, the universe as a whole? The more abstract our notions of value become, the more universal they are, the more the significance of the individual person is threatened. This significance of the individual person can only be asserted by the assertion of concrete particularity, by the assertion of particular contingent differences which may not make any difference in terms which can be generalized or derived from some more basic principle, but which are nevertheless the terms of the concrete particularity of individual human existence. This point is illustrated by the contrast to utilitarianism, which in its uncompromising universality deprives all individual differences, and thus the individual himself, of moral significance. Utilitarianism posits that it is the sum total of happiness that counts, and how

* This argument has the odd entailment of making my basically Kantian thesis about the importance of persons and about the moral norms which express that importance depend on what Kant would call contingent facts. I regard this as Kant's problem, not mine, and also I see in this an explanation of why the categorical norms I offer are much more material than those Kant proposes.

happiness is distributed among persons is a secondary, an instrumental matter. So also an ethic of excellence, which makes the advancement of knowledge or of the arts the primary criterion of the good, is ultimately indifferent to the human actors who are the contingent vehicles of these excellences. In such systems, a moral agent must view not only his own happiness or excellences as being adventitiously and irrelevantly his own (he is like a trustee with whom these values are deposited because they must be deposited somewhere), but even his capacities, dispositions, tastes, and pleasures are just the raw materials out of which this abstract value is to be fabricated.

The contrasting view gives content to the notion that it is the individual person who is the ultimate entity of value, so that even a person's happiness is only important because it is that person's happiness. Happiness is not a kind of undifferentiated abstract plasma waiting to be attached to a particular person but the aim and outcome of individual *choice,* the success of the self in realizing its own values through its choices and efficacy. Accordingly, the maintenance of the integrity of the individual as the locus of valuation and choice is more important than the abstractions of happiness, pleasure, or excellence. These latter are, after all, rather the *objects* of individual valuation. And if the primacy of the individual is to be maintained, if it is individuality, personality, which is the point of departure of ethical judgments, then the "irrelevantly" particular must be allowed significance.

The integrity of the person as the center of moral choice and judgment requires that we find room for the inescapably particular in personality, that we avoid disintegrating universality. The absolute norm "Do no harm" expresses this centrality of the person on both ends of the relation: it gives special prominence to the physical person as the object (victim) of the relation, and it makes the person as agent both more responsible for what he does directly or intentionally and less responsible for what merely comes about as a side effect of his purposes. If, as consequentialism holds, we were indeed equally morally responsible for an infinite radiation of concentric circles originating from the center point of some action, then while it might look as if we were enlarging the scope of human responsibility and thus the significance of personality, the enlargement would be greater than we could support. For to be responsible equally for everything is to have the moral possibility of choice, of discretion, of creative concretization of one's free self wholly preempted by the potential radiations of all the infinite alternatives for choice. Total undifferentiated responsibility is the correlative of the morally overwhelming, undifferentiated plasma of happiness or pleasure.

Direct Harm It is a natural point of departure for any containment and highlighting of personal responsibility to give special prominence to that which we accomplish by touching, that which is accomplished by our physical bodies. Our ethical constructs attach a peculiar importance to that which is done directly, immediately, because it is through such actions that we first learn about our capacities and our efficacy. As we touch and produce results in the world by touching, we learn that we are able to produce results and that we as individuals are different from the results we produce. It is by touching that the notions of acting and efficacy develop in us. It is by touching that we learn that we are different from the world, that we become acquainted with our identity, and that we become acquainted with our capacity for causal efficacy. Willard Quine has suggested this same intuitive connection between touching and cause: "Of these two wayward idioms, the causal and the dispositional, the causal is the simpler and the more fundamental. It may have had its prehistoric beginnings in man's sense of effort as in pushing. The imparting of energy still seems to be the central idea. The transfer of momentum from one billiard ball to another is persistently cited as a paradigm case of causality in terms of the flow of energy."* To be sure, an objection might be raised that in stabbing, it is the knife, not the hand, that makes the contact. And what of dropping a stone on somebody or running him over in a truck? The idea of direct harm is approximate and intuitive,

* *The Roots of Reference* (LaSalle, Ill.: Open Court, 1973), p. 5. A possible linguistic recognition of the special nature of certain ways of bringing about results in the world, those ways that are more direct, is found in the fact that transitive verbs like "melt," "break," "kill," "shatter" have a different grammatical functioning from the terms some might suppose to be their equivalents, "cause to melt," "cause to break," "cause to die." For instance, "one can cause an event by doing something at a time distinct from the time of the event. But if you melt something, then you melt it when it melts . . . . [Thus] (20), but not (21), is well-formed.

"(20) John caused Bill to die on Sunday by stabbing him on Saturday.

"(21) John killed Bill on Sunday by stabbing him on Saturday" (J. A. Fodor, "Three Reasons for not Deriving 'Kill' from 'Cause to Die,'" *Linguistic Inquiry* [1970]: 433).

which does not matter since it is indeed only a springboard to the concept of *intentional* harm—and intentional harm can work in very remote and indirect ways. For the moment, suffice it to say that the dagger appears quite naturally as an extension of the hand. So might the stone or even the truck appear as extensions of the person, as extensions of direct physical efficacy. The limits are vague and to a degree conventional.

Physical harm inflicted directly, personally as it were—in the language of the classical Roman law, *damnum corpore corpori datum*—provides a paradigm for the kind of relation between persons which is the subject of the categorical prohibition. And, though the discussion has been concerned so far explicitly only with one side, the agent's side, of the relation encompassed by the norm "Do no harm," the argument is symmetric. The same factors, which identify the importance of the particular embodied person for the purpose of anchoring the causal chain of responsibility in the immediate and direct *production* of results, operate as well to bind the person of the victim with peculiar closeness to what he *suffers* in his physical person.

The Analogy to Benefit A man's life is full of particular affections and concerns. He loves his children, is fond of his friends, is moved by the suffering of a particular person, even a stranger. In Part III, I consider at length decisions to benefit particular persons rather than some abstract, impersonal mass of persons. I anticipate that discussion briefly now because the claim of a special right to benefit those who are close to us is symmetrical with the claim that direct harm, harm to those close to us, is absolutely wrong. Now, I believe that to condemn any preference for particular persons as morally invalid, to require us to treat all human beings with strict impartiality, would leave the very concept of human welfare with a remarkably poor content: there would be no room for concern based just on the fact of relationships with others. To the extent that personal concern is grounded in, say, affection or friendship, such concern would imply an improper preference, a departure from impartiality. The individual would become a kind of dimensionless locus of his own hedonistic and self-centered pleasures on the one hand and a source of completely generalized concern for all the other such loci on the other. Such total impartiality conflicts with a sense of one's own individuality. Indeed, it is but another version of what I have called the reduction of disintegrating universality. A full account of just how much impartiality we must show in benefiting others will depend on a theory of rights and of justice. Here I assert only that the maintenance of a properly rich and articulated moral life must allow us to maintain some reserve for relations with particular persons. But those persons can be the subject of our particular concern only if we have somehow made contact with their concrete, particular features.

The argument for a right to benefit specially certain identified persons (as opposed to humanity in general) is not directly translatable into an argument condemning with special stringency the harming of an identified person in a direct and immediate way. The natural obverse of the benefit argument would seem to be the case of treachery, where one harms those who trust him or to whom one has a special obligation. But that is not at all the paradigm of direct, personal harm. Rather, a direct attack upon anyone, even a stranger, is the baseline of that primitive wrong. And thus the point of departure is a point on the spectrum which in respect to *benefit* seems a most attenuated form of relationship: "mere" propinquity. Now, propinquity is indeed a necessary condition, a natural precursor, of personal relations. We cannot enter into personal relations with those with whom we have not come into contact. (Affinities contracted by correspondence or telephone are, after all, parasitic on the paradigm of a friend as someone we have encountered personally.) But even though propinquity is such a natural precursor of relations of special care, it does not follow that something especially *bad* arises out of what might be considered a mere refusal to take up the invitation to deeper involvement that propinquity offers. When we refuse aid to the stranger in our path, this is not obviously *worse* than refusing aid to some unknown, unseen, random stranger who may need our help as much. And if one can decline the invitation to enter into a relation of benefit with a particular stranger, how does the case of benefit help to show why plunging a knife into a stranger bears a greater burden of justification than increasing the level of radiation only so much as will doom one additional person of the world's population to death by cancer?

The distinction between benefit and harm arises in this way: If everyone who passed us by in a crowded street had a claim to our special *and positive* concern, a claim to be specially benefited, then little would be left over for those undoubted and strong cases—affection, kinship—in which a special claim to benefit seems justified. Nor would the problem be significantly less severe if we limited the strangers' claims to those strangers who asked for our help. The intrusion on our ability to limit and control the numbers and identities of those who have a privileged call on our help could be as bad in the latter case as in the former. If propinquity were recognized as a sufficient, not just a necessary condition for special relations of benefit, then the particular would indeed soon all but disappear in the general after all. But these problems are not with us in respect to harm. *It is not the victim who chooses the agent, but the agent who chooses the victim.* The agent retains control of his circle of concern; it cannot engulf. In direct harm, the agent focuses on the victim, knowing that his actions will impinge directly on him. It is the agent who makes the victim an issue and who must therefore take account of his particularity.

Thus some choice, some special circumstance, must single out the face in the crowd to whom the agent will stand bound by the special bond—for if he stood specially bound by everyone he met, in the end there would be no special bond to anyone. In the case of benefit, something has to reach out to particularize the beneficiary of the relation other than the general fact—applicable across too indefinite a range—of a susceptibility to benefit. If a stranger can say to me, "You might have benefited me," I can always reply, "No more than countless other persons." In harm this problem does not exist. The conscious, volitional infliction of harm directly by my person upon the person of the victim *ipso facto* sufficiently particularizes the victim. I cannot in general and always say, "If I had not harmed you, I would have harmed someone else," for usually it is open to me to harm no one at all.*

Now, I do insist that the direct impingement be conscious, a volitional gesture. If I harm you directly but inadvertently—through carelessness or even against my will, as when pushed—this may or may not create a relation such that I am to be blamed, must apologize or try to make it up to you, but I have not made a conscious decision to inflict harm on your person by

* I put to one side the case in which, unless one directly harms X, he will harm Y, as where a trolley driver approaching a junction has a choice between running down several persons on one or another of the two alternative tracks. See Judith J. Thompson, "Killing, Letting Die, and the Trolley Problem," *Monist,* April 1976.

my person. It is that decision which is the subject of the absolute norm "Do no harm." And it is from that decision that I shall now build out to deal with the issue of intentional but possibly indirect harm.

FROM DIRECTNESS TO INTENTION

Directness is invoked to limit and make practicable the norm "Do no harm." I have argued that without some limitation it is not possible to conceive of the norm as expressing a categorical wrong: we would be forced either to have recourse to consequentialist weighing or to risk paralysis, obsession and contradiction. Stabbing someone or running him down are cases of direct harm proscribed—unless excused or justified—by the absolute norm. But really there is no great problem about such cases of direct harm if the harm is caused knowingly and as a result of deliberate action. We do not get into the difficulties about intended means and side effects in these cases of direct harm. Recall the question from the first chapter, whether a distinction could be made between shooting a guard to assure a prisoner's escape and dynamiting a hole in a prison wall knowing that this would also kill the guard stationed on top of the wall. Or consider the distinction between deliberate bombing of civilian areas as part of a campaign of terror and bombing of a military target, causing civilian casualties. In the first case of each pair the absolute norm applies, because the deaths are intended means, not mere side effects. Intention, not directness, provides the distinction in such cases. And this is plain if we consider a case in which there is no hint of directness, as when I send my victim's mother poisoned chocolates which I expect her to serve to him. The intention is sufficient to invoke the categorical prohibition, and directness is not necessary. Direct harm deals with both too easy and too limited a range of cases. The complexities encountered in cases of more remote harming scarcely arise where the harm is direct.* The effects we produce directly are generally the first

* It is hard to imagine how an agent might knowingly and directly harm another but not as a means to his end. Well, I suppose the case might arise. For example, I am running very fast along a railroad platform and there you are standing in front of me. If I stop or try to get around you I might miss my train, so, because I don't stop, I knock you under a train passing on the other track. I did not knock you off the platform as a means to my end. I just kept running irrespective of whether you were there or not. I have done it directly. The case is unusual.

steps in a planned chain of causality radiating out from our persons. The problems about unwanted reverberations, the "mere" side effects, begin further out, after the causal sequence has left the range of our immediate person. It is to those more classically troubling cases that I now turn.

The more remote cases are, of course, crucial. Man's technical progress from the spear to the radio-actuated Mars lander epitomizes the history of his attempt to extend his efficacy in precisely targeted projects beyond the range of his own body. So, just as the concept of directness gathers its moral force from its connection with the primitive fact of personal efficacy, the concept of intention corresponds to the equally human phenomenon of planned and contrived *distant* efficacy. Direct efficacy may be the first experience of efficacy, but as intelligence is essentially human, so the mastery of increasingly complex causal processes is of the essence of intelligent agency. The *person* may be invested at first in direct efficacy, but his *intelligence* is invested in his remote projects and his person invests his intelligence. Thus planned results are the natural extension of direct results, and intention of directness.

If you would grasp the fundamentality of intelligent purposive action, consider the difference between two states of affairs, both removed from the physical and temporal proximity of the person and both equally beneficial to his ultimate goals and situation. One comes about without any intervention on his part, though he well knows that processes lead to the result. The other he brings about: he considers what he wants, he takes stock of the resources at his command and of the laws by which events unfold, he charts the course and then acts, setting the whole thing in motion. In both cases there is the result and there is the desire, but in the second there is purposive action, plan, intention. The two cases are basically different courses of events. Initiating one is the intimate, personal fact of immediate action, direct efficacy. But that is not all. Intelligence, foresight, the channel dug for events by our minds in imagination, carries that first intimate thrust forward and invests the final results with the same personal attachment as was present at the outset.

This is not an argument, it is a picture, a picture of what it is to be a human being in the world of events. And it is according to this picture that we can see why means are different from concomitants. For means are part of our plans and thus are invested with our persons in a way that concomitants are not.

The means we choose are the steps along a way we have mapped out in advance. Concomitants just happen; they belong to the domain of naturally occurring processes in which we might intervene if we choose. And of course we are sometimes responsible for what just happens, but really no more responsible for what happens as a concomitant of our plans than we are for what just happens because we choose not to act at all or to concern ourselves with other things. Directness is the kernel of personal investment from which we set out. From it, the world of events takes two courses: (1) the course of events in which we are, through plan and purpose, equally as invested as in the outset and (2) those sequences of events which radiate out from the starting point in the infinite concentric circles of mere causality. If we were responsible in the fullest measure for the second, then disintegrating universality would be upon us. If we were *not* responsible for the first, then the power of our reach would to that crucial extent be truncated. The special responsibility we bear for our projects is an appropriate recognition of our special involvement in those projects.

Thus the considerations explaining the absolute characters of the norm "Do no harm" in the case of *direct* harm must be generalized to the case of *intentional* harm. Direct harm describes a wrongful relation between two particular persons, just because it so intimately involves their particularity. Intended harm is wrong for closely analogous reasons. The harm, of course, on the victim's side of the relation is the same, but my account of the significance of intention shows why the agent's personal investment in his fellow's harm is just as great as if he produced it directly. It was the agent's very plan to bring about that harm; he formed a project in his mind and included the victim's harm in that project. Thus the intended injury is a result of personal agency, while in the case of a side effect or accident the injury is the product of natural causality (even if some human actions appear in the causal chain). Another person, who after all has the same capacity for reflection and the same concern to maintain his integrity, his person, as I do, has chosen to make my body, my person, a means to some end of his own.

None of this should be understood to excuse the evil of moral callousness, of disregard of the harm which our projects produce as a side effect, or of the harm which we might by some affirmative effect have avoided. I agree that our increased capacity to produce (or avoid) distant harm extends the range of our moral responsibility for all of those results. Starving populations in distant lands are our concern. Nothing I say here should be taken to deny this. I argue for a complex, not for a myopic sense of responsibility. The absolute norm forbids direct or intentional harm, but it does not excuse all other harms. The norm does not, however, forbid those harms absolutely. (As I have argued, it could not coherently do so.) There are duties of concern and beneficence toward all human beings, but they are not absolute. They allow for weighing and calculation—inevitably—as the absolute norm does not. Often these are impersonal duties to abstract persons and so they can be fulfilled in abstract ways— through governments, institutions, and the like. As we see next, very little can override the absolute norm "Do no harm," but the duty to care for abstract humanity may be overcome in many ways. Finally, there can be no doubt that my argument for an absolute prohibition of direct or intentional harm must operate to some extent at the expense of the interest of all those others who do not come into this specially stringent circle of concern. For there must be instances where only by doing intentional harm could I ward off greater harm from perhaps many others. And still I must do no harm.

COMPLETING THE STRUCTURE: DEFENSE

There is an obvious objection to the proposal that "Do no harm" is an absolute norm: the categorical judgment cannot plausibly be asserted in the face of our tolerance of direct, intentional injuries inflicted in sports, medical treatment, punishment, and combat. Harm is inflicted directly, though not as a means or an end, when we push through a crowd on some urgent errand. It is inflicted in protecting property and warding off dangers. Any theory which would always condemn such actions is obviously extreme and unacceptable.

Consent, authorization, defense of legitimate interest must be accommodated somehow in our moral deliberations. Now we might assign some weight to the negative term, here the physical injury, and recognize these justifications as positive terms to be weighed and balanced off against the negative term. But this is precisely what I have said must not be done. If consent and self-defense were to enter the arguments simply as counterweights, then they would enter the argument in exactly the same way that good purposes enter the argument when the harm is produced unintentionally or when the harm is just something we have failed to avoid. And that would destroy the distinctiveness of the thesis regarding the categorical norm. Thus consent, duress, self-defense do not just constitute excuses and justifications (which is the traditional and familiar point about them) but they must exist in a peculiarly close theoretical relationship with the very wrong they serve to qualify. Whatever theoretical explanation can be offered for giving the norm categorical status must itself provide the basis for the particular qualifications of that norm. These generalities are well illustrated by the example of defense as a justification for intentional harm. The system of justification, it will be seen, not only makes more plausible but fills out the substantive concept of harm as a paradigm of a forbidden relation.

Defense of the Person Physical harm is permissible if it is intended as a means of defense against a proportional physical harm. Thus the absolute norm is qualified even further than by its limitation to intentional or direct harm, for here is a case of permissible *intentional* harm. Some writers, wishing to maintain the absoluteness of the norm (at least insofar as it applies to the harm of killing), believe they are forced to argue that intentional harm (killing) is not permissible even to defend against harm (death), and that in cases in which we seem to sanction this, the death of the aggressor is only an unintended side effect of some lesser defensive purpose—to stop the aggressor, to disable him. This explanation would thus disaggregate what naturally appears as a unitary event into different aspects—stopping the attack and killing the attacker—so as to absolve the defender from the charge of having intended the death of another as a means to his end. In Chapter 1, I noted this kind of move, which would allow one to say that in exploding the fat man from the mouth of cave the intention was merely to blow him to bits, his death being a mere side effect. If this move were indeed generally available, then the meaningfulness of the means/side-effect distinction and thus of the concept of intention in absolute norms would be severely undermined. It is ironical, therefore, that just this disaggregation gambit should be urged by those who are seeking to *maintain* the absoluteness of the norm. But since self-defense will be shown to fall outside the norm altogether, this kind of maneuver is unnecessary.

The defender does indeed intend to kill; the death of the aggressor is the means to the defense, even though (as is often the case with intentional harm) the defender may prefer to have some less drastic means available to him. The case illustrates a general point about the disaggregation gambit: that the supposed indeterminacy in the concept of intention must be considered in the context of the norm in which it is invoked. Here the norm forbids intentionally producing harm as a result. If the disaggregator offers stopping the aggressor as the means to his defensive purpose, then we may ask what are his means to accomplish that subpurpose of stopping. Let us say the defender shoots, stabs, drops a large weight on the aggressor. In any such case I think no answer can plausibly be offered which does not include harming the aggressor as the means to the sub-end. For it is inadmissible to say that one intends to put a bullet through a man, stab him, crush him, or blow him to atoms but does not intend to harm him. All of these things just *are* harming him.

So the means/side-effect distinction remains intact and the absolute norm with it. The reason defense against an aggressor is permissible is not because the harm is not intended, but because it is not wrong to intend harm in the case of defense. What is wrong about intentionally harming is the relation it asserts between agent and victim. The agent is using his victim's *person* as a means to an end, and this is what constitutes the offense against respect, the offense against the person of the victim. The agent's principle of action, though it need not deny the human bond in general, would exclude the victim from it. And here is the special offense. But in the case of self-defense, the defender asserts no moral priority over his attacker, for the defender's intention is sufficiently justified by an assertion that his (the defender's) person, while of no greater moral significance than the attacker's, is of no *less* consequence either. The reciprocity of interests and the similarity between the actor-defender and the victim-aggressor are crucial. Self-defense describes a form of relation whose structure we may affirm.

All this is straightforward and familiar. The inquiry into self-defense is intended primarily to illustrate a method and to give content to some very general ideas. Now let us take the argument for self-defense further by considering intentional harm to protect against values other than physical integrity or to defend against an aggressor who is acting on a mistaken or insane belief that his conduct is justified, or indeed an aggressor who is not acting intentionally at all.

Defense of Other Values I own some valuable object which another tries to take from me. What may I do to protect my interests? American law provides in general that I may use whatever force short of deadly force is reasonably necessary to protect my property against immediate loss. Or I am walking on the sidewalk and a bully insists I walk in the street to humiliate me. May I insist on my right if I know this may provoke perhaps a deadly attack, and may I then use deadly force in my defense? The answers to these questions will depend to a great extent on the general social context. It is not surprising that in some times and places even deadly force has been authorized to protect property. On the other hand, a person threatened with deadly force anywhere but in his home is usually required to retreat if he safely can before using deadly force, but no common-law jurisdiction deprives a man of the right to defend himself—if need be with deadly force—on the ground that he might have avoided the occasion of the attack in the first place by acceding to a threat or yielding some right. Now I am not primarily concerned with law but with morals, and the law is significant as it illuminates these moral questions.

A consequentialist would see in the legal and moral judgments a trade-off between the value of bodily integrity and, for instance, the value of property. Indeed, it is a feature of consequentialist analyses not only of defense but also of prevention and punishment to allow the advantages to the wrongdoer and the harm to his victim to enter into the balance on an equal footing and to ask only which quantity is larger. As a result, consequentialism comes up with peculiar concepts like "the optimum level of crime," which is supposed to be the point where the benefits to wrongdoers from their criminal activities begin to be greater in amount than the harm suffered by victims—as if these quantities were in principle entitled to equal consideration. The correct analysis, of course, is more complex, taking into account not only the relative value of life versus property but also the fact that the aggressor against property is acting wrongly, is violating the rights of the defender. In other words, we do not just balance the two values, but also take account of the fact that values are attributed to persons in particular relations.

Consider a schematized version of the encounter: The defender warns that he will inflict bodily injury if necessary to protect his property, and only after this warning is defied does the defender inflict injury. I assume further that the aggression is against a substantial value and that the aggression is wrong and known to be wrong. The defender's action differs from wrongful infliction of harm not because there is a substantive value (the property) to be balanced against the injury he inflicts, for that fact is usually present and I have argued that it is insufficient, but because the "aggressor-victim" himself intends a violation of the agent's rights. It is the threatened violation of the defender's rights which is crucial. Since I have made no point of the concept of rights so far (rights are the subject of Part II), suffice it to say now that we are assuming that the invasion of the actor's property interest would be a wrong toward him in the same sense (though not necessarily to the same degree) as would the earlier paradigm case of intentional physical harm. And thus an agent who inflicts injury on a robber does not affirm a principle asserting moral superiority to the robber any more than he does when he defends his person. Nor does he assert that the robber's person is available to him for his ends—only that his (the defender's) rights are not available for the robber's ends.

Though this may seem obvious, how would we answer the doubter who insists that in this case too one intentionally uses the injury of another to further (protect) some end of one's own? The robber would use the actor here by violating his rights, would subject his victim to this unjust use. The defender, by resisting, intends to inflict injury to be sure, but all this may also be correctly characterized by saying that he intends to protect his rights. Thus, far from asserting a moral superiority to the robber, far from implying a degrading relation to him, the actor intends to prevent just such a degrading relation from coming about. This intention of the defender to prevent wrong may not do the whole job, but at least the shoe is on the other foot: the actor's intention is capable of a statement which seems consistent with the arguments used to account for the norm "do no harm." Now we must see if this new thrust must not itself in turn be contained. Imagine this as an argument:

(1) Robber to actor: "You must not intentionally hurt me."

(2) Actor to robber: "But you are not an innocent object of my intention; I am preventing a violation of right by you, and you yourself need the notion of right to make out your claim against me in the first place."

Is there a third move in their dialogue, or is that the end of the argument? What of the use of deadly force to save an object of trivial value? There is, I think, room for further specification.

One way the actor's defensive force might be justified is by the notion of consent. The case presupposes an encounter in which the robber is squarely faced with the choice: if you go on, I will do this. Thus it might be said that the robber himself chose physical injury in pursuit of his victim's property, and we may suppose that in general consent justifies the breach of an absolute norm. Now it may be objected that this is a very odd sort of consent; this is not like consent to surgery, for instance. Surely the robber would *prefer* that he get the property without suffering hurt. (The patient would prefer to be rid of his appendix without being cut open.) But he is given a choice and what happens is according to that choice. And if we reflect further, we will see that reliance on a supposed choice by the victim is an irrelevant irony only in those cases where the undesirable alternative has been unjustifiably imposed on that victim. The highwayman's "Your money or your life" does not provide a case of justifying consent since the highwayman has no right to take your money. The whole thing never gets going other than on a basis of wrong. In my case, however, it is the robber's victim who is putting the alternatives, and since the robber is not entitled to his victim's property, a fortiori the robber cannot complain if he is told that his personal intergrity depends on giving up something to which he has no right.

But we do on occasion feel justified in preventing someone from choosing to suffer death or maiming for some trivial end—even if the attainment of that end injures no one. Should we not hesitate as well to allow this extension of the notion of consent to justify grave harm inflicted by a victim defending against a trivial transgression? There are, of course, theorists who are persuaded that an adult should be allowed to consent even to death for whatever reason the consenter wishes, and I would suppose that these theorists might feel least impelled to insist on some limit of proportionality to the right of defense. And though this difference of philosophy may account for some variation in conclusions regarding the limits of defense, a second reason may also come into play. We assume from the outset that whatever harm is inflicted is necessary to defend the imperiled value. But if society by police and courts can assure that the threatened property will eventually be restored, then recourse to force is no longer necessary. And of course the extent to which a society is willing and able to give such assurances will vary.

Defense against an Innocent Aggressor This notion of waiver or consent may work well enough where the aggressor/victim is knowingly violating the right of the actor, but what of this case?

V. A and B have a violent quarrel at the conclusion of which B rushes off threatening to get his gun, which is just downstairs, and to shoot A. Moments later, C, who has heard the noise and rushes to lend assistance to A, runs up the stairs and bursts into the room. A, believing this is B returning to kill him, knocks C unconscious as he enters. (Adapted from *Crabtree v. Dawson,* 119 Ky. 148, 83 S.W. 557 [1904].)

A thought that the kind of argument I offered to justify self-defense covered him, but he was wrong. Should that matter? Not at all, if the issue is the moral condemnation of A for his original act. For he acted just as we would have him act, had the facts been as he believed them to be. And if there are no grounds for condemning the way he came to that conclusion—for instance, negligently—then how can we say to him that he chose wickedly? The fact that C is entirely innocent in this case does require some acknowledgment. We may well argue that it is unfair for the whole (or any part) of the burden of the loss in this unfortunate incident to fall on C, but that goes to compensation afterward. If we judge the actor's *choice,* if we ask how he should choose in the situation that confronts him, then from that perspective we can urge no different action on him than in the paradigm case of self-defense. So, though this case is unfortunate, it is not difficult.*

A difficult case is this one:

VI. D attacks A, insanely thinking that A is a dangerous killer or a wild animal. A, fully aware of D's delusion, defends himself using deadly force.

---

* This analysis does permit the possibility that C, seeing that he is about to be attacked, will justifiably defend himself against A before A realizes his error, so that we will have a fight between two persons, both acting justifiably. This is unfortunate but in no sense a contradiction in the theory. Indeed, it is a possibility in *any* theory which judges the morality of an action from the perspective of the actor's factual perceptions. Now what if A realizes his mistake as C begins his justified, deadly counterattack in self-defense? May A now defend against what he now knows to be (1) a justified counterattack by C and (2) a counterattack provoked by his own mistaken earlier attack? I am inclined to hold that in that case A should desist even at risk to his life, because to do otherwise is to allow him knowingly and intentionally to cast the burden of his own mistake onto an innocent party. Since he could not have initially seized C as a shield against B's attack, I would incline against further violence to C for the same reason. See generally Robert Nozick, *Anarchy, State and Utopia* (New York: Basic Books, 1974) , pp. 34–35, and Lawrence Alexander, "Self-Defense and the Killing of Noncombatants," *Philosophy and Public Affairs* 5 (1976) : 408–415.

This case differs from V in that A can perfectly well see that D is suffering from an insane delusion and thus knows that D is acting just as we would want anyone to act if the facts were as D honestly (but insanely) believed them to be. Indeed, we might get a different version of this same problem if we looked at case V from C's point of view. Imagine the same facts as in V except

> Va. C turns in time to meet A's attack, understands at once A's mistake, but can only prevent harm to himself by striking and gravely injuring A.

The difficulty is, of course, that the innocent aggressor unlike the robber does not choose to "use" A unjustly, and so he does not waive his right to A's respect of his (the aggressor's) physical integrity. Indeed, one might say that the innocent aggressor is more like E in this case:

> VII. E is leaning against a railing high above A. The railing unexpectedly gives way. E falls and A can save himself only by raising his arms and deflecting the weight of E's fall, thereby seriously injuring E. If E had fallen on A, E probably would have sustained little if any injury.

In VII this "aggressor" E endangers the actor, but not intentionally or knowingly and directly. The encounter is not one in which there is invoked the kind of paradigmatic human efficacy of which I have been developing the picture. In the paradigm case of self-defense the intentions of the two parties meet squarely: the actor knows what the aggressor intends, and the aggressor knows that the actor knows, and so on. We might say that the aggressor in cases V, VI, and VII in one way or another is like a natural force which the actor fends off rather than a person against whom he defends himself. But has our example of a categorical norm grown too weak in this process of refinement? "Do no harm" turns out to mean something more like "Respect everyone's physical integrity," with the word "respect" bearing a heavy burden of casuistry. Consider these cases:

> VIII. An assassin, who for some reason cannot get to his victim himself, threatens to kill your child unless *you* kill his chosen victim.
> IX. A retarded and sickly child is the only available donor of a kidney for an otherwise normal sibling. The donor would surely not survive the removal of his kidney.

In both of these cases our means/concomitant analysis would clearly designate the harming of the victim or donor as intended, a means toward a laudable end. If the absolute norm means anything, it surely would forbid the harm in both cases. But how are we to distinguish these killings from the killing of the innocent aggressor in VII? The degree of the victim's innocence is the same in all these cases. They show that we must go further than the concept of respect. For why is it not a violation of respect to fend off the falling body in VII, while it is a violation to inflict harm in VIII and IX? The answer lies in the concept of defense. The actor does not defend himself *against* his victim in either VIII or IX. Note first that in cases V through VII the victim is going to do something to the actor, who must act to prevent this. In VIII and IX the victim threatens nothing. But this is only a first approximation, since the very claim that might be made in VIII and IX is that there is indeed a threat in the sense that if the action against the victim is not taken, the actor or someone close to him will die. How is this piece of sophistry to be blocked; why do we feel so sure it *is* mere sophistry? If we consider the concepts of attack and defense as in some sense symmetrical, we will get the answer we need. Defense is defense against an attack, and an attack is itself intentional. The victims in VIII and IX do not intend harm.* The unjustified attack creates a relation, a relation of wrong, between the attacker and his victim, which is different from the relations in which the victim stands to the rest of the world, and in particular it is different from the relation in which any person stands to those other persons who might, if they chose, take affirmative action to confer a benefit upon him, to help him out of a predicament. The victim of a robbery stands in a different relation to his robber than to the priest and the Levite who "passed by on the other side." It is only as to those to whom one stands in the relation of victim to aggressor that a right of defense arises.

The falling victim is still difficult. Now in case VII the falling

---

* Philippa Foot offers this variant of case IX:

IXa. There are six persons in a hospital. Five can be saved by manufacturing a substance, which will produce a poisonous gas as a by-product, and that gas is sure to kill the sixth.

She argues that negative duties are more stringent than positive duties, so that the killing of the sixth person is as much a violation of a negative duty as carving him up so that his organs may be used to save the other five. My proposal would distinguish the cases, holding IX but not IXa to be intentional.

victim may harm directly but he does not *do* harm; certainly there is no intention. The falling victim has got himself into a situation where either he is going to be treated as an inanimate object—a falling body—or he will insist on his humanity, but then he is estopped from denying the human character of the effect he is about to produce. This is not completely satisfactory, but at least we do not even begin to go down this road with the potential victims in VIII and IX. If there is a problem about VII, it is because we are at a conceptual border. The falling body should be treated like the fat man stuck in the mouth of the cave; killing one is as bad as killing the other. And perhaps this shows that direct killing of the fat man may after all be permitted if we can just bring ourselves to view it as a defense against his blocking the way, which becomes a kind of attack. And certainly one can attack in this way. Suppose someone puts his hand over the sole air vent in a room which holds me prisoner? So case VII, like that of the fat man, may be a borderline case, but not because we doubt that the killing is direct or intentional, rather because we are not sure whether the victim is a threat in such a way as to justify killing in defense. Mere moral innocence will not block the right of defense, as we saw in Va and VI.

The exceptions I have produced under the rubric of defense do not require the conclusion that what we have here after all is just a value to be weighed up against other values. If the process were one of balancing values, then we have the value of life present on both sides of the balance in all five cases. And in the case of the person who defends himself against an attack which he might have avoided by yielding some lesser right (such as property), any *balance* favors the thief-victim. Yet it is not a question of the balance but of the relation. What justifies the apparent breach of the norm in the case of defense is that the actor inflicts harm lest the victim himself inflict harm on the actor (or another).

There are many other contours to be sketched before we have a full map of the country in the neighborhood of this norm. There are concepts such as consent, therapeutic injuries, punishment, actions in war. All of these, like defense, are limitations on the absolute prohibition. They are called into play when the norm is called into play, that is, to justify knowing, direct or intentional hurts. When we move to unintended and indirect harm, whether foreseen with certainty or only as a possibility, we are in a different realm altogether. The norm switches out of its absolute mode and balancing is the order of the day. Consider these cases:

> X. L is seriously ill in a hospital. The doctors operate on him in order to transplant his heart into M, his liver into N, and his two kidneys into O and P, thus saving four lives.
>
> Xa. Same as above, except the doctors withhold a readily available beneficial medicine so that L will expire and his organs may be used to save M, N, O, and P.
>
> XI. Q is dying of a disease which can be cured by giving him 4 cc of a certain medicine—less will not be effective. R, S, T, and U are also ill and can be saved with only 1 cc each. The hospital has only 4 cc available and administers them to R, S, T, and U.

Cases X and Xa are instances of intentional harm—one through an act, the other through an omission. Being intentional, they invoked the norm in its absolute mode and, being unjustified, they must be condemned. Case XI, however, is unintended harm, harm as a concomitant, so the norm switches out of its absolute mode, and a balance of values becomes appropriate. Note that the values in the balance are the same in all three cases.

Finally, I do not hold that a violation of the norm in its absolute mode is always worse than an egregiously wrong decision in the balancing mode. Consider this case:

> XII. W sees X drowning. The only life ring is freshly painted, and fearing to soil his clothes, W goes in search of help instead of throwing out the ring, knowing that thereby X is more likely to drown. X does drown.

Compare this to X and Xa. Though those choices are wrong, violating the norm in its absolute mode, I see no reason to say that what is done there is for that reason to be condemned more severely than W's behavior in XII. An egregiously disproportionate balance in favor of harm is as wrong as intentional harm. Causing harm as a mere side effect of one's projects or the conscious failure to render a benefit can on occasion be just as heinous as a violation of the absolute norm—or more so. The identification of those occasions, however, proceeds from different considerations than those grounding and qualifying the absolute norm "Do no harm." In particular, we must have an understanding of our affirmative obligations (to help, to avert harm from others) . That understanding requires a theory of rights, which is the subject of Part II, and a theory of the duties and relations of benefit, which is the subject of Part III. But whatever duties we are found to have to benefit others, a powerful constraint is implied by the analysis of this chapter: no amount of good we might do can justify intentionally harming innocent persons.

A further point of perspective: The norm "Do no harm" refers only to physical harm. There are other injuries (and other wrongs) a person may sustain: to his reputation, to his property, to his liberties. Physical harm is less abstract than these; it is more closely tied to the basic, animal facts of our existence. That is why it was appropriate to develop the concept of directness, which refers to this primitive physicality from the agent's point of view, and that is why also the norm has both intuitive power and a lack of conceptual neatness, a lack of analytic resolution just in that domain of directness. But it was worth bothering with directness, because we were able to build out to the more general, more intellectual concept of intention. And it is the concept of intention which has general applicability to the class of categorical norms.

3

On Lying

A GOOD MAN does not lie. It is this intuition which brings lying so naturally within the domain of things categorically wrong. Yet many lies do little if any harm, and some lies do real good. How are we to account for this stringent judgment on lying, particularly in the face of the possibly trivial, if not positively beneficial, consequences of lying? Is it the act of lying itself which moves us? This seems implausible, since, as we shall see, the act is defined in part in terms of its intention and that intention is to produce a particular consequence—belief in a false proposition. Is it then consequences which make lying wrong? But the consequences may be good. The strong intuitive distaste, together with the puzzles about explaining what is wrong about lying, makes lying a testing case for the thesis that there are such things as right and wrong, and not just the good and bad of consequentialism.

The case of lying advances the analysis of right and wrong for the additional reason that lying is essentially intentional. The concept of directness has no obvious application to the case of lying as it does in the case of physical harm. It makes no moral difference whether I look you in the eye when I lie to you or lie to you on the telephone, by mail, or through a third person. For whatever point might be made about directness in lying is systematically overwhelmed by the fact that lying is necessarily intentional. Speech, meaning, communication, and therefore perversion of these in lying are so paradigmatically intentional that there is no need to dig down into the primitive, perhaps irrational, facts of directness or immediacy to begin the argument about the moral quality of what is done. The link between intention and lying is so strong that certain of the problems regarding means and side effects which have concerned us cannot arise in the same way in respect to lying. There is no way in which one's own lie can be a mere side effect of some other intention that is pursued. One can only lie intentionally—it is not possible to lie inadvertently or as the known but unwanted side effect of some other purpose. To be sure, it is possible to create erroneous impressions as a side effect or inadvertently, but then one is not lying. Thus the lie is always an end in itself or a means, a chosen means, or it is not a lie at all.

Now, I readily concede that this is merely a preliminary point, a point about usage, as it were, since the creation of erroneous beliefs might be argued to be what is bad about lying, whenever anything is bad. And so it is certainly true that the case of lying is not dispositive evidence for the soundness of the means/side-effect distinction. Yet it is striking that a common, deep, and strong moral intuition—that lying is wrong—is limited to an act which can only be performed intentionally. For there is no corresponding intuition that inadvertently (though knowingly) creating a false impression is categorically wrong. Thus the argument for the judgment that lying is wrong will illustrate further the working of categorical moral judgments and will deepen the connection between the form of these judgments and their contents.

LYING DEFINED

A person lies when he asserts a proposition he believes to be false.* This is the root conception, which I shall refine as necessary to make out the claim that lying is wrong. Any assertion may be analyzed into a *statement, X* ("It is raining outside my window now"), together with an *assertion* that X is true. This analysis may seem to run the danger of infinite regress. For now we must find an analysis of the assertion that X is true that does not in turn consist of the *statement* that X is true together with

* See "The Intent to Deceive," by Roderick Chisholm and Thomas Feehan (*Journal of Philosophy* 74 [1977]: 143–159). Their central emphasis on assertion is identical to mine, which is not necessarily remarkable given the fact that the authors are heavily influenced, as am I, by Augustine's and Kant's discussions of lying. We differ principally in that they find a way to treat as not lying at all some cases which seem to me to be cases of justified lying. But my reasons and theirs are close and the difference is largely one of form. There are many useful and intriguing refinements and distinctions in their essay which my purposes in this work do not lead me to pursue.

the assertion that X is true is true. The difficulty is raised by the distinction between a statement (or an utterance) and an assertion. This is the distinction between saying X to test the register on a recording machine, or saying X as a philosopher's example, on the one hand, and saying X *and meaning it* on the other.

What is it to assert the truth of something? Note first that it is entirely sufficient simply to assert X, because to assert X *is* to assert its truth. And what is it to do that? As a first approximation: to assert X is to utter X in a context such that the utterance is intended to cause belief. But I can cause belief in a proposition without asserting it. I can, for instance, leave clues (perhaps false clues), the purpose of which may be to get you to believe X, and perhaps even to get you to believe that I want you to believe X. But by leaving such clues I have not asserted X. The further element, which seems constantly to slip away from us, is institutional or conventional. Assertion is indeed seeking to cause belief, but it is seeking to cause belief in a particular way. It is, one might say, inviting belief by reference to or in the context of the institution of asserting—or more abstractly, the institution of communication.

But to account for assertion by invoking the institution of asserting hardly seems to break us out of our circle. Asserting, then, is like promising. No analysis will get to the heart of what it is to make a promise if that analysis speaks solely in terms of statements of future intentions plus the intention that the statement be accepted and relied upon. What is distinctive about promising slips away in such explanations, just as what is distinctive about asserting slips away. Similarly, there is the apparent circularity of arguing that a promise intends to induce reliance by reference to the institution of promising. In both cases we must recognize an institution which preexists the assertion (or promise), such that the particular statement is understood by both parties as a move intentionally made in reference to that particular institutional background. And the intentional reference to a general institution in these cases is no more circular than the intentional reference to a game when one makes a particular move in that game. Now the institution which I have in mind in respect to assertions is the simplest, most general, most pervasive of human institutions: it is simply that institution by which people, when they make statements to each other, invite belief, and not belief based *on the evidence* of the statement so much as belief *on the faith* of the statement. To make an assertion is to give an assurance that the statement is true. The analogy to promising is very close. An assertion may be seen as a kind of very general promise; it is a promise or assurance that the statement is true. It is offered not as evidence of the speaker's state of mind but as a deliberate act on the speaker's part on which the hearer is intended to rely.

Every assertion is an intentional act made with the specific intention not only that it be believed, but also that it be understood as an intended move within the assertion game. So we can see why every lie is also intentional. A lie invites belief in an assertion which the speaker knows to be false. That is why my saying that it is raining outside when I know it is not, but when my sole purpose is to test my dictating machine, is not a lie. I am asserting nothing, and therefore I am asserting nothing false. What if my false utterance should be overheard? It is still not a lie. What if it is overheard and believed to be true? Once again it is not a lie, since I did not assert it to the hearer, believing it to be false. Indeed, I *asserted* nothing. What if in a lecture I use a hypothetical example involving a scandalous accusation against a particular person? What if that accusation is heard by somebody who does not appreciate its hypothetical context and thus believes it? And what if I knew or should have known that someone would hear my remarks and believe them? Would I have lied to that person? If the last case could stand as a lie, then indeed we would have an example of an unintended lie—a lie either through inadvertence or as a known but unintended concomitant of some other plan or project. But I would not call that a lie. The requisite intention is missing. I do not for that reason say that my conduct is blameless. It may be very wrong of me to risk damaging the reputation of another person for an insufficient reason, even though I do not do that damage by lying about the person.

This definition of lying should help to explain why one can lie otherwise than through the use of words. Surely, if a person nods assent to a proposition, this should stand as an assertion of the truth of that proposition. Under appropriate circumstances, even remaining silent may constitute an assertion, although one needs to be quite careful in defining the circumstances. If you know that your silence will be taken as assent, and you know that the other person knows that you know this, and you intend your silence to be so understood, then your silence can be a lie. If all the conditions are met except the last, that is, if you know all of these things but remain silent out of indolence or indifference, then you may be responsible for the beliefs which you have engendered, but you have not lied.

Every lie is a deception, but the reverse is not true. Imagine that I leave a letter containing false accusations against somebody on my desk where I know that you will read it. Imagine, indeed, that I know you will read it because I know you are an unconscionable snoop and will read the mail on my desk even though it is clear you have no right to do so. I have intentionally deceived you into believing the truth of the allegations falsely asserted in the letter, but I have not lied to you. I have not lied to you because I have not asserted anything to you. Though I have caused a false belief in you and have done so intentionally, I have not done so by reference to the institution according to which you know and I know that you know, and you know . . . that I make assertions, inviting belief by you.

What of the case in which a person asserts something which he believes to be false though it is in fact true? This too is a lie. My account of assertion implies that the speaker believes his statement to be true. For what would be the sense of giving assurance of the truth of a statement by asserting (rather than simply uttering) it, but *not* at the same time making the subsidiary assertion that one believes the principal statement to be true? It follows that the man who says something he believes to be false, which however turns out to be true, is indeed lying and not just attempting to lie. For instance, a government official might state that one of our citizens has been arrested and ill-treated in some foreign nation. He might make this statement to justify a policy hostile to that foreign country. The official has no information and does not believe that this arrest has taken place. Unknown to him, however, there has been such an arrest. I would say that this official has lied. He has not lied about the fact of the arrest, since he has made a true statement. He has, however, surely lied about the state of his beliefs, and the public who heard this statement, if they later discover that it was made with a belief that it was false, would rightly feel deceived.

Finally, an assertion need not be believed to be a lie. A lie may be disbelieved because the hearer has contrary information, but even though he does not believe the truth of the speaker's statement, he may still believe in the speaker's sincerity. Thus in the example I have just given, if a particular hearer had independent grounds for knowing there had been no arrests, his judgment of the speaker and the speaker's purposes would reasonably depend on whether he, nevertheless, believed the speaker to have been sincere though mistaken. The truly marginal case—perhaps we might call this an attempted lie—is the case in which the hearer not only does not believe what he is being told, but does not even believe that the speaker believes it.

Summarizing, then: A lie is an assertion believed by the speaker to be false. The complexity of the concept of lying is captured by the concept of assertion. Assertion is a paradigmatically intentional concept. Indeed, one might call a lie a perverse assertion. I now consider why lying is not just bad but wrong.

THE EVIL OF LYING

The evil of lying is as hard to pin down as it is strongly felt. Is lying wrong or is it merely something bad? If it is bad, why is it bad—is it bad in itself or because of some tendency associated with it? Compare lying to physical harm. Harm is a state of the world and so it can only be classified as bad; the wrong I argued for was the *intentional doing* of harm. Lying, on the other hand, can be wrong, since it is an action. But the fact that lying is an action does not mean that it *must* be wrong rather than bad. It might be that the action of lying should be judged as just another state of the world—a time-extended state, to be sure, but there is no problem about that—and as such it would count as a negative element in any set of circumstances in which it occurred. Furthermore, if lying is judged to be bad it can be bad in itself, like something ugly or painful, or it can be bad only because of its tendency to produce results that are bad in themselves.

If lying were bad, not wrong, this would mean only that, other things being equal, we should avoid lies. And if lying were bad not in itself but merely because of its tendencies, we would have to avoid lies only when those tendencies were in fact likely to be realized. In either case lying would be permissible to produce a net benefit, including the prevention of more or worse lies. By contrast the categorical norm "Do not lie" does not evaluate states of affairs but is addressed to moral agents, forbidding lies. Now if lying is wrong it is also bad in itself, for the category of the intrinsically bad is weaker and more inclusive than the category of the wrong. And accordingly, many states of the world are intrinsically bad (such as destruction of valuable property) but intentional acts bringing them about are not necessarily wrong.

Bentham plainly believed that lying is neither wrong nor even intrinsically bad: "Falsehood, take it by itself, consider it as not being accompanied by any other material circumstances, nor therefore productive of any material effects, can never, upon the principle of utility, constitute any offense at all" (*An Introduction to the Principles of Morals and Legislation,* ch. 16, sec. 24). By contrast, Kant and Augustine argued at length that lying is wrong. Indeed, they held that lying is not only wrong *unless* excused or justified in defined ways (which is my view) but that lying is always wrong. Augustine sees lying as a kind of defilement, the liar being tainted by the lie, quite apart from any consequences of the lie. Kant's views are more complex. He argues at one point that lying undermines confidence and trust among men generally: "Although by making a false statement I do no wrong to him who unjustly compels me to speak, yet I do wrong to men in general . . . I cause that declarations in general find no credit, and hence all rights founded on contract should lose their force; and this is a wrong to mankind" ("On a Supposed Right to Tell Lies from Benevolent Motives," in *Kant's Critique of Practical Reason and Other Works,* translated by T. K. Abbott [London: Longmans, Green, 1973]). This would seem to be a consequentialist argument, according to which lying is bad only insofar as it produces these bad results. But elsewhere he makes plain that he believes these bad consequences to be necessarily, perhaps even conceptually linked to lying. In this more rigoristic vein, he asserts that lying is a perversion of one's uniquely human capacities irrespective of any consequences of the lie, and thus lying is not only intrinsically bad but wrong.*

---

* "The greatest violation of man's duty to himself merely as a moral being (to humanity in his own person) is . . . the lie. In the doctrine of Law an intentional wrong is called a lie only if it infringes on another's right. But . . . in ethics . . . every deliberate untruth deserves this harsh name. By a lie a man makes himself contemptible . . . and violates the dignity of humanity in his own person. And so, since the harm that can come to others from it is not the characteristic property of this vice (for if it were, the vice would consist only in violating one's duty to others), we do not take this harm into account here . . . By a lie man throws away and, as it were, annihilates his dignity as a man. A man [who lies] . . . has even less worth than if he were a mere thing. For a thing, as something real and given, has the property of being serviceable . . . But the man who communicates his thoughts to someone in words which yet (intentionally) contain the contrary of what he thinks on the subject has a purpose directly opposed to the natural purposiveness of the power of communicating one's thoughts and therefore renounces his personality and makes himself a mere deceptive appearance of man, not man himself.

Finally, a number of writers have taken what looks like an intermediate position: the evil of lying is indeed identified with its consequences, but the connection between lying and those consequences, while not a necessary connection, is close and persistent, and the consequences themselves are pervasive and profound. Consider this passage from a recent work by G. F. Warnock:

> I do not necessarily do you any harm at all by deed or word if I induce you to believe what is not in fact the case; I may even do you good, possibly by way, for example, of consolation or flattery. Nevertheless, though deception is not thus necessarily directly damaging it is easy to see how crucially important it is that the natural inclination to have recourse to it should be counteracted. It is, one might say, not the implanting of false beliefs that is damaging, but rather the generation of the suspicion that they may be being implanted. For this undermines trust; and, to the extent that trust is undermined, all cooperative undertakings, in which what one person can do or has reason to do is dependent on what others have done, are doing, or are going to do, must tend to break down. . . . There is no sense in my asking you for your opinion on some point, if I do not suppose that your answer will actually express your opinion (verbal communication is doubtless the most important of all our co-operative undertakings). (*The Object of Morality* [London: Methuen, 1971], p. 84.)

Warnock does not quite say that truth-telling is good in itself or that lying is wrong, yet the moral quality of truth-telling and lying is not so simply instrumental as it is, for instance, for Bentham. Rather, truth-telling seems to bear a fundamental, pervasive relation to the human enterprise, just as lying appears to be fundamentally subversive of that enterprise. What exactly is the nature of this relation? How does truth-telling bear to human goods a relation which is more than instrumental but less than necessary?

"A lie (in the ethical sense of the term), as an intentional untruth as such, need not be harmful to others in order to be pronounced reprehensible; for then it would be a violation of the rights of others . . . A lie requires a second person whom one intends to deceive, and intentionally to deceive oneself seems to contain a contradiction.

"Man as a moral being (*homo noumenon*), cannot use his natural being (*homo phaenomenon*) as a mere means (a speaking machine), as if it were not bound to its intrinsic end (the communication of thought)." (*Tugendlehre* [428–430], translated by Mary J. Gregor, *The Doctrine of Virtue*, Philadelphia: University of Pennsylvania Press, 1964.)

The very definition of lying makes plain that consequences are crucial, for lying is intentional and the intent is an intent to produce a consequence: false belief. But how can I then resist the consequentialist analysis of lying? Lying is an attempt to produce a certain effect on another, and if that effect (consequence) is not bad, how can lying be wrong? I shall have to argue, therefore, that to lie is to intend to produce an effect which always has something bad about it, an effect moreover of the special sort that it is wrong to produce it intentionally. To lay that groundwork for my argument about lying, I must consider first the moral value of truth.

Truth and Rationality A statement is true when the world is the way the statement says it is.* Utilitarians insist (as in the quotation from Bentham above) that truth, like everything else, has value just exactly as it produces value—pleasure, pain, the satisfaction or frustration of desire. And of course it is easy to show that truth (like keeping faith, not harming the innocent, respecting rights) does not always lead to the net satisfactions of desire, to the production of utility. It may *tend* to do so, but that tendency explains only why we should discriminate between occasions when truth does and when it does not have value—an old story. It is an old story, for truth—like justice, respect, and self-respect—has a value which consequentialist analyses (utilitarian or any other) do not capture. Truth, like respect, is a foundational value.

The morality of right and wrong does not count the satisfaction of desire as the overriding value. Rather, the integrity of persons, as agents and as the objects of the intentional agency of others, has priority over the attainment of the goals which agents choose to attain. I have sought to show how respect for physical integrity is related to respect for the person. The person, I argued, is not just a locus of potential pleasure and pain but an

* This definition is derived from Alfred Tarski via Donald Davidson, "Meaning and Truth," in Jay F. Rosenberg and Charles Travis, eds., *Readings in the Philosophy of Language* (Englewood Cliffs, N.J.: Prentice-Hall, 1971). See also Gottlob Frege, "The Thought: A Logical Inquiry," and Michael Dummett, "Truth," both in Peter Strawson, ed., *Philosophical Logic* (Oxford: Oxford University Press, 1967). The difficulties in arriving at a satisfactory conception of truth do not touch the moral issues that I discuss in this chapter. Indeed, I suppose that any of a large class of definitions might be substituted for the one I used in the text and my substantive argument would go through without a hitch.

entity with determinate characteristics. The person is, among other things, necessarily an incorporated, a physical, not an abstract entity. In relation to truth we touch another necessary aspect of moral personality: the capacity for judgment, and thus for choice. It is that aspect which Kant used to ground his moral theory, arguing that freedom and rationality are the basis for moral personality. John Rawls makes the same point, arguing that "moral personality and not the capacity for pleasure and pain . . . [is] the fundamental aspect of the self . . . The essential unity of the self is . . . provided by the concept of right" (*A Theory of Justice* [Cambridge, Mass.: Harvard University Press, 1971], p. 563). The concept of the self is prior to the goods which the self chooses, and these goods gather their moral significance from the fact that they have been chosen by moral beings— beings capable of understanding and acting on moral principles.

In this view freedom and rationality are complementary capacities, or aspects of the same capacity, which is moral capacity. A man is free insofar as he is able to act on a judgment because he perceives it to be correct; he is free insofar as he may be moved to action by the judgments his reason offers to him. This is the very opposite of the Humean conception of reason as the slave of the passions. There is no slavery here. The man who follows the steps of a mathematical argument to its conclusion because he judges them to be correct is free indeed. To the extent that we choose our ends we are free; and as to objectively valuable ends which we choose because we see their value, we are still free.

Now, rational judgment is true judgment, and so the moral capacity for rational choice implies the capacity to recognize the matter on which choice is to act and to recognize the kind of result our choices will produce. This applies to judgments about other selves and to judgments in which one locates himself as a person among persons, a self among selves. These judgments are not just arbitrary suppositions: *they are judged to be true of the world.* For consider what the self would be like if these judgments were not supposed to be true. Maybe one might be content to be happy in the manner of the fool of Athens who believed all the ships in the harbor to be his. But what of our perceptions of other people? Would we be content to have those whom we love and trust the mere figments of our imaginations? The foundational values of freedom and rationality imply the foundational value of truth, for the rational man is the one who judges aright, that is, truly. Truth is not the same as judgment, as rationality;

it is rather the proper subject of judgment. If we did not seek to judge truly, and if we did not believe we could judge truly, the act of judgment would not be what we know it to be at all.

Judgment and thus truth are *part* of a structure which as a whole makes up the concept of self. A person's relation to his body and the fact of being an incorporated self are another part of that structure. These two parts are related. The bodily senses provide matter for judgments of truth, and the body includes the physical organs of judgment.

The Wrong of Lying   So our capacity for judgment is foundational and truth is the proper object of that capacity, but how do we get to the badness of lying, much less its categorical wrongness? The crucial step to be supplied has to do not with the value of truth but with the evil of lying. We must show that to lie to someone is to injure him in a way that particularly touches his moral personality. From that, the passage is indeed easy to the conclusion that to inflict such injury intentionally (remember that all lying is by hypothesis intentional) is not only bad but wrong. It is this first, crucial step which is difficult. After all, a person's capacity for true judgment is not necessarily impaired by inducing in him a particular false belief. Nor would it seem that a person suffers a greater injury in respect to that capacity when he is induced to believe a falsity than when we intentionally prevent him from discovering the truth, yet only in the first case do we lie. Do we really do injury to a person's moral personality when we persuade him falsely that it rained yesterday in Bangkok—a fact in which he has no interest? And do we do him more injury than when we fail to answer his request for yesterday's football scores, in which he is mildly interested? Must we not calculate the injury by the *other* harm it does: disappointed expectations, lost property, missed opportunities, physical harm? In this view, lying would be a way of injuring a person in his various substantive interests—a way of stealing from him, hurting his feelings, perhaps poisoning him—but then the evil of lying would be purely instrumental, not wrong at all.

All truth, however irrelevant or trivial, has value, even though we may cheerfully ignore most truths, forget them, erase them as encumbrances from our memories. The value of every truth is shown just in the judgment that the only thing we must not do is falsify truth. Truths are like other people's property, which we can care nothing about but may not use for our own purposes. It is as if the truth were not ours (even truth we have discovered and which is known only to us), and so we may not exercise an unlimited dominion over it. Our relations to other people have a similar structure: we may perhaps have no duty to them, we may be free to put them out of our minds to make room for others whom we care about more, but we may not harm them. And so we may not falsify truth. But enough of metaphors—what does it mean to say that the truth is not ours?

The capacity for true judgment is the capacity to arrive at judgments which are in fact true of the world as it exists apart from our desires, our choices, our values. It is the world presented to us by true judgments—including true judgments about ourselves—which we then make the subject of our choices, our valuation. Now, if we treat the truth as our own, it must be according to desire or valuation. But for rational beings these activities are supposed to depend on truth; we are supposed to desire and choose according to the world as it is. To choose that something not be the case when it is in fact the case is very nearly self-contradictory—for choice is not *of* truth but *on the basis of* truth. To deliberate about whether to believe a truth (not whether it is indeed true—another story altogether) is like deciding whether to cheat at solitaire. All this is obvious. In fact I suppose one cannot even coherently talk about choosing to believe something one believes to be false. And this holds equally for all truths—big and little, useful, useless, and downright inconvenient. But we do and must calculate *about* (and not just *with*) truths all the time as we decide what truths to acquire, what to forget. We decide all the time not to pursue some inquiry because it is not worth it. Such calculations surely must go forward on the basis of what truths are useful, given one's plans and desires. Even when we pursue truth for its own sake, we distinguish between interesting and boring truths.

Considering what truth to acquire or retain differs, however, from deliberately acquiring false beliefs. All truths are acquired as propositions correctly (truly) corresponding to the world, and in this respect, all truths are equal. A lie, however, has the form and occupies the role of truth in that it too purports to be a proposition about the world; only the world does not correspond to it. So the choice of a lie is not like a choice among truths, for the choice of a lie is a choice to affirm as the basis for judgment a proposition which does not correspond to the world. So, when I say that truth is foundational, that truth precedes choice, what I mean is *not* that this or that truth is foundational but that judging according to the facts is foundational to judging at all. A scientist may deliberate about which subject to study and, having chosen his subject, about the data worth acquiring, but he cannot even deliberate as a scientist about whether to acquire false data. Clearly, then, there is something funny (wrong?) about lying to oneself, but how do we go from there to the proposition that it is wrong to lie to someone else? After all, much of the peculiarity about lying to oneself consists in the fact that it seems not so much bad as downright self-contradictory, logically impossible, but that does not support the judgment that it is wrong to lie to another. I cannot marry myself, but that hardly makes it wrong to marry someone else.

Let us imagine a case in which you come as close as you can to lying to yourself: You arrange some operation, some fiddling with your brain that has no effect other than to cause you to believe a proposition you know to be false and also to forget entirely the prior history of how you came to believe that proposition. It seems to me that you do indeed harm yourself in such an operation. This is because a free and rational person wishes to have a certain relation to reality: as nearly perfect as possible. He wishes to build his conception of himself and the world and his conception of the good on the basis of truth. Now if he affirms that the truth is available for fiddling in order to accommodate either his picture of the world or his conception of the good, then this affirms that reality is dependent on what one wants, rather than what one wants being fundamentally constrained by what there is. Rationality is the respect for this fundamental constraint of truth. This is just another way of saying that the truth is prior to our plans and prospects and must be respected whatever our plans might be. What if the truth we "destroy" by this operation is a very trivial and irrelevant truth—the state of the weather in Bangkok on some particular day? There is still an injury to self, because the fiddler must have some purpose in his fiddling. If it is a substantive purpose, then the truth is in fact relevant to that purpose, and my argument holds. If it is just to show it can be done, then he is only trying to show he can do violence to his rationality—a kind of moral blasphemy. Well, what if it is a very *little* truth? Why, then, it is a very little injury he does himself—but that does not undermine my point.*

---

* Distinguish from this the frequent and important instances where one refuses to receive certain truths: the man of honor who will not read scandalous accusations about another's private life, the judge who will not

Now, when I lie to you, I do to you what you cannot actually do to yourself—brain-fiddling being only an approximation. The nature of the injury I would do to myself, if I could, explains why lying to you is to do you harm, indeed why it is wrong. The lie is an injury because it produces an effect (or seeks to) which a person as a moral agent should not wish to have produced in him, and thus it is as much an injury as any other effect which a moral agent would not wish to have produced upon his person. To be sure, some people may want to be lied to. That is a special problem; they are like people who want to suffer (not just are willing to risk) physical injury. In general, then, I do not want you to lie to me in the same way that as a rational man I would not lie to myself if I could. But why does this make lying wrong and not merely bad?*

Lying is wrong because when I lie I set up a relation which is essentially exploitative. It violates the principle of respect, for I must affirm that the mind of another person is available to me in a way in which I cannot agree my mind would be available to him—for if I do so agree, then I would not expect my lie to be believed. When I lie, I am like a counterfeiter: I do not want the market flooded with counterfeit currency; I do not want to get back my own counterfeit bill. Moreover, in lying to you, I affirm such an unfairly unilateral principle in respect to an interest and capacity which is crucial, as crucial as physical integrity: your freedom and your rationality. When I do intentional physical harm, I say that your body, your person, is available for my purposes. When I lie, I lay claim to your mind.

Lying violates respect and is wrong, as is any breach of trust. Every lie is a broken promise, and the only reason this seems strained is that in lying the promise is made and broken at the same moment. Every lie necessarily implies—as does every assertion—an assurance, a warranty of its truth. The fact that the breach accompanies the making should, however, only strengthen

receive unauthorized information about a matter before him. These do not involve deliberate espousals of falsity. There is, after all, a proper domain of secret, private truths and of things which are none of our business.

* It may be the case that every instance of any intentional injury to another person constitutes a wrongful relation (is wrong), but I am not prepared to argue that. I would rather examine the circumstances of this one kind of injury, lying, and show how that is wrong. In Part II, I shall argue that every intentional violation of a right is wrong, but to make use of that proposition requires a theory of rights, which is not yet in hand.

the conclusion that this is wrong. If promise-breaking is wrong, then a lie must be wrong, since there cannot be the supervening factor of changed circumstances which may excuse breaches of promises to perform in the future.

The final one of the convergent strands that make up the wrong of lying is the shared, communal nature of language. This is what I think Kant had in mind when he argued that a lie does wrong "to men in general." If whether people stood behind their statements depended wholly on the particular circumstances of the utterance, then the whole point of communication would be undermined. For every utterance would simply be the occasion for an analysis of the total circumstances (speaker's and hearer's) in order to determine what, if anything, to make of the utterance. And though we do often wonder and calculate whether a person is telling the truth, we do so from a baseline, a presumption that people do stand behind their statements. After all, the speaker surely depends on such a baseline. He wants us to think that he is telling the truth. Speech is a paradigm of communication, and all human relations are based on some form of communication. Our very ability to think, to conceptualize, is related to speech. Speech allows the social to penetrate the intimately personal. Perhaps that is why Kant's dicta seem to vacillate between two positions: lying as a social offense, and lying as an offense against oneself; the requirement of an intent to deceive another, and the insistence that the essence of the wrong is not injury to another but to humanity. Every lie violates the basic commitment to truth which stands behind the social fact of language.

I have already argued that bodily integrity bears a necessary relation to moral integrity, so that an attack upon bodily integrity is wrong, not just bad. The intimate *and* social nature of truth make the argument about lying stronger. For not only is the target aspect of the victim crucial to him as a moral agent but, by lying, we attack that target by a means which itself offends his moral nature; the means of attack are social means which can be said to belong as much to the victim as to his assailant. There is not only the attack at his moral vitals, but an attack with a weapon which belongs to him. Lying is, thus, a kind of treachery. (*Kind of* treachery? Why not treachery pure and simple?) It is as if we not only robbed a man of his treasure but in doing so used his own servants or family as our agents. That speech is our *common* property, that it belongs to the liar, his victim and all of us makes the matter if anything far worse.

So this is why lying is not only bad (a hurt), but wrong, why lying is wrong apart from or in addition to any other injury it does, and why lying seems at once an offense against the victim and against mankind in general, an offense against the liar himself, and against the abstract entity, truth. Whom do you injure when you pass a counterfeit bill?

What about little pointless lies? Do I really mean they are wrong? Well, yes, even a little lie is wrong, *if* it is a true piece of communication, an assertion of its own truth and not just a conventional way of asserting nothing at all or something else (as in the case of polite or diplomatic formulas). A little lie is a little wrong, but it is still something you must not do.

Justified Lies

I have argued from the nature of lying to the values of truth and back to the proposition that lying is wrong. It is important to be quite clear what the second leg of my journey was: *Lying* is wrong. I have not argued for an obligation to further or promote the truth. To urge such an obligation, to urge that it is wrong to fail to pursue and to promote truth wherever possible, would be absurd in ways that I have sufficiently indicated. My previous argument certainly does show that promoting truth is *good,* other things being equal, but the value of truth must be balanced against all other goods and bads with which it competes. Its weight as truth may at times be very light. Accordingly, both Augustine and Kant, though they conclude that it is wrong to lie even to save an innocent victim from his would-be killer, urge that every possible device short of lying be used to conceal the truth in that case.*

In his essay "On a Supposed Right to Tell Lies from Benevolent Motives," Kant hurls thunderbolts of moral indignation at the following argument by Benjamin Constant:

> The moral principle that it is one's duty to speak the truth, if it were taken singly and unconditionally, would make all society impossible. We have the proof of this in the very direct consequences which have been drawn from this principle by a German

---

* Withholding truth may be our chosen means of doing injury. Imagine that I have placed arsenic in the sugar bowl. Obviously it is part of my plan that my victim remain ignorant of this substitution. Or I may just know that the sugar bowl has come to contain poison (not through my doing at all), and because I wish the sugar-user to die, I withhold the warning (information) for that very reason. I act wrongly in these cases, but not particularly because of my relation to the truth. The wrong I do, I do because of the harm.

philosopher, who goes so far as to affirm that to tell a falsehood to a murderer who asked us whether our friend, of whom he was in pursuit, had not taken refuge in our house, would be a crime.

It is a duty to tell the truth. The notion of duty is inseparable from the notion of right. A duty is what in one being corresponds to the right of another. Where there are no rights there are no duties. To tell the truth then is a duty, but only towards him who has a right to the truth. But no man has a right to a truth that injures others.

Kant readily acknowledges that he is the German philosopher whom Constant has in mind and in the passage quoted earlier in this chapter undertakes to refute Constant's proposal. Augustine refers to exactly the same case in his treatise *De mendacio*. Having argued that God destroys all who tell lies, he asks:

> If this truth be granted, who of those who assent will be shaken by such argument as are given by those who say: "What if a man should flee to you, who by your lie can be saved from death?" . . . In very truth, some are indignant and angry if someone is unwilling to lose his soul by telling a lie so that another may grow a little older in the flesh. Would these people say that we should submit to theft or adultery, if someone could be freed from death by our theft or adultery? Such persons do not realize they compel themselves to admit that in order, as they say, to save a life, one must yield to the sinful advances of a man who brings a rope and threatens suicide if his desire is not granted. If this proposition is absurd and wicked, why should anyone defile his soul with a lie so that another person may live corporeally, since if, for that same purpose, he would give the body to be defiled, he would be convicted of base wickedness by the judgment of all. (*De mendacio,* chs. 6, 13, in *Treatises on Various Subjects,* Fathers of the Church, vol. 16, ed. Ray J. De Ferreri [New York: Fathers of the Church, 1952], pp. 67–68, 83–84.)

Augustine considers this case several times in his treatise and always comes back to the conclusion that, even for such an urgent motive and to a wicked auditor, a lie may not be told. And though his reasoning is laced with quotations from Scripture, secular versions may be given of two crucial arguments alluded to in the passage I quote. First, the frequent references to lying as defilement might fairly be given the following interpretation: If lying is (absolutely) wrong, then to treat lying as something which is simply bad, undesirable, but to be traded off to procure other goods, to avoid worse harms, is to pursue good ends by impermissible means. To use a Kantian formulation, the violation of the categorical imperative is inestimably worse than any harm one may fend off by such a violation, since the categorical imperative and our obligation under it are what found our moral nature. Any violation for a mere contingent good trades what gives us moral status at all for something which has moral status only insofar as it is attributable to a moral being. This, then, is the Kantian version of the notion of gaining the whole world but losing one's soul. Second, there is a very sophisticated perception that allowing a justification for lies in such a case would admit a principle by which wrongdoers could get us to do anything at all simply by threatening to do a marginally worse thing. But if the blackmailer knows you adhere to a moral principle categorically forbidding certain things, the blackmailer will know in advance that certain threats will not work. This in turn would deprive wrongdoers of an important range of facilities for accomplishing their purposes.

These two arguments engender a third, which also appears throughout Augustine's essay on lying: that we are responsible for the wrongs we do ourselves and not for those which by our wrong we fail to prevent others from committing. This argument is necessary, as we have seen, to maintain the distinction between the wrong and the bad. The category of the wrong speaks in the first or second person, but not in the third person: it tells me what I must not do, and I violate it just by doing the forbidden thing. But though the norm is universal in its application, a violation by another person is not a wrong except in relation to that other person. In relation to me it is bad, so that my lying to prevent a wrong by another is a case of my doing wrong in order to prevent something which *from my point of view* is a bad. To be sure, what the other will do *is* wrong, but it is *his* wrong.

The question remains whether the case of the liar and the would-be assassin is a valid instance of these formally correct arguments. I am extremely uncomfortable with Augustine's and Kant's rigoristic conclusions in this case. There may be something heroic about the man who will not lie, but follows Augustine's advice:

> If, however, you do know where he is, whether he is actually where he is being sought or elsewhere, when you are asked whether he is there or not, you must say: "I know where he is but I will never disclose it." For if you do not answer in regard to one place and say that you will not betray him, it is as though you are indicating that place with your finger, since a definite suspicion

is aroused. If, however, you acknowledge at the very outset that you know where he is but you are not going to tell, then it is possible that the investigator will turn his attention from that place to you, in an effort to induce you to betray where he is. Whatever you suffer for this act of fidelity and kindness, then, is not only judged as unmerited but even as praiseworthy. (*De mendacio,* ch. 13.)

But surely such heroism is not morally required. The failure to follow this path is not wrong. Any conclusion as harsh as Augustine's and Kant's cannot be accepted without a struggle. A struggle is necessary in the context of my argument, since I have already concluded that lying is not merely bad but wrong.

The most promising approach is indeed the one proposed by Constant, when he argued that the would-be assassin has no right to the truth. Kant responds that Constant misses the absoluteness of the stricture, misses the defilement (as Augustine might put it). I agree with Kant insofar as he says that there is a wrong in lying over and above any wrong (or injury) one does *by* lying. Kant and Augustine go too far because they do not conceive of lying as an essentially relational wrong. As for the defilement, it seems equally in order to speak the language of defilement whenever one does wrong, as for instance when one hurts an *unoffending* person—and there the relational character of the wrong is quite clear.

The way out of the dilemma, then, runs through the relational character of lying. What would you say, first, of this admittedly trivial case: You and I agree that over a defined period of time, or within a limited context (when we are playing poker, for instance) we will feel free to lie to each other. Surely the statements we make to each other pursuant to this agreement are lies only in a rather special sense, if at all. They are communications which quite explicitly do not carry with them the assurance of their truth. Our communications within the context of the agreement do not invoke the general social institution of truth-telling, and thus I see no reason why what is said in this context, if untrue, should be condemned as wrong. Nor are we engaged in a kind of mutual self-deception such as I condemned in the example of brain-fiddling, since we are not creating a situation where each binds himself to accept as true a statement by the other which the other believes false. On the contrary, we explicitly recognize that the *statements* are *not* to be taken as assertions of truth. Rather, the statements are like moves in a game, which people should be entitled to play. And so we do no wrong in "lying" in the context of such an agreement, at least so long as the agreement is sufficiently limited as not to overturn or even threaten to overturn the general institution of truth-telling between us or between other persons.*

Now let us consider in schematic form what is involved in the case of the person who lies to protect a victim from a would-be assassin. (a) The assassin asks a question which it is in the liar's (or his friend's) interest not to answer. (b) Moreover, the liar knows the assassin does not have a right to the answer, since the assassin would use the information to commit a wrong and there is no general right to information as such. (c) The assassin knows that the liar knows that he (the assassin) has no right to the answer. And finally, (d) the liar cannot (because of the structure of the colloquy, or whatever) not answer, and this too is known to both parties. Propositions (b) and (d) are crucial. It is right to lie here, because it is right that the assassin be prevented from getting something from the liar to which he is not entitled. The assassin is seeking to force (morally force) his interlocutor to give him something (the truth) to which the assassin is not entitled; or more precisely, he is attempting to force the liar to assist him in what both of them know and each of them knows the other to know is a wrong. But if the liar lies in this circumstance, is he not at least as free from blame as any member of the liar's club? In the liar's club, when A "lies" to B, B knows that he may not expect the truth from A, and A knows that B knows, and B knows that A knows that . . . If this is sufficient to take the case out of the general prohibition against lying, is not the liar in our schematized case of the assassin a fortiori also free of blame?

Now there are several related objections to be made to this argument justifying the liar. First, is my argument not inconsistent with the proposition that a wrong cannot be justified just because it would prevent a wrong of an equal or greater degree by another person? But that objection begs the question by assuming the lie to the assassin is wrong. Lying to the assassin

---

* Note that my use of a consequentialist argument regarding the possible ill effects of such an agreement does not contradict the general nonconsequentialist nature of my argument. Specifically, my argument is that there is a moral right (nonconsequentialist) to enter into lying clubs, so long as these clubs do not have the consequence of undermining the institution of truth-telling. On the other hand, lying outside of a lying club is morally wrong because of its inconsistency (nonconsequentialist) with the institution of truth-telling.

is not like intentionally injuring one innocent person (say, cutting off his arm) in order to protect another innocent person against some greater harm (the loss of both arms). For, in the case of the liar and the assassin, the lie is told *to the assassin,* to the would-be perpetrator of the greater wrong. Indeed, the justification here follows a fortiori from the analogous justification of intentionally harming an assailant in self-defense or defense of others, since it is questionable whether the untruth here is even always a lie. But when I shoot my assailant in self-defense there is no doubt that I have shot him.

Second, there is the objection implicit in Kant's argument that when one lies (even in a case such as this) the harm is in no way done to the would-be assassin but to humanity in general and specifically to the institution of contracts. This institutional argument against lying to the assassin begs the question. It is only if the sanctity of the institution of truth-telling is taken to extend to cases like the assassin's that a moral right to lie to the assassin would wrongly imperil that institution. But I have presented an argument why the institution need not, indeed should not, be so extended. My argument, far from depending on some exploitation of the assassin by the liar, builds on the reciprocal appreciation that the assassin has no right to the truth which he seeks. Though the Kantian might go on to support his rigoristic strictures by arguing that such an exception is liable to abuse, that it introduces a dangerous laxness into conduct, that potential liars will unconsciously see in it a self-deluding and self-regarding encouragement to their mendacity, this is a tack which the Kantian can take only at the cost of abandoning the nonconsequentialist interpretation of his original position. For arguments about abuse and self-delusion might relevantly be urged by the *consequentialist*. The Kantian is at most entitled to ask what the consequences would be if moral agents, acting in good faith, took the maxim being proposed by the agent for his own actions as the general definition of their moral duties. And when the argument switches into that mode, there is simply no room for the proposition that though an exception may be correct in principle, it cannot be admitted because the morally infirm will abuse it. One might as well argue against a right of self-defense on the same grounds.*

* This response to Kantian rigorism about lying is in fact a version of a parallel problem in Kant's *Rechtslehre*. In that work Kant builds up an obligation to obey the law from principles of moral autonomy and natural

Finally, there is the objection that this line of argument may prove too much. If, for instance, it is argued that no one has a right to the truth when his having that truth would be on balance worse, then it would follow that one might lie whenever on balance it seemed better to do so. Thus any assertedly categorical argument against lying would collapse into consequentialism after all. Consider this case:

> XIII. The prosecutor asks the public defender, whose client has just been found guilty, whether the client was in fact innocent, for in that event the prosecutor would press for a lenient sentence. If the defender believes his client is guilty, to reveal that belief would be a breach of duty to the client. To say nothing, to evade, or to protest would be taken as the equivalent of admitting a belief in the client's guilt.

Does the prosecutor have the right to the truth in this case? May the defense attorney lie? Unlike the assassin, the prosecutor will not make wrongful use of the information. (To recommend leniency on his best judgment of the case is part of the prosecutor's job.) But still we can say he has no right to the information. He knows that he has put the defense attorney into the dilemma of choosing between a lie and the breach of fiduciary obligation. As a matter of professional ethics the prosecutor's question is improper. It is as if he were seeking to steal the information by breaking into the defender's files. He has no right to the truth for that reason and a lie is justified. Contrast this case:

> XIV. It is not the assassin but the assassin's honorable mother who asks about the intended victim's whereabouts. Though she would be horrified to think she had assisted a killing, you have reason to believe that the assassin can cleverly worm the information out of his unsuspecting mother.

---

right, and then comes to the extraordinary conclusion that these starting points require an absolute and exceptionless obligation to the law, even the law of a tyrant, irrespective of whether that law infringes in some particularly important way upon natural rights. Kant comes to this repellent conclusion in much the same way that he comes to his rigoristic conclusion in the case of the assassin: he is unwilling to allow an individual moral agent the occasion to consider and apply to his own conduct some qualifying or excusing condition upon the general rule. He is unwilling to allow it because of the possibilities of abuse, but he fails to see that by relying on an argument based on the dangers of abuse he switches the whole basis of his argument from the moral and nonconsequentialist to the causal.

If the lie is authorized, we are getting closer here to a pure consequentialist theory. The mother would neither knowingly abuse the information (as would the assassin) nor does she try to get the information by means she knows are wrong (like the prosecutor). We may assume that if she knew of her son's plans she would not wish to possess the information. The case is analogous to that of the emergency use of another's property when there is no time to get permission. And, as in that case, perhaps you should make up for the imposition as soon after-wards as possible with a full explanation. But what if she lets you know she really does want the truth regardless of the risks? We must ask why she insists on having the information. Does not her insistence make her an accomplice after all? What if she foolishly believes she can keep the secret or talk her son out of the murder? Well, your best judgment may be that this is foolish and that she *should* want to be kept in the dark. Is that case like this one?

XV. A chief of state believes that his nation's strategic position depends on going to war with a certain foreign country. He also believes that the citizens and their repre-sentatives would not support a declaration of war, though he believes they *should*. So he creates an incident provoking an attack by the foreign power, lies about it, and thus procures the declaration of war.

The difference between the two cases is that in the case of the mother she would for no sufficient reason be assisting a wrongful venture—perhaps unwillingly—but she has no right to do that. So you do her no wrong if you prevent her from doing what she should want to have no part of. The citizens and their represen-tatives, by contrast, have a right (a constitutional right, it may be) to declare war or not. The lie impedes that exercise of right. The mother is not like an innocent hostage whom you harm on orders of a wrongful aggressor to protect other innocents from greater harm. Rather, she herself would be the (unwilling) agent of harm. Perhaps we might say of her what we said of E (the falling body) in case VII in Chapter 2.*

* A possible objection: Does not my argument come down to saying that it is permissible to lie to the mother because in the case hypothesized she should want to be lied to, she should want to be deceived? She is like a secret agent who wants to have false information so that when he reveals it under drugs or torture to the enemy the enemy will be fooled or at least will not have learned the truth. But if that is the tendency of my argument, why

These cases may now be generalized. In XIII and XIV but not in XV the person lied to has himself initiated the encounter by asking a question or otherwise intentionally trying to get the speaker to reveal his mind. Moreover, the difficulty in all cases except XV arises because the questioner asks in a situation in which for one reason or another it is not possible to withhold an answer—that is, even a failure to respond will be taken as an answer. Now, I may have a duty not to reveal a certain fact, as where revealing the fact might lead to great harm or where I have promised to keep it secret; and in other situations I have a right to keep a fact secret or private. Where another initiates an encounter (as by asking a question) intended to *force* such a fact out of me, and thus to force me to do wrong or to yield a right to him against my will, it is he, not I, who abuses the mutual institution of truth-telling. And where the questioner is subjectively innocent (he does not know that my telling him the truth would be a breach of duty or the relinquishment of a right) I am entitled to treat him as a moral man, that is, I am entitled to presume that if he would want to place me in that situation regardless, then *ipso facto* he is not innocent. Now all such cases contrast with those in which it is I who initiate the encounter, proposing the lie. This is case XV. Here the lie is like an attack on an innocent person. I seek the hearer's confidence and then abuse it; I seek his confidence in order to abuse it. In cases XIII and XIV I have not sought the questioner's confidence, but

---

does it not contradict my earlier conclusion that it is irrational to want to be lied to? I have been careful to say that what the mother should want is not to be deceived, but rather not to have the truth. For there is indeed a contradiction about wanting to be deceived about a particular piece of information. There is no contradiction at all about someone saying, "Don't tell me about *that!*" Now, in lying to the well-intentioned but garrulous mother you are seeking to comply in the only way possible with her presumed wish not to have the information. There is no need to presume a wish on her part to be deceived. You are, to be sure, complying with that wish by lying to her. It is the only way it can be done. And it is lying in order to withhold the truth that I say is justified in this case—not lying in order to deceive. The fact that one must lie in order to conceal the truth is due to a defect in the mother, who would not want to assist her assassin son but cannot help herself. That is why she is like the person who in falling would crush an innocent person in the street below: either we take that person seriously as a willing agent, and then we can defend against him, *or* we can treat him as *pro tanto* an impersonal force, which we can fend off. In the mother's case it would be like "lying" to a misprogrammed computer.

respond to an unjustified assault upon my right or duty to remain silent.

The notion of non-innocence is not to be interpreted so widely that this argument collapses once again into a purely consequentialist one. Specifically, I do not mean that any person is non-innocent (in the sense that lying to him is justified) whenever lying to him would lead to a net increase in utility. Rather, his non-innocence is established by the encounter in which the issue of lying to him is raised: he is non-innocent in that he provokes my lie by leaving me no choice but to lie or to yield a right, violate a duty. He is not non-innocent because he is a bad man generally, or because he has committed many unpunished wrongs and plans even more. The same point holds in respect to defensive force against physical harm—to oneself or to others: I cannot claim justified defense if I harm a man just because he is a bad man in general, because he has done wrong in the past, or even because he is likely to do wrong in the future. Another's person does not become generally available to me for my purposes, even my beneficent purposes, just because he is a bad man in general or because he has evil purposes. So also I may not lie to a bad man any more than to a good, and the justification for lying I have proposed does not depend on innocence in general at all, as case XIV shows, but innocence relative to the encounter. And if I may not lie to an evil man in general, but only to an inquirer (good or bad) who leaves me no choice between lying and breaking a duty or relinquishing a right, so of course I may not lie just because the sum of good consequences would be greater as a result of my lie.

It is reasonable to hold, then, that lying is wrong, while recognizing limitations and qualifications of that absolute stricture. As in the case of harm, the boundaries are drawn by reference to the very principles which ground the absolute norm they qualify. The exceptions I present are narrowly drawn. There may be others. I have not sought to be exhaustive but to show that one can at once argue that lying is wrong and at the same time argue that it is not always wrong. I emphasize again that in this part, I have also not sought to present an exhaustive catalogue of wrongs. Rather, harm and lying are important examples of how the concept of wrong works. Implicit in the rest of my argument is the assumption that there may be other wrongs as well.

II

Rights

4

Rights—The Economic Analysis

RIGHTS

RIGHTS AS *Absolutes* Rights are a different way of look-
ing at the moral absolutes discussed in Part I. Rights consider the same moral phenomena from the point of view
of the victim. It is wrong to harm an innocent person or to lie to
someone, and this leads us to say that an innocent person has a
right not to suffer intentional harm, not to be lied to. But rights
are not merely the obverse of what we most naturally think of as
wrongs. There are property rights, rights to a jury trial, the right
to freedom of speech, the right to vote. In respect to these entities,
it is their aspect as rights which comes to mind first, and the wrong
of violating these rights presents itself as the secondary or correlative concept. But whether the right or the wrong seems primary,
the way in which the entity operates in a moral argument is the
same. A claim of right blocks the appeal to consequences in
justifying violations of a right, just as such an appeal is blocked
in the case of wrongs. And in general, it is wrong to violate a
right. The reason for having two concepts is that it is more
natural and informative in some cases to emphasize the
"victim's" side of the relation—as in the right to vote, or the
right to freedom of speech—while in others it is the violator's
conduct which is more salient, as in lying or harming. In the
latter instances, it is simpler just to designate the act as wrong.
To speak of a right not to be harmed (or, more pompously, a
right to physical integrity) or a right not to be lied to is at best
awkward, and at worst invites confusion about such matters as
the kind of intentionality involved in the harming. Since the
crucial inquiry will be into the contents, boundaries and limita-

81

tions of the moral entity, that aspect—as a wrong or right—will be chosen which is most likely to illuminate the inquiry.

Now, it is a commonplace that some rights are rights only against certain categories of persons, and this is a notion which can be perfectly well accommodated in the general framework I have been offering. To take an example I shall recur to often, the right to freedom of speech is a right against governmental (and certain other) actors only, not against all persons generally. The government may not take action for the purpose of silencing my expressions of opinion, but a newspaper or publisher can perfectly well refuse to print my views for precisely this reason. On the other hand, my right to physical integrity extends pretty much to all actors. (It may be that those "rights" like physical integrity which are best developed as wrongs are just those rights which one has against all men in general.) A further distinction is that between positive rights and negative rights. Positive rights are rights *to* something and include such things as a claim under a contract or a minor child's claim to support by his parents. A negative right is a right *not* to be treated in certain ways, a right not to be the object of certain actions, wrongful actions.

Rights and Intention   These conjugations of the concepts of right and wrong and of positive and negative rights articulate with the claims of Part I regarding the intentionality of wrong. If I have a right that you do not harm me physically, you wrong me in respect to that right only if you harm me intentionally. On the other hand, positive rights present the problem of intentional omissions generally. If you owe me a sum of money so that I have a right to be paid, do I not have a right that you make a positive effort to get the money to me? But how strenuous must that effort be? To be sure, you must not intentionally avoid payment, but is that all? This seems too weak, just as it may seem too weak to say that my right to physical integrity or to the security of my property entails no more than that you should not intentionally invade these rights, while leaving you free to take risks, perhaps very large risks, of injuring me or my property. These are serious doubts, but in the end they support the soundness of the categories I have offered. For if my right against you to the security of my property means that you do me wrong if you take even a chance of damaging that property in the pursuit of some other end, then that right is too intrusive, potentially barring you from the pursuit of any goals—since everything carries some minuscule risk of producing the untoward result.

More plausibly my right imports a categorical prohibition on your making its violation your end or means, but as to unintended though foreseen infringements the degree of protection will vary with the right.* It is likely that the fact that a right is invoked will require a greater degree of justification for foreseeable but unintended impositions than when a mere interest is endangered. And one might express this by saying that one has a right—a positive right—that a certain measure of care be taken not to infringe right-protected interests.

Rights as Moral Privileges Finally, the concept of right has an affirmative, power-conferring aspect which also relates to the forms of judgment discussed in Part I: A person exercising a right may to some extent be dispensed from weighing the unintended consequences of his actions so long as what he does intend is the pursuit of a right. I want to do something. It is not wrong, but it has (bad) unfortunate concomitants. Do I have to weigh these, and forbear if the balance is unfavorable? Usually yes, *unless I have a right to do whatever it is I am doing.* If I have a right to marry whom I want (who wants to marry me), then this

---

* In the case of freedom of speech, the government is not foreclosed from putting the media under general regimes such as the tax, antitrust, or labor laws, even though such regimes have an effect on expression. In such cases it might be said that the regulation is not of speech but of the business enterprise which does the speaking, and any effect on speech is a side effect of this business-regulatory purpose. A more serious difficulty arises when the regulation of speech is the very means of accomplishing some other purpose, as in efforts to limit noise by banning or limiting the use of sound trucks or to control littering by limiting pamphleteering. Constitutional law has evolved a number of conceptual devices for dealing with such cases, including the balancing test and least restrictive alternative test. Both of these fall short of recognizing the right as absolute; rather, they are devices for giving the interest very great weight at best. Perhaps, however, an absolute right might be discerned after all—a negative right not to have the *contents* of one's speech limited—and this absolute right operates like other absolute rights. It has boundaries, and the function of casuistry is to fix those boundaries, rather than to determine the weight of the interest. Thus the concepts of fraud, obscenity, and defamation may be viewed as sketching out such boundaries in much the same way that self-defense or consent sketches the boundaries of the wrong of harming another. In this view, what the courts treat as the right is at once wider but less categorical than the right I suggest. Perhaps the right protected in law is so conceived in order to erect a non-categorical buffer zone around the inviolate kernel of the right. That kernel expresses a central aspect of respect for the intellectual integrity of the person. The broader but more porous concept in law also protects wider but vaguer notions related to the integrity of the political process.

just means I do not have to consider how our happiness compares to the unhappiness our marriage will cause my rivals or hers, our parents, the neighbors. Do we not readily discern this form of argument behind the rejection of the claims of outraged neighbors and puritanical strangers not to be upset by unorthodox sexual behavior? They may be pained and upset, truly, and the pleasures on any particular occasion may be quite slight—maybe no pleasure at all—but that is not the point. Sometimes it is said that the neighbors have no right to be hurt and so no right to complain. But people just are upset or pained, and it seems odd to speak of a right to be hurt or not. The right is the right of people to choose whatever forms of sexual activity they please, and not a right of people to be upset about it or not.

The basic notions of positive and negative rights combine to yield this secondary manifestation of a right as a privilege. Roughly, the privileged status of certain exercises of rights is a function of the logically prior judgment that intentional interference with the exercise of the privilege—even after calculation of the balance of advantage—would be wrong.

Rights and Interests I am aware that in one familiar terminological system I would be accused of confounding what are called rights, privileges, and powers. I do not adopt that terminology, since I am interested in all moral entities which set certain interests of persons apart and mark them for special treatment, a treatment other than that which would be accorded those interests if they were simply taken into account in a consequentialist balance aimed at accomplishing the greatest good. If the intentional violation of a particular interest is absolutely wrong, then obviously something very special is going on and I would say this interest has been designated a negative right. If a certain interest must be served, no matter what, or if a certain level of effort must be made to serve that interest, then that interest is a positive (or claim) right. And if an actor is permitted to disregard entirely or to a limited extent some or all of the bad side effects in his pursuit of a particular interest, then too I say he has a right to pursue that interest.

I put these types of cases together because they share one important characteristic: they accord a special significance to the interests they designate, so that those interests enter into moral arguments other than just as consequences in the world to be weighed along with other consequences. Rights enter into moral arguments in more complex ways, which both formally and in terms of their contents show their relation to the categorical wrongs of which they are the correlatives.

Yet it is the case that rights are *also* interests, or at least they protect or express interests. Indeed, in consequentialist analyses rights appear only as interests, more specifically as those interests which in a particular or general striking of the balance have ended up as carrying the day over competing interests. In the system I propose, rights have a prior status. When a person asserts a right he is doing more than announcing an interest to be taken into account. After all, every interest must at least be taken into account. And since an interest is a potential pleasure or pain, the utilitarian must always consider it, just as a business-man must consider any potential revenue or cost. The assertion of a right is categorical. Thus a right is not the same as an interest, though there is an interest behind every right. In general, one asserts an interest when one proposes that a particular action or decision would indeed be beneficial to oneself. One says, "Here is some good that your decision can do, so please do this for me." Or one says, "Since you are seeking to maximize utility, here is some good which your decision might do which you should weigh along with all the other possibilities, as you decide what the best thing to do overall might be." A claim of right, however, is peremptory. It says that because I have this right you must do (or forbear doing) this thing irrespective of whether recognizing my right would maximize the sum of advantages. It is this logical feature of the concept of rights which explains why rights are said to be so important in establishing our moral status vis-à-vis others, for rights state what we can (morally at least) expect from others. To the extent that we make a claim grounded upon the inclination of the grantor or dependent on the utilitarian sum of advantages, we make the claim to a moral notion which is in no way committed to granting it. The value within that notion is the maximization value. When we make a claim of right, however, we make that claim not to and on behalf of some general moral notion to which that claim is understood to be subordinate, but on our own behalf. Rights are peculiarly personal.

In the balance of this chapter, I present and criticize the economic analysis of rights. This is a recent, sophisticated elaboration of utilitarian thinking, promising detailed conclusions on specific questions of rights. Because it is so subtle, powerful, and comprehensive, no consideration of rights can ignore it. The critique of the economic analysis of rights will point the way to my own substantive theory.

THE ECONOMIC ANALYSIS OF RIGHTS

This most comprehensive recent treatment of rights began with the analysis of legal rules and rights offered by the economists Ronald Coase and Harold Demsetz. Although their work was originally formulated to account for a range of problems at the intersection of law and economics, an exposition of their views and of the implications drawn from those views will show their general applicability.

The Coase Theorem I shall start with a brief exposition of Coase's theorem, and then go on to show how this theorem has been applied and generalized to a wide variety of legal and social phenomena. I shall refer to the Coase theorem as CT, and the generalized economic analysis of rights as EAR.

Consider four cases:

I. A wheat farmer (F) and cattle rancher (C) are adjoining landowners. C's cattle are inclined to stray onto F's land, trampling and eating his wheat. If, as would be the case at common law, the owner of animals is liable for damage done by those animals when they stray onto another's land, then it would seem that F's rights are recognized in law and he is protected—if his wheat is trampled and eaten he may sue for compensation. If, on the other hand, the rule is that the owner of the animals is not liable for such damage, so that if the farmer wishes to protect his crops he must fence at his own expense (this is the rule in the Plains States of the United States), then it would seem that it is C who has broader and F who has lesser rights.

II. Homeowner (H) lives next to manufacturer (M), whose factory smokestack emits quantities of noxious soot flakes. These land on his lawn and flower beds, darken the clothes hung out on the washing line, and find their way into the house in the form of particularly unpleasant dust. It would seem that if H has a right to the "full enjoyment" of his property and M has no right to send anything, no matter how small or light, across the property line, then it will be M who must pay to put soot suppressors on his stack, or must pay H so that H can buy an electric clothes dryer and air filtration system for his home. And indeed, if H cannot only sue M for damages but can obtain an injunction against the soot deposits, and if M cannot practicably prevent the escape of soot, M may have to close down his factory, possibly relocating elsewhere. On the other hand, if M has the right to send soot into the air on his own property, irrespective of where it comes down, then it would seem that H is much worse off, has a more restricted range of rights, and it may be H who ends up moving away.

III. If a rapist (R) is held to commit a civil and criminal wrong on the person of his victim (V), then this implies that V has a right to the integrity of her person, a right to control access to her body, and R can accomplish his purpose consistently with that right only if he obtains V's consent. If, on the other hand, R is free to have his way and V must bargain with him to obtain whatever measure of security from assault she wishes, then it is R who has the rights in respect to V's body.

IV. A motorist driving in a residential district, his mind on other things, fails to notice a curve in the road and strikes an elderly gentleman strolling on the sidewalk near his house. Because of his age, the pedestrian is unable to dodge the car, and also because of his age the bone fractures heal slowly and imperfectly, leaving him a cripple in need of assistance and attendance. If the driver (D) must compensate the pedestrian (P), then P might be said to have a right to walk on the sidewalk free of the threat of injury from automobiles—or perhaps from negligently driven automobiles. If, on the other hand, P must bear the burden of his injuries himself, this entails the judgment that D has the right to drive where and how he pleases—provided only he does not choose to injure P as a means or an end.

It is the striking and counterintuitive thesis of the Coase theorem that it makes no difference in respect to the attainment of efficiency whether we accord to F the right that C's cattle not trespass on his wheat fields (with an action for damages against C if they do) or C the right to allow his cattle to stray wherever they are able to go; whether we accord H a right to an atmosphere uninvaded by M's soot or M a right to spew soot into the air wherever it may fall; whether we give V a right to the security of her person or R a right to make use of those persons he may fancy; whether we put the burden on D to drive carefully, making him liable for the consequences if he does not, or on P, who would thus have no recourse against the driver who caused his injuries. This remarkable theoretical conclusion is the product of a line of reasoning which, though it involves a number of steps and some rather special assumptions, makes its crucial move at the outset by questioning the "naturalness" of assigning responsibility or rights to any particular party in these cases.

It is, I believe, the most remarkable insight of CT that in every situation where there is a question of a definition of rights and liabilities there is no "natural" way of making the assignment: every determination of the boundary between the mutually impinging parties implies a normative judgment and therefore stands in need of justification. The naive assumption, on the contrary, holds that he who acts, he who imposes, he who disturbs the status quo, is the one who must purchase the right to do so. The person in passive possession, in the naive view, is the one whose assent must be obtained. It is thought self-evident that C, M, and R are the ones who are imposing, it is they (or in the case of C, his cattle) who are acting, while it is F, H, and V who are "just sitting there," and whose passivity should be respected.*

* Consider, for instance, this remark of E. J. Mishan: "Indeed, the virtue of the Pareto principle resides in its alleged neutrality: if A habitually amuses himself by throwing smoke bombs through B's window, but agrees to desist on payment of $25 a week, both are made better off if B chooses to pay it rather than continue to suffer these depredations . . . Thus, the fact that whether A successfully compensates B, or whether B successfully compensates A, a Pareto improvement is effected, is all too frequently believed illustrative of the cardinal virtue of an economic principle that is above and independent of the law. If the smoker's enjoyment is reduced by abstaining for the sake of the nonsmoker, each interferes with the enjoyment of the other. The conflict of interest, it is concluded, is symmetric in all relevant respects, and the determination of which of the parties ought, if possible, to compensate the other is either held to be of no interest to economists, or else may be settled by reference to the distributional implications . . . But this apparent ethical dilemma, at least, does not stand up to scrutiny. In accordance with the liberal maxim, the freedom of any man to smoke what he chooses would, indeed, be conceded—but with the crucial proviso that his smoking take place in circumstances which do not reduce the freedom of others. Insofar as it does, the freedom of the smoker is not symmetric with that desired by the nonsmoker who merely wishes to breathe unpolluted air, and, in the pursuit thereof, and unlike the smoker, does not reduce the amenity of others . . . The conflict of interest does not arise, therefore,

Though I agree with the intuitions which would tend to assign the rights to the passive party, it is the major achievement of CT to put into question this commonsense set of judgments and, by showing that they may be reversed, to force us to offer an ethical justification for them. It is worth seeing, moreover, that CT challenges us to explain not only why our land is ours, or our automobile, but why our teeth, blood, kidneys, ideas, and labor are our own. We should welcome the opportunity to clarify our intuitive, strongly held judgments and to discover an ethical content where before there seemed only to be questions of natural causation.

Now, CT concludes that who of each pair of competing actors is granted the protection of rights (or of a liability rule) is immaterial. But CT reaches this conclusion only by defining the inquiry in a special way: (1) the actors in each case are assumed to be able to bargain freely, costlessly, and effectively among themselves, and (2) all we care about is bringing about the most efficient utilization of resources. The definition of efficiency is that made familiar by neoclassical economics under the term Pareto-efficiency: an allocation of resources among competing uses is efficient if no change in that allocation may be effected which would improve the situation of any of the parties without worsening the situation of any other of them. It is obvious that if bargains can indeed be struck freely and costlessly, then the situation between the parties must inevitably come to rest when no more bargains profitable to at least one of them and harmless to the other can be proposed. And to close the argument: it can make no difference to the achievement of efficiency (so defined) whether one or the other of the parties starts out holding the rights; if a favorable deal can be made, by hypothesis, it will be. If the farmer has the rights, so that the rancher must keep in his cattle or pay compensation to the farmer, they will bargain about whether it is more advantageous for the farmer to grow less wheat or sell his land or for the rancher to limit his herd or fence

from reciprocal effects and does not imply equal culpability. The conflict arises from the damage inflicted only by one of the parties on the other. It follows that, unless the law is altered to provide comprehensive safequards for the citizen's rights to certain fundamental amenities, the range of voluntary agreements that are, or might be, entered into within the existing legal framework cannot be vindicated, at least not on ethical grounds, by reference to invisible-hand arguments." "Pareto Optimality and the Law," *Oxford Economic Papers* 19 (1967) : 279–280 [footnotes omitted].)

them in. And if you give the benefit of the rights to the rancher, so that his cattle are entitled to roam at will, it will still be the case that a bargain about the size of the herd, the planting, or fencing will be reached. In fact, if you give the rights to the farmer on Mondays, Wednesdays, and Fridays and to the rancher the rest of the week, once again they will come to an efficient bargain, or no bargain at all if the status quo happens to be efficient.

This much of CT follows inexorably from the definitions and premises, so inexorably indeed that the conclusion appears trivial. There is, to be sure, another aspect of CT which is much less obvious (therefore much more interesting) but also the subject of considerable controversy. This second part of the Coase theorem holds that not only will the parties reach an efficient solution no matter how the rights are assigned between them, but they will reach the *same* efficient solution. Thus, if farmers and ranchers, victims and rapists could indeed bargain freely and assume the bargains would be kept, then this second leg of CT holds not only that it would be equally efficient to give ranchers and rapists the rights as to assign the rights to victims and farmers, but that the same pattern of conduct would end up being agreed upon, irrespective of what was the starting place for the bargaining. Fortunately, whether the second leg of CT holds or not is not important for my purposes. We do need to notice, however, that who is assigned the rights will surely make this one difference: the party assigned the rights will be better off at the end of the bargaining than if he were not assigned those rights. For, obviously, if you must pay to be free of rape, you will end up poorer than if you could demand payment as recompense for suffering it, and this is true even if we agree both situations are equally "efficient" and even if the same amount of raping and refraining from rape would be agreed to under either assignment of rights.

The crucial term in the Coasean analysis is, of course, efficiency. One is inclined to say that if efficiency is to be defined as merely any result which could not be improved upon by free bargaining, then we should not be much concerned with efficiency. But the definition is far from arbitrary; instead, it is a direct response to the problem of defining a workable standard for maximizing welfare. The Benthamic formula, requiring the choice, among all available alternatives, of that one in which the sum of the pleasure of all individuals is highest runs into a well-known difficulty: how can one person's pleasures and pains be compared to those of another so as to allow the overall summing on which the utilitarian standard depends? This has come to be called the problem of the interpersonal comparison of utilities. The neoclassical economists, despairing of any objective mode of achieving this intercomparability, seized upon Pareto-optimality as a criterion of choice, which allows one to ignore this difficulty. The argument is straightforward. So long as any change is possible which improves the situation of anyone at all while worsening the situation of no one, such a change must be appropriate on utilitarian grounds—that is, in terms of people's actual preferences—and without any recourse to the problematic comparisons by which one person's loss is judged to be out-weighed by another's gain. The other side of this Pareto gambit is to hold that movements improving one person's situation at the expense of another cannot be justified in an objective way. So where no further changes of the first sort are possible and any change would have to be of the second sort, no objective grounds exist for arguing that this state of affairs can be improved: it is Pareto-optimal; it is efficient. The link with bargaining is straightforward, too. For if bargains are truly costless, fully available, and effective, then the situation where no improvement for one party is possible except at the expense of another must correspond to the situation where no further room for bargaining exists. Bargains are struck only where both bargainers have something to gain. And it does follow inexorably that if bargains can be freely struck, then efficiency will indeed be attained however the initial assignment of rights is made.*

Where Bargains Are Not Costless: The Economic Analysis of Rights The Coase theorem that the assignment of rights is irrelevant to the attainment of efficiency, where bargains can go forward with perfect ease, is obviously of doubtful relevance to the question of assignment of rights in the real world, where

---

* It has been suggested that even where bargaining is free, that is, in the absence of transaction costs, parties may not bargain to an efficient outcome if they engage in strategic behavior which "goes wrong," so that an un-reconcilable standoff ensues. See Donald Regan, "The Problem of Social Cost Revisited," *Journal of Law and Economics* 15 (1972) : 427–437; and Robert Cooter, "What Is the Public Interest?" Unpublished doctoral dissertation, Harvard University, 1975. This objection may be met by considering this risk as itself a transaction cost, though of a very special kind.

bargaining is constrained in a variety of ways. The operative significance of CT is as a model which will allow questions of rights to be determined under less than ideal or model conditions. It is this application of CT in real-world conditions to yield criteria for the assignment of rights which is the work of the burgeoning hybrid discipline of what I shall call the economic analysis of rights (EAR).

The economic analysis of rights seeks to discern which assignment of rights in the real world of costly and impacted bargaining best approximates the attainment of efficiency, that Pareto-optimal situation which would obtain in the frictionless world of costless bargaining. Harold Demsetz offers the example of the assignment of territorial trapping rights to competing Indian trappers, after the European demand for fur had produced a temptation to overtrapping. If the Indians had been able without cost to reach and enforce limitations on their takes by bargains, no assignment of territorial rights would have been necessary (or perhaps such an assignment might have emerged naturally from the bargains). But individual bargains obviously could not be reached in sufficient time, nor could they be enforced, so efficiency was attained through territorial assignments by rules. Demsetz argues in the manner of Locke that the rules of the private property system in respect to farmland, inventions, and the like can be explained in a similar way, as being the systems of rights which in the world of costly bargains is most likely to attain efficiency. What, for instance, of the "right" to one's own labor? Why should that not belong to whoever believes he can make use of it rather than to the laborer? Not even there does the assignment of the right rise to any higher dignity than as a device for attaining efficiency. If another man's labor could be captured so that freedom from slavery would have to be purchased rather than the labor being purchased, a free-for-all of bargains with all the world would have to be struck by each worker with all potential enslavers. It would be far simpler—far less time and effort would be wasted on making and enforcing bargains—if the laborer owned his own labor and would have to make only one bargain at a time with a purchaser of his work. If, however, bargains could be instant, universal, and automatically enforcible, as in some complex system of computers, CT teaches us it would not matter how the rights were assigned initially.

The application of this argument to case III (Victim versus Rapist) should be clear. Due to the multiple bargains that would have to be made by potential victims with all potential rapists, it is far simpler, in a world where communication takes time and effort, to assign the rights to victims. Potential rapists are forced to communicate with their potential victims and strike bargains with them. Also we do away with the incentive to pretend to be a potential rapist who may seek payment from potential victims.*

And in general there is no preexisting moral or other judgment which tells us how to assign rights. Either the assignment is a matter of indifference or it is dictated by contingent circumstances which happen to suggest that efficiency is more likely to be attained in some particular way. Rights are not moral entities, but a device for attaining efficiency.

EAR and the Problem of Distribution   According to EAR the function of the legal system in making its initial assignment of rights and liabilities is to promote economic efficiency, that is, to simulate the outcomes of bargaining in the absence of transaction costs. The intuitive notion is that an efficient allocation of resources is one in which there is no waste. Now, it is crucial to recognize that the concept of efficiency which is used in EAR is completely indeterminate in respect to distributional questions. Where the process will come out (what will be the efficient solution) is a function of initial endowments and assignments of rights; that is, it is a function of the distribution with which the bargaining parties begin. A particular solution may be efficient, but if the initial endowments are somehow improper, then it is

---

* Richard Posner has taken the analysis a step further to show why certain acts, like theft and rape, are not only the occasion of civil liability but criminally punished as well: "The theft of an automobile may increase the value of resource use: the automobile may be worth more to the thief than to the owner in the sense that the thief, if unable to steal it, would have bought it. Theft is punished because it is inefficient to permit the market to be bypassed in this way. Only two parties are involved; if the automobile is really worth more to the thief, a sale can readily be arranged. We prefer this to his taking the car without the owner's consent. The taking substitutes for an inexpensive market transaction a costly legal transaction, in which a court must measure the relative values of the automobile to the parties" (*Economic Analysis of Law* [Boston: Little, Brown, 1973], p. 68). "Society does not want to deter only those rapes in which the displeasure of the victim is shown to be greater than the satisfaction derived by the rapist from his act. A simple damages remedy would therefore be inadequate" (pp. 357–358). And the reason that society makes this judgment is only because, as in the case of theft, it is inefficient to allow the market to be bypassed.

hard to see why the outcome of the process has any privileged claim to our approbation or to social sanction.

For those who insist that no objective judgments can be made regarding distribution, the attainment of efficiency may at least appear to have the virtue of offering a clear and unambiguous criterion of social policy. But this is a non sequitur. The obvious fallacy is to take a conclusion about social policy, which is a function of two independent variables—efficiency and just distribution—and to say that since we are unable to determine the value of the second variable, it is therefore reasonable to treat the conclusion as if it were a function only of the first.*

This indeterminacy about distribution was certainly recognized as a grave problem for EAR, and it is a problem for classical utilitarians as well. The most common resolution proposes making adjustments after the machinery has cranked out its efficient solution, by something called a lump-sum transfer, so that those who end up too well off must disgorge a sum of money large enough to make the losers in this process as well off as our ethical judgments require. What ethical judgments? Well, Bentham-like utilitarian ethical judgments if you want, that is, ethical judgments which purport to be able to compare somehow the total situations of different people and to be able to discern when the losses of one person are made up by the gains of another. So, if the outcome of the EAR process is to make one person—say a skilled worker—too well off relative to the consumer of that work (too well off in the sense that the sum of utility would be greater if the individual levels of utility were more nearly equal), we would then tax the skilled laborer and

* Perhaps as a result of an inchoate understanding of this objection, some theorists appear to argue that EAR is not put forward in a normative sense at all, but rather as an analysis describing how institutions work or would work if they were rational. But this analytic-descriptive version suffers from another defect. If rational men are concerned about distributive justice and things other than efficiency, then a model which takes initial endowments as given and defines efficient solutions from the starting point of those endowments will not describe the behavior of such actors. Finally, a possible move which has been attempted (most notably by Hochman and Rogers) is to translate concerns with distributive justice into substantive preferences, so that one of the things which the parties are said to be bargaining about is the distribution to others. Why this move does not work is a topic on which I cannot enter here. Briefly, it involves a category mistake, equating preferences and demands for goods with normative judgments about the distribution of those goods.

give the proceeds in cash to the less favored party. Indeed, this distributional twist to EAR purports to have an even wider range of appeal, a greater generality, since these lump-sum redistributions may be made to accomplish a variety of ethical goals. If you favor not the greatest happiness principle but, say, the principle of equality of happiness (which Bentham hoped would coincide with the greatest happiness but quite plainly need not) or some principle of reward for excellence, or even some advantages for membership in a favored group, all of this can be accomplished: Let the machine crank out its efficient solution and then make lump-sum adjustments to accomplish your desired ethical goal—whether it be maximizing happiness, creating equality, or rewarding some kind of excellence.*

The proponents of EAR claim striking advantages for this one-two play. It is, they argue first, the only analysis consistent with the assumption that each person is the only proper judge of what is good for him. We can and must make ethical judgments regarding distribution, but these are judgments about people's appropriate relative shares; they should not be judgments about what particular things a person gets. Thus to produce equality by giving everyone the same housing, diet, health care, or to attain the maximum by producing more of some particular good, to reward the excellent with vacations or gold watches, all of this is irrational. Though we concede a difficulty about interpersonal comparison of utilities, we make ethical judgments, distributive judgments anyway. Fine, that is inevitable. But it is irrational to use houses, diet, gold watches, or any particular thing as the units of our ethical or distributive metric, when we know that different people value these things differently. Whether our ethics tell us that people ought to be maximally or equally happy or that the best ought to be happiest, it is irrational to measure distribution by housing, which we know will *not* make all people

---

* The perfect lump-sum transfer is an economist's abstraction rather like the cost-free transaction. In theory, such a transfer has no effect on expectations or incentives. In practice, any approximation such as an income tax, a wealth tax, or an inheritance tax introduces major distortions. A true lump-sum transfer is like a tasteless, odorless, colorless gas. It comes once when no one expects it and never again—lest any one expect it and plan accordingly. See Paul Samuelson, *Foundations of Economic Analysis* (Cambridge, Mass.: Harvard University Press, 1947), pp. 247–248, and M. Polinsky, "Economic Analysis as a Potentially Defective Product," *Harvard Law Review* 87 (1974): 1677–79.

equally happy or reward most all those we want to reward. Indeed, if we give everybody the same housing, diet, and so forth, what is sure to happen (unless we forbid it) is that those who care more for food will start trading with those who care more for housing. And that would be odd, because the assumption was that all of the trading and bargaining had already been completed. If, however, lump-sum redistribution is in the form of cash, then the citizenry will be able to purchase what they want, what makes them happy.

What EAR comes to, then, is this: Efficiency is one thing, distribution another. Through a manipulation of rights assignments (liability rules), we assume that the allocation of goods in productive exchange is as good as it can be. Through lump-sum redistribution we assure that the benefits of this efficient, no-waste allocation are enjoyed by whatever ethical (distributive) formula appeals to our ethical or political sense. What is striking about this approach is the sundering of ethical decisions from decisions about rights. Or one might put the matter in this way: According to EAR, the only right that an individual has that is independent of the contingencies of what may be needed to attain efficiency (one might say the only moral or preeconomic right one has) is just the right to whatever distributional share of the efficient total our ethical norm assigns to him; but there are no rights to particular, concrete goods—at least no moral or preeconomic rights. Thus, in this view, what rights a person has (and here we might think not only of the cases of Householder, Victim, and Rapist, but also of political rights, civil liberties, and the like) is wholly contingent upon the economic analysis which seeks to promote efficiency. Rights cannot be thought of as expressive of the moral position which one has in entering into bargains or relations with others. Rights are the creatures of the contingent social situation and EAR. The only thing, therefore, that has a noncontingent, preeconomic character, the only kind of judgment which accords claims to individuals before and not after the bargaining process has taken place, is the distributive norm.

Applying this to the cases we began with, if the initial assignment of rights between, say, R and V or H and M is dictated by anything other than the attainment of efficiency, if the assignment of rights is dictated, for instance, by the judgment that the use made by R is somehow worse than the enjoyment of V in not having that use made, this cannot be justified under EAR. If it is

truly a more efficient solution to give the rights to R and not to
V, then the only objection we can offer is that some Vs will have
their total level of welfare diminished relative to what our
ethical, distributive norm demands. For instance, if our distributive norm is equality, then the assignment of rights to R may
mean that, for some Vs, income will sink below the level of
equality, while for some Rs it will rise above equality. In that
case we will be moved to flatten out these differences by lump-sum
transfers. But it is important to note that our ground for flatten-
ing them out will be only that the total income of the two parties
no longer accords with our distributive norm and *not* that somehow the advantage enjoyed by R is an unfair advantage. Moreover, for any V whose welfare is not depressed below the pre-
scribed value by such an assignment of rights, or for any R who is
not unduly enriched, no correction would be warranted. The
oddness of this result was well expressed by Mishan:

> While this explicit concern with distribution . . . may be seen
> as one of the redeeming features of the New Welfare Economics,
> the question of who, under the circumstances, ought to pay com-
> pensation must also be referred to ethical considerations, distinct
> from and possibly in conflict with those invoked in discussing
> the distribution of welfare. If my neighbor's weeding machine is
> eccentric enough to blow his weeds into my garden, I should not
> like to think that the question of who compensates whom is to be
> decided by reference to our relative incomes. ("Pareto Optimality
> and the Law," p. 279, n. 2.)

Now it should be clear that EAR sharply contradicts the
nonconsequentialist, categorical conception of rights. Under
EAR, rights are assigned *instrumentally,* in order to procure the
efficiency as a consequence. Thus EAR is a complete theory of
rights for legal systems. It is a complete theory because it purports to make room for any "rational" grounds for assigning
rights. In EAR such grounds are of two sorts, efficiency and
distribution, and the complete version of EAR claims to yield
determinate answers to all questions regarding legal rights and
liabilities. Specifically, EAR offers a criticism of those who might
find some other, perhaps intuitive, basis for assigning rights. If
one should argue on some intuitive grounds that, for instance, V
should have the assignment of rights, perhaps because people
should have a right to bodily integrity or because the forced
impositions of R are "wicked," EAR would respond that such
arguments are either wholly inadmissible or the confused ver-

sions of correct arguments under the theory itself. Why, a pro-
ponent of EAR would ask, should the class of Vs have a right to
bodily integrity? What, after all, is so wicked about the behavior
of R?

EAR offers plenty of good reasons for those assignments of
rights which seem intuitively clear to us,* but the reasons have
nothing to do with the inherent "rightness" of V's position or the
wickedness of R's. In a perfectly computerized world, for instance, where all information could be transmitted and acted
upon instantly and costlessly between any and all persons, according to EAR the rational basis for our present intuitions
regarding rights would drop away. This is because EAR provides
us with no basis other than efficiency and distribution for assigning rights. So far as efficiency is concerned, the basis for the
present assignment would change. Can our strong intuitions in
this matter relate to the distribution? Not, I believe, under a
consequentialist conception of distribution. It is one of the principal features of distributive norms that they are neutral (as
between the contents of individual preferences), providing only
a scheme for distributing the satisfaction of those preferences. It
would violate the constraints built into EAR to have, as a reason
for a particular pattern of distribution, a substantive judgment
on the rightness or worth of some particular preference. In this
respect, EAR carries forward Bentham's dictum that "prejudice
apart, the game of pushpin is of equal value with the arts and
sciences of music and poetry." Nor is it an answer to this to say
that pushpin hurts no one else while the activities of R certainly
impose upon V. The hurt to V is just a negative utility or
preference, and it is exactly the purpose of EAR to provide a
complete theory under which the conflicting claims of the various
parties may be arbitrated.

---

* Some of those are set out in the passage from Posner quoted above.
Additional reasons might look like this: If the rights were assigned to the
class of Rs, Vs would have greater difficulty in arranging for total security
beforehand, because they would not know from whom to purchase their
security rights. Further, there would be an incentive for persons to distort
their actual preference structures in order to pretend to belong to the class
of Rs in order to extort security rights from Vs. Finally, there would be
serious problems of definition in respect to the assignment of rights to the
class of Rs: would such an assignment mean that V is required to submit
unless she has purchased security rights, or would it mean only that R can
try to force his will if he can, but V may resist; if the latter, further inefficiencies may arise in respect to bargains intended to maximize the safety
which both R and V would desire in the possible ensuing melees.

It might be argued that all this has nothing to do with a *moral* theory of rights, that one might accept EAR solely as a theory to explain legal rights, to explain who should be made to compensate whom when competing interests have come into conflict, and to explain what conduct should be forbidden by the criminal law. Now what would the connection between a legal and a moral theory of rights be? The moral theory might itself be consequentialist, so that *moral* rights would appear as instrumental entities assigned as a function of some other primary consequentialist goal, such as the maximization of utility. This, indeed, is the standard utilitarian line on moral rights. But then the moral account of rights would just repeat in the moral domain the same analysis that EAR offered in the legal domain. Well, then, might our moral theory be deontological, recognizing categorical entities such as rights and wrongs, while our theory of legal rights was consequentialist? In this view, assault would be morally wrong, but an assailant might have a legal right to commit assault. But this ignores the connection between moral and legal theory. Moral theory must dominate legal theory in the sense that it judges what the law ought to be. To be sure, we may believe assault is categorically wrong morally, while concluding that we shall not devote resources to its prevention or to its prevention in every case. And this is a corollary of the personal nature of categorical judgments. When we fail to prevent a particular assault, we do not commit the assault; the assailant does that. What wrongs we choose to prevent is a matter of weighing and balancing just like the question of what good or bad we will do. But what if the law not only fails to condemn assault but goes on to condemn resistance to assault—by the victim or by those who choose to help the victim? At that point our legal system is no longer consistent with our moral system, which condemns the assault as categorically wrong. At that point we are using the force of law to restrain resistance to wrong, and that is the same as actively assisting the wrong. But if assault is a categorical moral wrong, then we may not commit that wrong or intentionally assist it, even if some consequentialist analysis (like EAR) holds that it is more efficient for the law to give assault rights to assailants. Thus a theory of legal rights, while it need not make every moral wrong a legal wrong, may not make it legally wrong to exercise a moral right or to resist a moral wrong. And therefore, though a theory of legal rights is not the same as a theory of moral rights, a thoroughgoing consequentialist theory of legal rights (EAR) risks contradicting a categorical theory of moral rights. And of course in any such conflict moral theory must dominate.

I shall offer a categorical, nonconsequentialist theory of rights, but I have so far only argued that such a theory is inconsistent with EAR. In the next section, I give detailed criticisms of EAR. Since it may easily be shown that any consequentialist theory of rights must take the form of EAR, by arguing against EAR, I argue against consequentialist conceptions of rights generally and thus open the way for an alternative theory. For EAR is nothing other than that theory which holds that rights are wholly instrumental entities, wholly instrumental to the consequentialist goal of attaining efficiency. Of course, EAR does not hold that rights are the only or even a necessary device for attaining efficiency. Rather, consequentialism holds if we do not need rights to attain efficiency, we do not need rights at all. And so I conclude that whatever may be said against EAR is said against any consequentialist analysis of rights at all.

Bargaining and Moral Foundations

It is, as we have seen, the most illuminating aspect of EAR—of any consequentialist analysis of rights—that no possession, no interest (not our lives, not our safety, our land, our ideas, our labor, our teeth, our kidneys) can be taken for granted as naturally ours. According to EAR, every apparently self-evident allocation of entitlements might have been otherwise and can only be finally validated in terms of its tendency to produce efficient results. This theory suffers from a crucial internal defect that prevents it from being what it pretends—a complete theory of rights. My objection is that the central validating process of bargaining in EAR must assume some background entitlements which guarantee the integrity of the bargainers as intelligent, free agents. Without this background, exchanges between individuals cannot be described as bargains or exchanges at all.

This general point can be introduced by considering the case of fraud—does a person have the right not to be defrauded, lied to? Is it wrong to lie and cheat? If everything is an appropriate subject of bargaining, nothing taken for granted, then there is no obvious reason why freedom from fraud should not be as open a subject for bargaining as anything else—no moral or preeconomic reason, that is. Fraud might be viewed as simply a lack of equality in respect to an initial endowment of information and thus would seem to refer not to some vice in the very process of exchange but to one of the things which the parties might bargain about. Now, the bargaining model does assume that each person is the best judge of what his best bargain will be—and that is just an entailment of the moral premise that efficiency maximizes preference, and preference is subjective. If he bargains for information, he is still the inevitable best judge of his own bargains. For the party without the knowledge knows that he lacks it, knows that the party with it has it, and thus is in a position to put a price on it. That, at any rate, is how the argument would go.

One is right to feel uneasy. The assumption of sufficient knowledge is crucial to the argument, and the fast shuffle by which ignorance is turned into sufficient knowledge is indeed suspect. True, one may imagine a market for information as for other things, and the bargaining model assumes that purchasers and sellers have complete information in this sense: that they know perfectly well what information is worth to them. I know what a particular, rather precise item of information is worth to me and thus I am able to strike a bargain about it. But the point about fraud is just that I think I have the information, but I do not. My ignorance is such that I do not even know how to value the information which I do not have. Under these circumstances, surely, there is no reason to assume that a process of voluntary exchanges will necessarily lead to an efficient outcome. It will lead to an outcome, but that is all.

Well, then, am I not just talking about a kind of "market failure" which requires us to use the more elaborate mechanisms of EAR to supplement CT? More specifically, should we not assign rights and liabilities so as to assure fully informed exchanges, perhaps by giving an enforceable right to information to the person most in need of it? That is how the thing would be done, and rights to information, like all other rights, would then be defined so as to assure efficiency. But I do not think this move does the trick. It does not work as well as it does in respect, say, to the right to make or to be protected from noise in one's home. Information is not just a good in respect to which bargains may be struck and initial endowments defined. Rather, it goes to the definition of the process which validates results as efficient. The theory assumes, as we have seen, that each individual is the best judge of his own welfare. But this assumption makes the possession of knowledge and the capacity to reflect upon it not the subjects of bargaining but the foundations for bargaining. If some minimal rational capacities and some minimum knowledge of the world are not present, then the result of a process of bargaining can no longer be seen as validating anything. At most it is the description of something that has happened—period.

The objection is fundamental. There is no obvious way to determine just how much knowledge and capacity for thought are sufficient to ground the market model. Indeed, there is not even a clear distinction between what one knows and a general capacity to deliberate. It is inconceivable that a person should be able to reason adequately about his preferences, and yet be ignorant of certain important general and particular facts about the world. In EAR, knowledge and rationality are treated both as conditions for making the theory work and as specific goods subject to the processes which the theory founds. What we have, in short, are pretheoretic goods, or *rights*, assumed to be necessary if the theory is to work at all. But in that case the theory cannot itself provide a neutral model for what rights should and should not be recognized and how goods should be allocated and distributed.

EAR assumes exchanges, bargains, valuations, and the rest. But valuation, exchange, and bargaining are not morally neutral processes. These are concepts which it would not make sense, for instance, to use in describing the transactions of ants, ions, or subatomic particles. To be sure, there are processes and exchanges that take place between such entities, but they are plainly not the processes envisaged by economic theory. The defect of economic theory is to assume that these processes can take place without any assumption whatever as to the substantive qualities of the actors engaged in the processes. This assumption is due quite naturally to the fact that the characteristics which the actors must have are very general and familiar. They are so general and familiar that one can easily fail to view them as characteristics at all. But they are. Without certain very substantial endowments, the human being would literally be incapable of the complex psychological processes which make the use of the terms "valuation" and "bargaining" at all meaningful in respect to that individual. The behavior of, for instance, a drastically brain-damaged child of three cannot without triviality be fitted into the model. Yet the endowments that must be assumed are by no means insubstantial, costless, automatic. Thus there is a whole crucial category of goods which must be assumed before the model can take hold, even though the model purports to be perfectly general, covering the allocation and distribution of *all* significant goods.

This point is illustrated also by the treatment in EAR of the problem of coercion and violence. Just as the picture of exchanges assumed by the EAR model requires *informed* choices, it also requires *voluntary* exchanges. To pick an extreme example, a taking by force could hardly constitute the kind of voluntary exchange on the basis of which we would be willing to conclude that the situation of both parties to the "bargain" has been improved. Though this might seem obvious, the position on this of EAR is in fact unclear. Once again, recall case III. It is part of EAR that freedom from violence—like freedom from fraud—is a subject for bargaining, but we are at a loss to know whether transactions involving force are to count as bargains validating their own results. The argument of EAR works well enough in determining some particular right or entitlement as the outcome of an actual or hypothetical bargaining process. Thus, for example, whether or not a particular territory is to be designated as "my" property and whether my prerogatives within that territory are to be defined as exclusive might very well be determined by bargains or by a decision mimicking what bargains would have brought about. But the parties to the bargains must be assumed to start from some position of security. If their land is not their own, then surely their house, or their body, or their teeth are their own. But have we not discovered that EAR holds that these things are themselves the subjects of bargaining (or of government fiat approximating the outcome of bargaining)? So it may well be said that one has a "right" to one's teeth, for instance, but only *as a result* of the EAR process of analysis.

If one's oranges, land, house, car, and, finally, even teeth are not one's own unless the process of bargaining wins them for him, and if, therefore, there is no basis for assuming, apart from the *outcome* of that process, that taking a man's teeth or twisting his arm is an interference with the bargaining relation (instead of simply just the exercise of it), then what is exempt from bargaining? Here again—as in the case of fraud—we come to an impossible dilemma: either what is called bargaining is in fact simply a description of how people behave (and why just people? why not tigers, sugar crystals, and electrons?) or some freedom from unconsented-to imposition must be assumed as a privileged starting point, a background against which the very concept of bargaining is defined. But if CT and EAR merely describe the process of exchange, they cannot yield determinate answers to questions about how economic exchange should be organized. And if a useful theory must assume prebargaining privileged starting points, then CT and EAR do not provide a complete account of rights and liabilities as the outcome of their processes, since they require the assumption of some rights before the process gets started.

This objection seems to me to be simply another manifestation of a difficulty, mentioned earlier, with the utilitarian analysis generally. Utilitarian analysis offers no way of giving substantive content to the concept of the person, all characteristics being available for adjustment as the optimific calculus might dictate, all attributes of the person being contingent. The person finally becomes an abstract point, to which pleasure and pain may be attributed, but with no dimension or shape of its own.

CONCLUSION

If only consequences count, there are no categorical wrongs. And if there are no wrongs, then there are no rights either. For what distinguishes a right from an interest is its insistent quality, and that quality is best captured by saying that to violate a right is not only bad (to be avoided), but it is wrong. On the other hand it is possible to hold that certain things are categorically wrong without thinking that any one has rights. Religion may define a whole host of wrongs without granting rights to anybody. Similarly, the wrongs I considered in Part I, though they are concerned with relations between persons, may be wrongs not because rights are violated in those relations, but because the relations offend some ideal of community. And so the development of a theory and system of rights will extend and specify the analysis of Part I. If certain wrongs—harm, lying—are correlated with rights in the victims, then we have learned more about the underlying basis of those wrongs: harming is wrong as it violates a right. Moreover, the analysis of the injury done to the victim of harm or lying suggests how a general theory of rights might go.

In this chapter, I have mainly explored a theory which is the very opposite of the theory of rights we want—under EAR, rights are secondary, instrumental entities determined by the contingencies of our primary purpose to attain efficiency. The indifference, the moral neutrality of EAR about acts like rape and theft, acts which seem to us both wrong and the violation of rights, are a sign of this secondary role of rights in EAR. The criticism of this instrumental view of (non) rights (?) as leaving the concept of person without sufficient content or foundation points the way to my affirmative account. For the theory of substantive rights I shall offer is elaborated from the concept of the person and what is necessary to establish the integrity of the person. In this theory, substance and form go together: a *substance* of personal integrity and a *form* which is the form of rights, rights as categorical entities morally tied by bonds of necessary argument to the person whom they protect and who is invested with them.

A NOTE ON COMPENSATION

I have not insisted on the distinction between condemning and therefore proscribing an act as wrong on one hand and compensation for one who is injured by the act on the other. They are not the same thing. For instance, we may conclude that a person who negligently, or even without any negligence, accidentally injures another in the operation of some dangerous and unusual piece of equipment should compensate the victim of the accident. We may conclude this without, however, also concluding that the actor is worthy of condemnation or punishment, or indeed without concluding that the actor did anything we would not have wanted him to do. Thus wrong is not a necessary condition for compensation. It is also not a sufficient condition, for there may be cases where a person does something which is morally or legally forbidden, which is wrong, but which, since it does not cause monetizable harm, may not be the occasion for any kind of compensation.

A large part of the literature on right and wrong and on EAR in particular has been especially concerned with problems of compensation. This is what the Coase theorem initially dealt with. In subsequent writings, particulary those of Becker, Calabresi, and Posner, that concern has been widened to other aspects of law, but the basic attitude toward right and wrong remains the same. Now, CT is often formulated not explicitly in terms of rights but rather in terms of liability rules: if the liability rule favors the farmer, then it is the cattleman who is liable and must pay compensation. From this I have concluded that it is the farmer who has the right not to be invaded by straying cattle and not the rancher who has the right to let his cattle roam at will. But this does not mean that economic theorists hold that it is morally wrong for the cattleman to let his cattle stray even deliberately. On the contrary, the point of CT is not to condemn that choice (or its complement) categorically, but to assure that it is made on the right calculation of cost and gain. Now, subsequent theorists of EAR have extended this analysis to criminal prohibitions. As the passage from Posner quoted earlier illustrates, however, whether something is a tort or a crime depends under EAR not on the moral quality of what is done but on the same kind of judgments which are invoked to determine whether assailants or their victims had the rights in the first place. Now, a theory of rights and wrongs cannot make its distinctions in this way. If intentionally harming an innocent person is wrong, then *that* is why the act should be condemned and compensation exacted. That the positive law may find it impracticable to enforce moral rights on all occasions presents a separate issue.

A theory of categorical right and wrong may nevertheless recognize a class of situations in which it is not the act itself which is wrong, but the refusal to pay compensation for the act. Thus it may not be wrong for me to take your car for use in an emergency, or maybe even for me to push you out of the way as I rush to catch a fleeing felon. It may not be wrong even if I know that, were there time to ask, you would not consent. But that such an emergency may permit my action even against your consent does not mean that I am also free to take the action and not compensate you for your loss. This is a complication which the formal structure can accommodate. If we can say that it is wrong to do X, or that a person has a right that no one intentionally do X to him, then it is also possible to say that it is wrong to do Y without paying compensation and that a person has a right not to suffer Y without receiving compensation. Some things are wrong even if we stand ready to pay compensation; others are wrong only conditionally.

There is a whole different range of cases regarding compensation which this prior discussion does not touch. These are the cases where an actor inflicts unintended injuries—whether negligently or without fault. There is no difficulty in principle in saying that it is wrong to act without giving sufficient care to the safety of others, so that one is morally culpable for doing so and bound to pay compensation if harm results. The difficulty inheres only in the specification: what is sufficient care in all the particular circumstances? I have not so far been concerned with such judgments. Case IV (Pedestrian-Motorist) is indeed intended to raise that problem, and in Chapter 6 I shall deal with it in detail. Finally, there are cases in which the conduct would have been culpably heedless if engaged in by an ordinary person, but the actual perpetrator for some reason or another was unable to appreciate the risky nature of what he was doing. In that case, if we require compensation it cannot be as a concomitant of the judgment that the actor made a morally wrong choice, that he was culpably heedless. He thought he was doing what we would say was proper. He could not help it. In such a case, criminal or moral condemnation would be preposterous—though it occurs— but what of a requirement to pay compensation? That stands on a different footing. The injured party is also innocent, but in addition to being innocent the injured party did nothing which counts as taking more than his share of the world's goods or the world's stock of risk and safety. So perhaps the person who did harm but could not help it is like someone who takes a risk which is only proper if he stands ready to compensate those who are hurt—such as a careful operator of dangerous machinery. Or our hapless actor may be like someone who takes and loses my umbrella, thinking it is his own. He is not a thief either morally or legally, nor need he even have been careless, but he still has to pay me for my umbrella.*

* Richard Epstein would generalize this last category to include—at least prima facie—every case of infliction of harm or loss, intentional, negligent, non-negligent or morally faultless. In his view, every imposition upon me deserves compensation. I have already argued why I do not believe this to be the case. See *An Anatomy of Values* (Cambridge, Mass.: Harvard University Press, 1970), ch. 11, where the concept of the risk pool is introduced to argue that we all stand ready to accept a certain measure of risk in return for the liberty of pursuing our proper purposes while imposing incidental risks on others.

5

Positive Rights

RIGHTS ARE categorical moral entities such that the violation of a right is always wrong. But this formal tie does not yet yield any substantive content for a theory of rights. Though every violation of right is a wrong, we cannot assume without argument that every wrong creates a right in him whom the wrong injures. What needs to be shown is that the underlying moral theory requires not only that certain things be judged wrong, but also that this judgment is fully realized only if we put the reins of the wrong into the (potential) victim's hands, only if we recognize his right in the premises. I have already argued that the moral integrity of the individual requires that lying and intentional physical harm be seen not just as undesirable consequences but as wrongs. The presentation of the economic analysis of rights permitted a first glimpse of an affirmative theory passing from wrongs to rights. I have criticized EAR for not providing a firm moral foundation from which choice (bargaining) could go forward. The process of bargaining on which EAR depends to validate social arrangements—actual or hypothetical—can have the moral significance claimed for it only if the bargaining goes forward from a starting point and against a background which is morally acceptable. And at the very least the integrity of the participants in the bargaining process must be respected: we must assume respect for their physical integrity and for the integrity of the intellectual process by which choice is made. The first connects with the wrong of doing physical harm, the second with lying. If bargaining is to be morally significant, it cannot be *about* these things but rather must assume them. And this suggests at once that the wrongs of harm and lying are indeed also violations of rights, since they deny

108

the principles of the victims' moral integrity. EAR is right to emphasize bargaining to the extent that bargaining is the metaphor for the exercise of choice, but EAR is wrong to the extent that it fails to see the need for a moral foundation for choice. That is what a theory of rights must do.

Rights, then, recognize and protect (protect morally, of course—they do not protect against wrong conduct, only wrong arguments) the integrity of the person as a freely choosing entity. But what follows from this general proposition—what particular rights are entailed by this conception? The rhetoric of rights has proposed a bewildering menu of rights. Some are very general, like the right to respect or to the pursuit of happiness. Others are more or less specific—the rights to health, to education, to a job, to a lawyer in a criminal case, and recently even the right to keep a pet.* In this profusion, some limitation and order are necessary or else the concept of rights will fall of its own weight. There just cannot be convincing philosophical arguments supporting all of these rights. That is why some theorists have retreated to a formal position, holding that the only morally (as opposed to legally) grounded rights are those that assure the moral validity of the conditions under which the political process defining and redefining legal rights goes forward. The only moral rights in this view are political rights: the right to vote, freedom of speech and assembly, the rule of law. These political rights then guarantee that whatever comes out of a political process that respects these rights is itself for that reason alone right. This purely political conception of moral rights seems too weak, however. Certain impositions on the person strike us as violations of right no matter how free the victim of the impositions might have been to participate in the political process and no matter how perfect the process that authorized such impositions. Furthermore, even such rights as freedom of expression or freedom from arbitrary arrest, which may be explained as necessary to acceptable political processes, seem to rest on a broader ground. We respect a man's right to read, write, or preach for reasons which go beyond the value of free public debate in insuring wise or fair legislation. Respect for the integrity of the person and of the mind surely contributes to a better political process, but even if and when it does not, it still

* This reference is due to Ruth Macklin, who reports that welfare recipients in a Canadian city had claimed this right in arguing for increased payments to allow them to buy dog and cat food. *Hastings Center Report* 5, no. 6 (October 1976) 31.

has categorical weight. Thus the problem of deriving the content of a system of rights remains.

In this chapter I shall be concerned primarily with positive rights, claims *to* particular things. I conclude that the principal positive right that we have against those with whom we live in general communities—cities and states—is just a right to a fair share of that community's scarce resources. Rights to particular things are derivative. They may be derivative from negative rights or they may be derivative from obligations, as where the beneficiary of a promise has a right to the promised performance. And rights may be derivative from the right to a fair share itself, for if that right accords me a certain level of income, then I have a right to that income and to all the things which I can lawfully acquire with that income. In this chapter I shall develop the argument that the right to a fair share is the primary positive right. And in the next chapter I shall show how this positive right articulates with the more numerous negative rights thus forming a system. The distinction between positive and negative rights is crucial to my enterprise.

POSITIVE AND NEGATIVE RIGHTS

A positive right is a claim to something—a share of material goods, or some particular good like the attentions of a lawyer or a doctor, or perhaps the claim to a result like health or enlightenment—while a negative right is a right that something not be done to one, that some particular imposition be withheld. Positive rights are inevitably asserted to scarce goods, and consequently scarcity implies a limit to the claim. Negative rights, however, the rights not to be interfered with in forbidden ways, do not appear to have such natural, such inevitable limitations. If I am let alone, the commodity I obtain does not appear of its nature to be a scarce or limited one. How can we run out of people not harming each other, not lying to each other, leaving each other alone? Consider the right to speak freely as an example. If this right is asserted against government, it might be objected that the recognition of the right imposes costs upon the community and thus runs up against limits of scarcity as surely as does any purported right to a share of material goods. But this objection depends on a misunderstanding. My right to freedom of speech is not a right to be heard, much less a right to have my views broadcast and applauded. If my right implied those things, then certainly it would be the equivalent of a positive right and would run up against the limits of scarcity. Since, however, the right is a right not to be interfered with in speaking, the scarcity limitation does not arise in any such obvious way. But what if others would deprive me of my freedom of speech—a hostile mob, for instance? Surely it is the case that in asking for protection against that mob I make an affirmative claim upon the scarce resources of the community. But this objection misses the point too, for the fact that I have a right to freedom of speech against the government does not also imply that I have a right that the government protect my exercise of that right. Threatened by a mob, it is not my right to freedom of speech which I can claim against the government, but my right to protection against those who would assault me. That is a right which I share with persons who are threatened with assaults for quite different reasons, reasons which may in no way be connected with the exercise of a right. And the claim to protection against unauthorized violence is, of course, a clear example of a positive right.

Consider a case of a negative right which is not a political right, not a right against the government. Grant me a plausible but as yet not fully established proposition: that in my case III it is the victim (V), not her assailant (R) who has the rights on her side. Let us call this the right to physical integrity. Now the economist will surely point out that whether or not somebody will be assaulted is at least in part a function of things like street lighting, police protection, sentencing practices of judges, and rehabilitative programs in prisons. And since these all cost money, is not this most obvious case of a negative right once again shown to be limited by the natural, pervasive fact of scarcity? This objection ignores the distinction between what is done to a person and what is allowed to happen. The right that I have posited on behalf of the victim is not the positive right to enjoy freedom from assault; it is a right not to be assaulted—a negative right. And that is a right that the assailant (R) violates, but the government when it fails to do *everything* that it might to prevent all possible assaults, does not violate. That is not to say that in failing to provide police protection or other benefits, the government does not ever violate rights. The government may, for instance, violate the right of a particular citizen or category of citizens to an equal share of governmental concern. That, however, is a positive right. Even when the government does violate such positive rights it does not violate the right to bodily security. It is not the government which commits the assault. That right is violated by the assailant himself, alone.*

This distinction between positive and negative rights takes up the argument about categorical norms. We saw that no system could accommodate, without risk of self-contradiction, multiple absolutes, unless those absolutes were limited by the concept of intention. It could not, for instance, be absolutely wrong to kill an innocent person unless it was intentional killing which was meant. Otherwise what could we do when not killing one person means endangering or failing to avert danger from another? Only by using the concept of intention could such dilemmas be averted. Now an analogous argument must be made in order to maintain the distinction between positive and negative rights. The intuitive notion is that negative rights do not run up against the problem of scarcity, do not involve competing claims to limited resources, since they require only forbearance from certain actions—harming, lying, falsely arresting, stealing. Just as we can avoid doing any number of intentional wrongs without risking conflict, so too scarcity does not put any limit at all on our ability to avoid violating negative rights—provided we understand a negative right as the right not to be wronged intentionally in some specified way. We can fail to assault an infinity of people every hour of the day. Indeed, we can fail to lie to them, fail to steal their property, and fail to sully their good names—all at the same time.

It is natural to object that if negative rights are important constraints on choice and action—as they surely are—then they cannot be costless. Good purposes may become more difficult or

* An interesting casuistic distinction: If the government withholds, say, police protection from a certain speaker or category of speakers in order that a mob should violently silence that speaker, does the government violate merely the positive right to provide protection, or does it *now* itself violate the speaker's right to freedom of speech? We can either say that in this instance government does indeed violate, through the agency of the mob, the right which the citizen has against it—and that is in accord with my analysis of an intentional omission. But we can do the job just as well the other way. So long as there is a right to any call for protection at all, whatever basis a government may have for limiting that affirmative claim upon it for protection, one basis which it may *not* use is its desire to restrict the speech of the claimant. The illegitimacy of this basis for apportioning of the scarce resource has its ground in the negative right against the government. So it comes to the same thing, only this way around we establish the government's violation of its affirmative duty, of the claimant's affirmative right via the route of his negative right.

even impossible to pursue if certain means—those violating rights—are prohibited. A dam providing irrigation and power for thousands may be unaffordable if we respect the property rights of those to be flooded. The validation of a new drug or the discrediting of an established but harmful surgical technique may be impossible without deceiving the subjects in clinical trials about the risks and purposes of the treatment they are receiving. A campaign of terror bombing may be the only way to force a stubborn enemy into an early surrender, avoiding far greater expenditures of lives and resources. In all these cases negative rights impose what the economists call opportunity costs, and opportunity costs are just as real as the factor costs involved in using up a scarce resource to meet competing positive claims. By asserting a negative right, one person makes it more expensive to respond to the claim of a positive right of another.

Honoring negative rights is costly. But the distinction I am making does not depend on the hypothesis that negative rights are costless in the economist's sense. Rather, my point is that it is logically possible to treat negative rights as categorical entities. It is logically possible to respect any number of negative rights without necessarily landing in an impossible and contradictory situation. That does not mean that respecting negative rights will not be burdensome, just as meeting positive claims is burdensome. Positive rights, by contrast, cannot as a logical matter be treated as categorical entities, because of the scarcity limitation. It is not just that it may be too costly to provide a subsistence diet to the whole Indian subcontinent in time of famine—it may be simply impossible. But it is this impossibility which cannot arise in respect to negative rights.

There are ways of defining negative and positive rights which appear to avoid the force of this argument. Thus it might be said that I have a negative right not to be deprived of a minimal diet (or not to have my portrait *not* painted by Salvador Dali). And, indeed, every positive claim might be cast in terms of a negative right not to be *deprived* of the good claimed. But the availability of this gambit does not in fact threaten the logical distinction between positive and negative rights. Nor does it threaten the point that only positive rights, not negative rights, are necessarily limited by scarcity. Negative rights are related to categorical wrongs in the sense that the violation of every negative right is a wrong. But a wrong can only be inflicted intentionally. Take the case of an alleged right not to be deprived of a decent diet. This

negative right, if it is one, is only violated if I intentionally
deprive you of a decent diet, either as my means or my end. But
if I just do not give you enough food to live on because I happen
to be feeding someone else, or because I am sleeping and feeding
no one, then I am not intentionally depriving you of food.
Indeed, it is perfectly clear that I do not deprive you of food as a
means to my end of sleeping instead of farming. The deprivation
is obviously a mere concomitant of my intention if anything is.
Now this is not to say that I cannot intentionally deprive you of
food. And this is just a corollary of the point that an omission
may itself be intentional, the chosen means of accomplishing a
chosen end. Thus if I fail to feed an infant in order that it die,
that is wrong in itself. If I grow flowers instead of corn on my
land, because I like flowers, you may starve, but I do not starve
you. I do you no wrong unless I have an affirmative duty to feed
you, and that duty does not arise simply because you will starve
unless I grow corn on my land. I may have a right to grow
flowers. Or at any rate, I surely have a right to do something else
with my life than devote it wholly to feeding those whose starva-
tion I might prevent if I worked at it night and day.*

The Sources of Positive Rights

Respect for persons, for their integrity as free, rational, incorporated agents is the basis of the wrongs already discussed and of
the negative rights to be developed. Does not respect for persons
also ground some structure of positive rights, does not respect for
persons require affirmative care for their situation, does it not
require a positive contribution to their welfare? If we are morally
bound to go further than just avoiding harm, if we are morally
bound to relieve the distress or to further the goals of our fellow

---

* This objection reminds us that not every intentional imposition is a
wrong. I have offered detailed arguments that certain specific intentional
impositions were wrong. Those arguments cannot by any means be extended
to every intentional imposition—for instance, not to every intentional imposition on another's property. That is why, also, one cannot turn anything
at all into a wrong and also into a violation of a negative right by utilizing
verbs like "neglect," "ignore," or "deprive" to make it look as if a failure to
benefit was just a case of active harm. For even if such a gambit could not
be blocked in a formal way—and I am not sure it can—the point about
categorical wrongs and negative rights is not just a formal point. Not every
untoward result that might be cast in the form of an active imposition is for
that reason alone wrong or a violation of right. The harm or imposition
must also meet certain substantive conditions.

man, does this further obligation not ground positive rights in those whom we are thus bound to benefit?

That respect for persons grounds affirmative obligations is quite clear in the Kantian theories from which much of my analysis derives. Kant argues for a duty of beneficence in *Foundations of the Metaphysics of Morals* [424]:

> A fourth man, for whom things are going well, sees that others (whom he could help) have to struggle with great hardships, and he asks, "What concern of mine is it? Let each one be as happy as heaven wills, or as he can make himself; I will not take anything from him or even envy him; but to his welfare or to his assistance in time of need I have no desire to contribute." If such a way of thinking were a universal law of nature, certainly the human race could exist, and without doubt even better than in a state where everyone talks of sympathy and good will, or even exerts himself occasionally to practice them while, on the other hand, he cheats when he can and betrays or otherwise violates the rights of man. Now although it is possible that a universal law of nature according to that maxim could exist, it is nevertheless impossible to will that such a principle should hold everywhere as a law of nature. For a will which resolved this would conflict with itself, since instances can often arise in which he would need the love and sympathy of others, and in which he would have robbed himself, by such a law of nature springing from his own will, of all hope of the aid he desires. (Translated by Lewis Beck [Indianapolis: Bobbs-Merrill, 1959].)

Now, we really cannot tell how far Kant would have this duty extend. There are several possibilities. He may mean no more than that we have the duty to relieve the fortuitous distress of another when we can do so without great inconvenience—in other words, we have a duty to avoid gratuitous callousness. At the other extreme, this may be the start of an argument which in the end would require a person to share with everyone less fortunate than he, right up to the point where all good fortune is equally divided. The correct interpretation of Kant's position is, I believe, vaguer but more reasonable than either extreme. Although Kant's argument might seem to be grounded in self-interest—a kind of moral insurance—in fact the appeal is wider. Kant seems to me to be arguing that the facts of mutual interdependence and common humanity make it unreasonable to adopt a principle of indifference to the situation of others. He speaks of love and sympathy and thus urges that the needs of others touch us—that we make them our own to some extent—and not just that we calculate how best to assure our own situation. Yet we are still left wondering what precise moral claims to our benevolent concern this gives to others.

John Rawls makes the same Kantian premises his point of departure in *A Theory of Justice,* and part of the interest of that work is its drive to give detailed content to the principles first set out by Kant. The most striking feature of Rawls's theory for these purposes is his proposition that differences in talents, endowments, good and bad luck must be considered as morally arbitrary, so that no person is entitled to the extra share arising from such natural advantage and no person is morally deserving of a lesser share by reason of a deficit in natural advantages. From this principle Rawls draws the conclusion that departures from equality can only be justified if they work to the benefit of the least advantaged.* Thus Rawls would permit differential economic rewards to draw out talent and effort, but only so far as those incentives would lead to an improvement in the situation of the *least* advantaged person over what the situation would have been in a regime of strict equality. This is the maximin principle. In short, for Rawls the source of our duty to share is simply the arbitrariness of not sharing.

Rawls's principal argument deals with the design of institutions and not initially with individual rights and obligations. Nevertheless, it follows that an individual within an institutional structure has a right to the benefits which Rawls's principles of justice accord him. Indeed, Rawls insists that the principles of justice are lexically prior to (that is, they may not be overridden by) considerations of efficiency or utility, so that the just allocation is (in my terminology) an entitlement or right, and its denial a wrong. Moreover, Rawls explictly holds that an individual has the obligation to cooperate in establishing just institutions and to contribute in accordance with their rules. Thus it would seem that the less advantaged have a moral claim to an affirmative contribution—what I call a positive right—and there is a corresponding moral duty that the better advantaged make this contribution. Just institutions operate as a kind of clearinghouse for these complementary rights and obligations.

Standing against this view is a thesis which has received its

* Or if such inequalities arise out of respect for the prior principle of equal liberty—a principle that includes liberty of conscience and expression, political liberty, and the protections of the rule of law.

most compelling recent statement in Robert Nozick's *Anarchy, State and Utopia*. Nozick argues that there are two conceptions of right or justice: (1) *an end-state or pattern conception,* which accords rights (or entitlements) according to some conception of what the proper configuration, the proper pattern of distribution, should end up being—such as equality, maximin,* the highest average utility, the greatest sum of utility, or perhaps some weighted average of equality and efficiency, and (2) *a historical conception,* Nozick's own, which asks only what our initial entitlements are, and what the proper modes of acquiring or transferring rights are. In this latter view, the actual configuration of wealth and misery at any moment is irrelevant. Not equality, or efficiency, nor any other ideal pattern of distribution is a ground for disturbing or criticizing any particular configuration, provided only that the modes of acquisition and transfer have been correct. In the historical view, there are no positive rights arising out of the mere fact of inequality or inefficiency. Indeed, in Nozick's view, there are no first-order positive rights at all.† There are no claims on another arising just out of a disparity of their relative situations—so long as the better favored had done nothing actively to harm his less fortunate fellow. Indeed, Nozick's ideal is exactly the one which Kant considers but rejects in the passage just quoted.

Nozick's claim might be understood this way: To recognize any first-order positive rights commits us to a pattern view, since positive rights are necessarily limited by the constraint of scarcity and therefore require some norm of apportionment. But the recognition of positive rights is incompatible with the recognition of the (negative) right which might roughly be characterized as the right not to be interfered with so long as one is not interfering with anyone else. And since for Nozick this right is the sum and substance of any proper system of rights, and since moreover this right is the essential guarantee of our moral integrity, any system of positive rights as well as any pattern theory must violate basic rights and therefore be immoral.

For all its starkness, this view is serious and important. One task I set myself is to show how one can recognize some positive

* Nozick classes Rawls among end-state theorists. That this may be an oversimplification of Rawls's theory is argued in Chapter 6.

† I say first-order to contrast with second-order positive claims, which arise out of freely contracted obligations or out of a duty to make reparation for a wrong.

rights (and therefore a pattern view in respect to them) without compromising the important kernel of integrity covered by the negative rights. I do not imagine that the system I propose can be shown to be a deduction from some set of self-evident or metaphysical principles. Rather, the theory must carry conviction by virtue of its richness and overall plausibility. Nevertheless, I should say something about my views regarding the source of positive rights. They are, I think, essentially Kantian.

Respect for our common humanity has provided the basis for the account of the categorical wrongs and the corresponding negative rights. Now, the same common humanity is the source of positive rights as well. The fact of our common humanity is so pervasive that to speak of obligations of debt and of gratitude to our fellow men is too weak. We incur debts as free agents, but our common humanity makes us the agents we are, helps to form the very notion of agency. Common human nature is not merely something which each of us possesses singly, though the possession is identical to all—like different examples of the same coin. It is also like a single thing which we all share, like the common thread that runs through each bead in a string. There are aspects of common humanity which we share because of the efforts of others to produce them: the fruits of common labor, the security of civil society, the riches of culture and civilization, the fact of language. These things bind us together not only because, like our bodies, we all have them and thus are enabled to recognize our fellows through them, but also because others have expended their energy in order to produce them for us. They bind us because they oblige us. They are the basis of positive claims. Thus it is inconceivable that respect for common humanity should compel the recognition of the negative rights of our fellow men even at disastrous cost to ourselves, while leaving us totally indifferent to their needs—needs which may be desperate and which we may easily be able to alleviate.

The issue for me is not whether there are positive rights and positive claims upon us, but what they are and what their limits are. A complete answer to those questions requires not only a fully developed economic theory but also a political theory to identify political rights. I shall offer less than that. I shall offer an account of the positive right to a fair share and then show how the recognition of this positive right fits in with and is constrained by the recognition of negative rights. I assume that one has at the least an obligation to meet some of the needs and perhaps the wants of those who coexist with him in cooperating units—economies, states, societies. And if we are under such obligations to our fellow citizens, then it follows that they do indeed have positive claims, positive rights within such units. This is, to be sure, an exclusively institutional conception of positive rights: the obligation is owed to the organized community and the positive rights are claimed from that community. This is not to deny positive rights and duties of beneficence in cases of individual need—the Good Samaritan problem. It is just that once the institutional case is taken care of, the individual case will be much easier to deal with.

NEEDS AND WANTS

The situation of our fellow men makes an affirmative claim upon us, and that claim supports an argument for positive rights.* I shall not concern myself with the formula for determining the amount of the contribution to meet this claim—whether it is maximin, equality, or whatever. Let us assume it is something like one of these, and for purposes of this discussion I shall use the deliberately vague term "fair share," so that the reader can then specify that fairness in terms of his favorite formula. My concern is with the things the preferred formula will measure: a fair share in respect to *what?* Is there a positive right to a fair share of everything, or just some things, and if just some things, which things? Even if we say there is a right to a fair share of everything, it is far from obvious what that means.

Subjective or Objective Standards What is it that we are seeking to distribute fairly? Is it happiness? If it is, then the result we are seeking to accomplish by redistribution is measured by a subjective standard. But there are grave difficulties in accepting a subjective standard of fair shares. Some people derive great happiness from the simplest pleasures—a thick slice of bread and butter, humming a tune, or perhaps even an opportunity to be of service to their fellow men. Others require the most extravagant expenditures of resources before they are

* Only if the basis of positive contribution were the utilitarian formula of maximizing the sum of happiness would the inference to positive rights be blocked. Though there would be a duty to contribute, no corresponding right would exist in any particular person, since the basis of the contribution would not be that person's situation but the general aim of maximizing utility.

moderately happy. A subjective standard makes the first group the hostages of the second. But if we move to an objective standard of fair shares, how do we avoid the absurdity of giving the same size overcoat to tall and short men, or overcoats to people who would prefer to go about cold in return for an extra ration of wine? Economists would, of course, immediately propose trades of wine for overcoats. That may be all right on some as yet unargued for principle, but it is not obvious why the resulting shares are fair.

Needs and Rights These difficulties have led a number of theorists (including myself on earlier occasions) to distinguish wants from needs. It has been asserted there is a right to health care, education, legal assistance, a basic diet, but not to smoked oysters, ballet seats, or silk shirts. Even though some people might want these latter things very much and be quite unhappy without them, they constitute mere wants, while health, education, and so on are needs. And it is to the satisfaction of needs that we have a positive right. The suggestion is plausible and attractive. It appears to connect with my arguments about the moral significance of respecting the integrity of persons as free, rational, but incorporated beings. And there is the great advantage that we can tell in a reasonably objective way what basic needs are and when they are satisfied: basic health care assures a person the preventive and curative measures generally available to permit full functioning during a normal life expectancy. A basic diet can be objectively designated, as can minimal needs for clothing and shelter. Our common humanity and the norms for our good functioning tell us what we mean by the satisfaction of need.

The needs of our fellow citizens are thought to make a peculiarly urgent claim upon us not just because they are susceptible to objective measurement but for the deeper reason that they relate to the development and the maintenance of the moral capacities of freedom and rationality, that is, the capacities to develop a conception of the good and to respect the moral personality of others. That we must maintain life and some modicum of vigor if these capacities are to persist is obvious and is a corollary of our corporeal nature. And the capacities for reason and for free, moral action cannot be taken for granted even where physical survival is assured. For these capacities to be present, the human animal requires certain conditions of nurture and instruction. Intelligence can be almost wholly thwarted by early neglect. It also seems that minimal conditions of care and affection are necessary if a capacity to relate to other human beings and to make a life among them is to develop.*

It is links such as these to the physical and moral integrity of the person that explain why needs—unlike wants—are thought to generate positive rights, rights measured in terms of their actual satisfaction. Health care is just one such need. Housing is a need, so is food. It takes little argument to add basic education to the list. And then there is protection against violence and

---

* It might be argued that whatever moral significance is attributed to these prerequisites for moral personality cannot extend beyond childhood, or beyond that time when moral personality has been finally established in an individual. Thereafter, whatever was needed to attain that full moral status is demoted to the level of a mere want. Consider the case of bodily integrity. The argument might be made that the maturing individual *needs* to have his physical integrity protected, for he must be allowed to come to believe both that there is a difference between himself and the rest of the world and also that this difference is not a threat to his survival. He must develop the sense of his body as being his, a sense that the bounds described by his body describe a basic, inviolate entity. But once his beliefs, attitudes, and capacities are finally established, why must we treat respect for bodily integrity as having any particular significance? Why does that integrity not represent simply another item of income and wealth? Similarly, a sense of the integrity of language, of truth is necessary to rationality, to a proper sense of our relation to objective reality. But again, once this concept has been developed and firmly established so that the corresponding moral capacities are truly present, why should truth represent any special constraint? The answer lies in the nature of morality itself. We confer upon the developing person the goods necessary to a moral sense not as we would confer other goods—clothing or medicines—but in principle. Our motives, the grounds for respecting the physical integrity of a child are as important as the actual respect. The principal necessities for the development of the moral sense remain necessities even after that sense has developed, and not just because the way adults treat each other would set a bad example to children, thus hindering their moral development (though this happens often enough). For we have grown up considering ourselves as embodied selves; we cannot now slough off this material husk of our identity and expect to have a complete, intact moral person left. An assault upon my body is an assault upon me. A principle which says that my body can be used is a principle which says that *I* can be used, and so correspondingly when I ask that my body be spared the calamity of serious illness, I am asking nothing less than that *I* be spared. And so neither positive nor negative rights may be viewed in an instrumental way, phasing out when no longer needed to procure a particular attitude. Thus negative rights may be explained in part by developmental needs, but they survive as rights after development is complete. So also *if* there were a positive right to health care, it too would survive into adulthood.

calamity. The list grows, so that one begins to wonder how anything is left over for wants. And this suggests the major objection to a theory of rights based on needs, however attractive it may seem at first. For though needs and their satisfaction have an objective quality, the fact is that any commitment, via the recognition of positive rights, to meet needs also makes us hostages to vastly varied and voracious needs.

Now, it would be absurd to argue that needs ground a system of positive rights to their *satisfaction* and then to go on to say that the measure of those rights is a fair share only of *effort* to meet those needs. After all, the two reasons for promoting needs above wants were our ability to be objective in comparing levels of satisfaction of needs, and the claim that as to needs it is their satisfaction which counts, even though the effort required to attain the same level of satisfaction may vary widely. Let us take the case of medical care, where sometimes enormous expenditures may in fact produce equality of results. The fact is that if we were to recognize a right to the satisfaction of our most unfortunate fellow citizens' medical needs, the drain on resources available to satisfy other kinds of needs (education, defense, housing) and also to satisfy all the residual wants of healthy, secure, educated persons would be staggering. Indeed, there is literally no end to the drain on resources that medicine might represent if we consider the various ways of prolonging life and restoring function which might be developed should we choose. To be sure, no standard would require us to spend money uselessly, that is, when it would procure *no* relief; but that is not much of a qualification, since there is always the possibility of devoting endless research funds to the development of relief measures which do not now exist. How to contain this voraciousness? If needs create rights to their satisfaction, how are we to prevent them from claiming so much that there is no energy left to pursue other goals?

Wants and the Concept of the Good The claim that needs have a special prior status rests on a mistaken conception of the importance of happiness and of the relation of the right to the good. I have emphasized the primacy of moral integrity, the primacy of the domain of the right over the good. To give this primacy to a person's needs over considerations of his happiness or the happiness of others appears to correspond to the priority of right and wrong over consequentialist considerations of better or worse. For if we associate needs with the right, with personal integrity and wants with happiness and the good, the argument for giving such a special exigent status to meeting needs seems on its way to being made. And yet the argument does not go through.

Moral personality consists, as Kant said, of the capacity to choose freely and rationally. But the capacity to choose implies a system of wants or ends, and so naturally moral personality implies a desire for happiness, a desire to choose and attain a conception of the good. So on the one hand, happiness has value and we are morally required to value the happiness of our fellow men. On the other hand, human happiness has moral worth only because it is the happiness of moral beings, and therefore happiness has moral worth only as it is pursued within the constraints of the moral law.* Rawls makes this same point by identifying happiness with each person's life plan, that is, the development and pursuit of a conception of the good. The constraints of right set the general conditions under which happiness or one's life plan is chosen and pursued. Respect for persons entails valuing the goods which moral beings have chosen because they have chosen them and attributing moral worth to human happiness because it is the happiness of moral beings. The right (freedom and rationality) establishes the moral foundations on which we build our lives.

Now, a claim to respect for physical and intellectual integrity implies a claim to the conditions under which a sense may develop of oneself as a free, rational, and efficacious moral being. But we cannot draw the conclusion that a person has a positive right to the fair satisfaction of his needs without regard to the burden this puts on others. On the contrary, we must stop short of the equal or maximin satisfaction of needs if such a goal would interfere excessively with the pursuit of happiness (the pursuit of *their* chosen life plan) by those called upon to make sacrifices to the possibly extravagant needs of the least fortunate. Just when the interference becomes excessive is, of course, the crucial question. All I wish to argue here is that any formula is in principle unsound which would make the *satisfaction* of needs the index of a person's fair share, without regard to the vastly

---

* By insisting in just this way on the moral worth of happiness, Kant does give moral status to what he calls contingent desires, and the whole engine is not deprived (as Hegel claimed) of the energy which some pursuits other than morality must supply to make it run at all.

varying costs, to the possibly immense burden of procuring that satisfaction. For it would be grotesque if our moral conception valued only the formation of the *capacity* to form a life plan and was indifferent to its *realization*. Although needs are objective (by definition) and are tied by arguments of philosophical necessity to moral foundations, and although no particular want has this moral status, yet the possibility of satisfying *some* reasonable system of wants, realizing some life plan, has the same moral status as do needs. That is why we cannot admit an argument which in principle holds the claim to happiness hostage to the possibly all-consuming needs of the least fortunate.

How, then, are we to bring the various aspects of a person's claims on his fellow man into some systematic relation, so that a theory of specific positive rights will emerge? We have seen that whatever our formula for judging those claims, for assessing the contribution we must make to each other's welfare, it would be unreasonable to use the subjective levels of satisfaction of wants—happiness—as the index. We have also just seen that there is a great problem about using as our index the satisfaction of objective needs. This seems to suggest that our fair-share formula should not apply to the *results* achieved by our contribution at all (objective *or* subjective results) but should apply rather to the actual amount of the contribution. But this is problematical too, if it is the end result, happiness, which concerns us.

THE SYSTEM OF POSITIVE RIGHTS

Money and Liberty Positive rights express the claims that men have on each other, by virtue of their common humanity, to help maintain and further their enterprise as free, rational beings pursuing their life plan. And the success of our life plans is intimately important to us; only our mutual willingness to respect the constraints of morality can be more important. Yet for all the importance that our life plans have, it cannot be that our claims on each other are a claim to satisfy our tastes and wants. In seeing why this is so, we learn something about liberty and point the way to a theory of positive rights.

I choose my life plan freely. It is what I make it, and that is why it would be hard indeed if I could design however elaborate an edifice I chose and then could force my neighbor to contribute to its construction. If my neighbor builds in wood, surely he can complain if he must contribute to my projects because his tastes are simple and mine grandiose. Nor should I be able to answer my neighbor's complaints by saying that it is not my fault that I have grandiose tastes while his are simple—that is how I was brought up, that is how I am made. For if I answer that way, there is nothing left to the idea that I am a free person, that my life plan is freely chosen. Though the system of wants I have constructed for myself is supremely important to me, it is after all I who have constructed it. And if it is more expensive to satisfy the system of wants that I have constructed than the edifice that my neighbor has constructed, then I have responsibly created a system of wants such that by insisting on its satisfaction I must deprive my neighbor of his satisfaction. And since it is I who have constructed the system, I cannot now complain about how expensive it is to realize. If I have a claim to assistance in the realization of my life plan, it is a claim to some fair share of objective resources out of which I can build what I want, but no more. The idea was clearly expressed by Lionel Robbins, when he argued (against the social agnosticism of those who denied the interpersonal comparability of utility) that money is a fair index of welfare just because of its neutrality, just because it represents no particular material good but rather the opportunity to obtain goods. Money is a generalized claim on the resources of the society as indexed by their scarcity relative to demand. And so a money measure in respect to wants (rather than our hypothetical index of actual satisfaction) is the correct measure, just because it measures the very thing we are after: the extent to which one man's realization of his system of wants will impinge upon the opportunities of others to realize theirs.

The idea seems to me particularly significant when one considers the most obvious objection which could be made to it: Surely a person cannot help his tastes any more than he can the state of his health; surely the condition of his preferences is as determined as the state of his genes. The contrasting conception I offer holds a man responsible for his wants by stating that he is morally entitled only to his fair share of *objective* resources for their satisfaction. Indeed, holding a person responsible for something means making him bear the consequences of the thing for which he is responsible. And accordingly we make a person responsible for his conception of the good by having him bear the consequences of that conception. One way of making him bear those consequences is by determining his fair share by an objective measure. Now, this argument in no way denigrates the satisfaction of wants. Indeed, our wants are the expression of the selves we ourselves in our liberty have constructed. The respect we are entitled to as regards our wants, as regards the conception of the good we create, depends on its source in our moral nature. It depends on the fact that as free beings we have freely chosen this conception of the good. But if we demand respect for this edifice because it is built on that substrate, on the foundation of our moral personality, on the foundation of our liberty, then we must accept the consequences and treat our wants as freely chosen.

But does this not make the problem of needs far more pressing? To respect the greater medical need of X seems entirely consistent with recognizing that X has the moral capacity to choose a system of wants. Surely there is no denigration of his moral status in recognizing that his kidney failure is a misfortune, not his responsibility. But there are many kinds of misfortunes—my favorite racehorse might be struck by lightning, my stamp collection destroyed by fire. Well, medical misfortune is a misfortune *to the person*. So though there is no doubt that money is a kind of universal solvent in terms of the resources which are called on to meet either wants or needs, the fairness of measuring one's positive rights to a fair share of the community's resources in money terms seems puzzling when it is needs that are in question. For where is the liberty not to have those needs? If a man's positive rights, his fair share, are measured by objective resources and not by levels of satisfaction, some great misfortunes may remain unassuaged. And when the disadvantage is medical or educational it is a disadvantage to the person rather than to something which the person has done or chosen.

The Insurance Principle Rawls offers as his formula for determining one's fair share an equal distribution of society's resources, except to the extent that departures from equality will serve to improve the situation of the worst-off representative man. Rawls avoids the problem of the voraciousness of needs by offering as examples of this worse-off category productive, functioning persons such as manual laborers. To some this seems a question-begging evasion of the gravest difficulty. Why does Rawls not choose as the example of the least advantaged, say, brain-damaged quadriplegics? I believe Rawls's move is perfectly reasonable and points us in the right direction. I now propose an argument for choosing money (which is the surrogate for claims on society's scarce resources precisely in terms of their scarcity) as the object to which the fair-share formula is applied—money, not particular goods, not results, not satisfaction, not wants, not needs. Thus, if our preferred fair-share formula were, for instance, equality, then it would be equality of money, of income and wealth, which we would try to achieve.

This is how the problem of needs would be resolved in such a scheme: Assume that each person has whatever money income is indicated by our norm of social justice. This represents his fair share of social resources, his fair claim on the benefits produced in common with all others. The amount spent on necessities, then, will be whatever amount each individual chooses to spend. Sudden, unexpected fluctuations in need would be taken care of by risk-pooling arrangements by which persons could insure themselves against disaster. The amount of social resources devoted to the victims of disaster would be precisely that amount which the members of the society themselves have determined. If I have a fair income, then I can save against medical need or I can purchase insurance with whatever benefit ceiling I choose, subject only to the constraint which my total income has placed on my ability to pay premiums. If I am someday denied some incredibly expensive therapy because its costs exceed my benefit ceiling, I cannot complain: I had during my healthy years made a deliberate choice to spend my share of resources on other things—housing, amusements, education, charitable contributions—so that now that the consequences of my choice have come home to roost, I should not be able to welsh on my bargain.

This conception has the virtue of recognizing the principle of autonomy; but there are objections to meet: the problem of children, who may have had no healthy years. One might simply see what provision parents generally make for their children and mandate a minimum level of protection for all children accordingly. A more serious objection asks whether it is fair to equate the income of someone who needs enormously expensive medical care with the income of a completely healthy person. Should not the fair situation be measured after basic needs have been taken care of? First we take care of a man's necessities, and then we distribute fair shares of income. This is what the distinction between needs and wants would require. But such a solution, unlike the insurance scheme, opens the potential for excessive demands by those with extraordinary needs. Moreover, there is nothing in the insurance proposal which assumes that expensive measures will *not* be available in the unlikely case that we need them: if the occasion of need is really very unlikely, then one ought to be able to purchase a very high level of protection for a small premium. If, on the other hand, the "need" is very likely to occur and very likely to be expensive—imagine some elaborate way to retard the effects of normal aging—then why should one complain if vast social resources are not made available for this purpose? Presumably, when we were younger we preferred not to forgo the consumption, preferred not to forgo the satisfaction of discretionary wants to the extent necessary to build up a fund to provide these measures. In a modest and undramatic way we have behaved like the mountain climber who accepts a certain measure of risk to life and limb in return for the fun and excitement of his achievement. Surely it must be right to allow reasonable people that choice. The insurance mechanism would do that.

The insurance model works well only because we have made the crucial initial assumption that the distribution of income is fair. This transfers the whole burden of the argument to the determination of a fair distribution of income. If we do not have a confident measure for this, then we cannot at all be confident that necessities would be procured by all at the appropriate level. Where many feel that income is not fairly distributed, while others question the appropriateness of governmental redistribution of income at all, there may be little else to do but to provide for necessities in kind. Unfortunately, this is an inherently unstable resolution, since there is no a priori measure for the proper level of meeting necessities. At best one might try to provide necessities at that level which each citizen would have chosen had he received some presumably fair share of income. But if we have a clear enough notion of what is a fair share of income, then why not just provide that measure of income itself?

THE DUTY OF BENEFICENCE

Let us pause to make explicit the implications, in terms of individual duties to our fellow men, of my conception of positive rights. If there are positive rights, then there must be corresponding duties. And it was with this question of duty, Kant's duty of beneficence, that the inquiry in this chapter began.

The basic, the primary positive right is a right to a fair share of money income—that is, to a fair share of the community's scarce resources. Now, this does not appear to be a right against any particular person, but rather against an institutional structure.

But if *no* person is under a duty, how is this right to be realized? The answer is that *all* members of the community are under a duty just as they all have a right, and that duty is to the community as the right is against it. Thus institutional structures are necessary to mediate these reciprocal rights and duties. The answer is essentially Kantian, for Kant posits in *The Metaphysical Elements of Justice* a duty to join with others in civil society. And Rawls in *A Theory of Justice* argues for a natural duty to work for the establishment of and to abide by the rules of just institutions. The institutional structures may be loose and informal if the community is itself small and homogeneous, or intricate and bureaucratic if the community is diversified, extensive, and complex. To some this conclusion may seem not sufficiently heartwarming, too impersonal, but that reaction is an antirationalist prejudice. That a crucial, human, natural duty should imply the existence of institutional structures is a symptom of the fact that institutions are implicated in the concept of human nature.

The duty to work for and comply with just institutions is neither trivial nor passive. It includes a duty on all citizens to come to a personal conviction as to what just institutional structures are and what fair shares (equal, maximin, whatever) should be provided by those institutions. It includes a personal duty to engage in political activity to establish these institutions and to assure that they collect and distribute fair shares. And finally, there is the personal duty not only to comply with the norms of existing institutions but also in appropriate situations to resist them in order to move them in the direction of justice. (The more favored one is by imperfect institutions, the greater is this duty.) These are personal duties and the concrete manifestations of concern for and solidarity with our fellow men. They are, thus far, more onerous and active than a mere duty to suffer passively any exaction by the taxing authorities. Furthermore, those duties connect in complicated ways with rights other than the right to a fair share. Fair shares emerge from just political institutions and usually represent reasonable compromises between opposing views. Thus political rights are involved in this institutional complex and their recognition is necessary to validate the justice of the scheme determining fair shares. And the political duty is therefore more than merely a duty to work for distributive rights; there is a duty to work for political rights as well.

The question remains, however, about concern and beneficence toward particular persons who may be in dire need despite the institutional structure and whose plight we are in a position to relieve. This is the Good Samaritan problem. Can we really escape Kant's demand by hiding behind institutions? The problem is serious, but it does not make a hole in the structure I have been proposing. Two kinds of situations must be distinguished: there is the anomaly, where generally just institutions exist but have failed to provide for this case, and then there is the case which comes up precisely because just institutions do not exist. As to the first, we might recognize a duty to lend assistance without endangering the discretionary space I have been arguing for. By hypothesis, the case will be rare. And we may assume that if the institutions are indeed just, devices will obtain for compensating the rescuer after the fact. Thus there is no difficulty about including, as part of the background conditions of just institutions, a set of corresponding rights and duties to relieve immediate, critical and anomalous needs. I work out the details of this argument in Part III and illustrate my conclusions by the examples of doctors and lawyers.

The more difficult problem, to which I have no satisfactory solution, is our duty to concrete persons who are the victims of unjust institutions. It seems insufficient to say that our duty is wholly discharged by working to change those institutions. And yet the duty we have to our fellow men is to contribute a *fair* share; it is not a duty to give over our whole lives. Can it be that we do wrong, violate our duty to contribute, when we refrain from a total sacrifice which is necessitated only by the plain violation of duty on the part of others? I cannot give an answer. I suggest that compassion and solidarity demand a great deal of us—and particularly if we are the (unwilling) beneficiaries of the unjust situation. But they do not demand everything.

Finally, the recognition of duties in respect to positive rights shows that there are wrongs in this area too. Specifically, the neglect of these duties is not just bad, it is wrong. And that is because the positive claims to concern and to a fair share are not merely claims, but rights.

CONCLUSION AND PROSPECTS

There is no simple way to recognize positive rights, that is, positive claims to scarce resources, except as part of an overall distributive norm which holds that our fellow citizens have a claim (based on common citizenship) to some fair share of the objective resources produced and available in our society. The basis for meeting positive rights is through a conception of a fair distribution of objective income. Any other system is either incoherent or paternalistic. In short, though there are secondary positive rights which derive from obligations freely undertaken (I have a positive right to that which you have promised me) or which derive from special situations (an infant has a positive right to be cared for by its parents) or from some previous violation of right (I have a positive right to the return of goods you have stolen from me), my primary positive right is to my fair share of the total pool of benefits resulting from the schemes of cooperation in our common life—that is, my fair share of income and wealth.

The conclusion may seem lame in view of my criticisms of the economic analysis for its failure to provide for particular rights with sufficient specificity and emphasis. Indeed, I have argued that the moral blindness and therefore the unacceptability of the economic analysis of rights cannot be cured solely by redistributing in the form of lump-sum transfers the presumably efficiently allocated maximal social stock. What has been the point, then, of arguing that the concreteness of our incorporated human situation entails a system of rights which is prior to, more fundamental than, these political, economic rights, more fundamental than the right to one's fair share? My answer will appear presently, for so far I have offered only the first half of my theory of rights. I have offered only a theory of positive rights. I shall go on to argue that however fair shares are determined, they can be determined, they can be collected and distributed only subject to categorical, inviolable negative rights. And that argument will draw on everything that has gone before.

6

Negative Rights

W E KNOW that the concept of a right implies that its violation is wrong. This much follows from the categorical nature of rights. I have argued for only one first-order positive right: a right to a fair share. Certainly it is easy to accept that the denial of that right is wrong, a wrong which expediency and the claims of the common good cannot justify. But this is a very general right. The system of rights gets its concreteness and specificity from negative rights. Negative rights give the system grit; they block the impression that, after all, the individual disappears, is submerged in the collectivity, receiving back from it as of right only his fair share. I do not propose any general negative right not to be imposed upon, not to have one's liberty or interests prejudiced. On the contrary, the negative rights I consider are very specific, and the requirement of intention further limits and specifies these negative rights.*

The arguments establishing intentional harm and lying as wrongs suggest why these wrongs conjugate quite naturally into rights on the part of the victims of the wrongs. Harm and lying are wrong because they involve the agent's using the victim for his own purposes, and I have showed why this is a wrongful use, why a misappropriation. The argument depends on a concept of attributes which must be respected to ensure the integrity of the person. Now, my arguments establish wrongs by reference to

---

* If there is a general negative right—a right to be let alone—it is the right not to be imposed upon *maliciously;* that is, a right not to be imposed upon by someone whose very end it is to harm or frustrate you. But malicious impositions are both so plainly wrong and so very hard to make out against the violator that I put them aside as not important to my thesis.

attributes of the victims which it is essential to protect; the arguments recognize that these acts have victims. Thus we can pass from harm and lying as wrongs to a right not to be intentionally harmed or lied to. The passage to rights is also authorized by the role that I have identified for a theory of rights: Such a theory serves as the foundation for the situation of the individual in his relations with other individuals and with the collectivity. I have argued that the reliance of the economic analysis of rights on a bargaining model to establish all rights was unsatisfactory insofar as it specified no secure foundation—secure, for instance, against recourse to force or fraud—on which the bargaining would go forward. With absolutely everything "up for grabs," the concept of bargaining loses any sense or heuristic power. Rights to physical and intellectual integrity, however, establish just the needed starting point from which bargaining might sensibly be imagined to go forward. Bargains struck on that basis can have normative significance, for they are the bargains of free and rational persons whose freedom and rationality are not themselves to be established by bargaining.

The conjugation of wrongs into rights does not, however, authorize the conclusion that the individual has a right not to *suffer* harm as an indirect and unintended or accidental concomitant of another's purposes. As to that, all that can be said is that the indirect and unintended harm must be weighed and considered as a bad. Security and knowledge may be the results of an enjoyment of the rights not to be harmed or lied to, but that is another question. The claims to security, to protection, and to education are positive claims, and insofar as these claims are related directly to rights at all, they are aspects of a person's fair share—just like claims to the satisfaction of other needs and wants. Just because a need relates to an interest (physical integrity) which is also related to a negative right, that need does not have any special status in the calculation of fair shares.

The most important thesis of this chapter deals with the relation between positive and negative rights, between negative rights and the value of those rights. But my general arguments would be unduly restricted (and rather tedious) if confined only to the two rights I have discussed in detail so far. There are other rights; I have simply not argued for them. There are personal rights: freedom of movement, freedom of speech and development of one's talents, sexual freedom, the right to privacy. There are political rights: the right to vote and to participate in government.* And there are legal rights, such as the right not to have one's liberty or property interfered with by the state except according to the processes of law, the right not to be subject to criminal prosecution except before a jury and with the assistance of counsel, the right not to be compelled to testify against oneself. I assume the existence of such a plurality of negative rights and thus will not confine myself only to those rights I have argued for in detail. I shall, however, argue for family rights and the right to liberty of motion, because these rights seem to me to grow out of the rights I have sought to establish. And it is important to see how rights relate to and articulate with each other.

NEGATIVE RIGHTS AND FAIR SHARES

Consider case III (Victim/Rapist), set out in Chapter 4. A clearer case of wrong, of a violation of right, could hardly be imagined. R's action should be condemned, punished. Whether or not such institutional steps are taken, it is at least clear that a moral person should not commit rape, however much he may want to, however much he thinks his own pleasure in such an act will exceed his victim's pain. We have seen that under EAR the assignment of rights is a technical, not a moral question. If V is assigned the right, it is on sufferance, as it were, because that assignment is most likely to be efficient for all concerned, not because of some intrinsic moral claim of V. Do we not just reject EAR then, especially if it offers such unsatisfactory explanations and possibilities?

Unfortunately, the deliverances of EAR are not so readily dismissed, for they are intimately tied into the question of fair distributive shares. And fair distribution is not a consequentialist principle at all. Distributive formulas are the basis for the positive right to a fair share of the community's scarce resources. In Rawls's formulation, for instance, no distribution of wealth, in-

---

* I shall not here go into the extent to which these are positive or negative rights. They have large negative elements—for example, if anyone can vote, then no citizen may be prevented from voting (except on conviction of crime or for some other grave reason), no citizen may be prevented from offering himself for election, and so on. And there are the usual questions about the associated positive claims to the enjoyment of these rights. *Must* the government, for instance, as a matter of right provide free transportation to the polls or financial assistance to candidates for public office? If it must, is this done as a recognition of rights or for some purpose of the polity as a whole?

come, or rights should be unduly influenced by the morally arbitrary accidents of natural advantage—the product of these advantages should be enjoyed by all on a fair basis. But what is to count as wealth? Notice that an assignment of rights to V over R gives V an advantage; it constitutes a form of wealth and a potential source of income, since V can now sell (or demand compensation for being forcibly deprived of) the rights which the liability rule has assigned. And, as the Coase theorem shows, there is an exactly corresponding disadvantage to R, who now must buy from V (or compensate V for taking) what otherwise he could take or get money for not taking. Now if the assignment of rights to V over R is merely instrumental, merely intended to promote efficiency, then distributive shares should not be affected and V should not enjoy tax-free, as it were, the advantage derived from this assignment. Should not all assets in principle be subject to redistribution in order to achieve fair shares? If V can enjoy the benefit of a right over R which she would otherwise have to pay for, without this counting as the enjoyment of scarce resources, is that not a case of someone having more than someone else as a result of an unearned natural advantage?

The difficulty can only be overcome if we recall that V's right not to be assaulted is a categorical moral right, not just an instrument of social expedience, and R's act is categorically wrong. The only way to accommodate these categorical judgments in the system of fair shares is to refuse to consider the constraint upon R as a deprivation, a disadvantage, to be taken into account in calculating R's fair share, and similarly to refuse to consider V's right as an advantage. So in effect we refuse to compensate for his disadvantage, refusing as well to charge such compensation (in the name of fairness) to V's account. And in general, all negative rights retain their force only if the advantages and disadvantages incident to respecting rights and avoiding wrongs do not come into the redistributive pool at all. When the fairness tax is assessed, these items are no part of the calculation. Thus, just as negative rights furnish the unbargained-for baseline from which bargaining in a bargaining model such as EAR would take place, so also negative rights are the foundation on which redistribution and fair shares must build. Both EAR and the various distributive formulas are devices for solving problems of economic organization—the problems of efficient and fair distribution. In both cases some foundation is necessary if the analyses are to be plausible and have heuristic power.

Negative rights provide that foundation. Thus negative rights and the positive right to a fair share have distinct scope and force. The resulting theory is more complex, but it is a richer theory because it accommodates both sets of notions.

Now it might be objected that a system of fair distributive shares can only be intelligible if all values are within its grasp, in principle assessable and redistributable. This objection assumes that we do not and cannot have available to us a more richly detailed moral theory than the fairness theory itself—for a pure and exclusive fairness theory makes no moral judgments at all except the one judgment about how goods and bads are to be distributed. But why should we assume that the repertoire of moral notions is so poor? All that needs to be done is to posit that moral grounds exist in terms of which certain "advantages" are not to be counted as advantages at all, certain "goods" and "bads" will not be allowed to enter into our calculations. Specifically, we can say that certain satisfactions—such as the satisfaction of R in successfully carrying out his assault or the satisfaction taken by cruel men, liars, and thieves in indulging their vices—simply do not count as goods in our moral calculus, even though they count as goods in the individual calculus of these vicious men. Conversely, the frustration of such satisfactions is not a negative quantity in any moral calculus. Now, those who would reduce the moral system to a fair distribution of wholly subjective states, with no judgment whatever being made on the quality of any particular subjective state except that it was pleasurable or painful, may well object to our ruling out certain "goods" and "bads" on moral grounds. The correct way to meet this objection is to offer a theory explaining why such exclusionary rules are invoked. But that is just what the argument for categorical wrongs and their conjugation into negative rights have sought to do.

So the solution to case III is determined by the theory of negative rights: the right is in V, and it is there irrespective of any judgments about the efficiency or inefficiency of the resulting regime, and irrespective also of any entitlements or positive rights, any obligations of the respective parties arising out of the consideration of their relative wealth and their appropriate fair distributive shares. Contrast this case to cases I and II (Farmer versus Cattleman, Homeowner versus Manufacturer). In both of these cases, one is inclined to leave the field to EAR—that is, to allow the assignment of rights to be determined on grounds of efficiency, with the appropriate redistributive judgments doing their work to make sure that the objective wealth of all concerned is appropriately adjusted. For I can see no argument in terms of which the reciprocity of the situations of F and C, H and M can be denied on prior moral grounds.* In those instances, the parties are disputing not about rights in their persons, not about the boundaries of self, but about their rights in the external world, property rights in the usual sense, rights to things which do not come morally preassigned to any particular self. It seems inevitable that such rights as those in cases I and II should be subject to social judgments of efficiency and fair shares. In both cases, one may view those rights as items of trade and commerce, whose value to the parties is fully expressed in monetary terms. And then it is a short way to a judgment that both the right and its obverse are appropriate items in any judgment regarding the relative income and wealth of the parties.

One might, to be sure, feel at least a hint of prelegal moral considerations in the case of the homeowner, and perhaps even in that of the farmer. It might be asserted that somehow the farmer has a right to the integrity of his fields that is analogous to the right of the victim in case III, but that is quite implausible. His land was, after all, obtained under some kind of grant—whether from a prior owner or from the government—and this grant could have been made subject to an explicit easement permitting just such incursions by the rancher's cattle. Or the whole dispute might be made to turn on who should pay the cost of fencing off the crops. The case of the homeowner is more difficult. For suppose that the right claimed by H's opposing party is not the right to pollute H's air but to install audiovisual transmitters in his bedroom. What this suggests is that the concept of "moral space," which I have developed to enclose the victim's body,

* I put aside the fact that in these cases neither C nor M intends the violation of F's or H's interests, but at most foresees them as concomitants of his pursuing his own interests. Even if it could be said that C or M intentionally uses the property of F or H as the means to his end, nothing would change. For what it means to use another's property is a function of how we define that property, and how to define the property right is just the question. A man's interest in his person and in the truth are not, however, the creatures of legal definition. A closer analogy to wrongful personal injury is intentional interference with property for the very purpose of causing harm, as in the case of spite, or as a way of extorting concessions. This corresponds to the wrong of maliciously harming another—as an end in itself.

might perhaps extend somewhat further. Indeed, I have argued elsewhere that the concept of privacy does refer to an argument—a moral, not an economic or distributive argument—for a certain measure of moral space extending well beyond the boundaries of bodily self. I shall not recapitulate that argument here; it is perfectly consistent with the thesis I am developing.

Now the homeowner or farmer may concede that his rights are the creatures of contract, custom, or legislative grant but argue that it is wrong nonetheless to unsettle his expectations merely because circumstances have changed and it is no longer expedient (efficient) to recognize these rights. This claim raises a general point about legal rights. Many legal rights do not express a recognition of moral rights but represent simply the legislature's or the courts' determination of how best to produce efficiency. Although such legal rights may have their source in expediency, if once couched by the law in the language of rights, they represent a bargain or a commitment to treat the relevant interests *as* rights. When society grants a legal right, it invites reliance on the grant as a grant of right—that is, it gives the grant categorical force. To violate that legal right then becomes wrong just as if the underlying interest itself had been a moral right, but for another reason: the grantee has been abused, but not because his land is like his person, but rather because his confidence has been abused. He has been asked to rely on the grant. Presumably society's purposes (to encourage development, for instance) were furthered if the grantee did in fact so rely. And now, having procured the benefits, society seeks to revoke the right. That is an abuse of the person too—not of his body, but of his trust and confidence. Thus a legal grant of right gathers categorical force similar to a promise. And, as in the case of a promise, it is a moral (not just a legal) question what the commitment in fact was and whether circumstances have changed so far as to render further performance unreasonable. So also in law it is a legal and a moral question how to interpret and when to abrogate a grant of right. For instance it is a fair question whether a grant was a grant of right at all; perhaps it was explicitly or implicitly given at the complete sufferance of the state. Property interests tend to have the status of grants of rights while commercial or competitive advantages do not.

Finally, even those legal rights which are the creatures of legislation, and which are granted only so long as the society deems expedient, operate in a categorical way in legal judgments until the law is changed according to the appropriate procedures. The principle of the rule of law says that any legal right must be treated categorically until it is changed by the due processes of law.*

NEGATIVE RIGHTS AND FAIR CONTRIBUTIONS

In this section I shall show how negative rights constrain not the determination of what should be allotted *to* an individual as his fair share, but rather what may be taken *from* an individual to provide a fair share to others. There can be no allotment of benefits to those less favored without a corresponding exaction from the more favored. Yet the actual obtaining of such a fair contribution may conflict with negative rights. Now, social schemes must not depend on violations of rights, must not use such violations as a means, even if the end of the scheme is to accomplish justice by assuring fair shares. This constraint is implicit in the proposition that the violation of a negative right is wrong: good purposes will not justify wrongful means.

I start with the easiest case: compelled donations of kidneys or other organs. From this I shall develop an argument to deal with a more difficult and important issue: compelled contributions not of bodily parts, but of talents, training, and effort. This issue will lead to a suggestion of how contributions to the social pool should be assessed and collected. If no assessment may be levied on bodily parts, talents, or other natural advantages, such as a

---

* For a recent illustration of these considerations, see *Flushing National Bank* v. *Municipal Assistance Corporation*, 40 N.Y. 2d 731 (1976), in which the New York Court of Appeals held invalid a state law declaring a three-year moratorium on the payment of notes of the City of New York, when the city had pledged its full faith and credit in contracting the debt and did in fact have revenues out of which to pay them. The language of the court is the language of rights: "By any test, whether based on realism or sensibility, the city is constitutionally obliged to pay and to use in good faith its revenue powers to produce funds to pay the principal of the notes when due. The effect of the Moratorium Act is, however, to permit the city, having given it, to ignore its pledge of faith and credit to pay and to pay punctually the notes when due. Thus, the act would enable the city to proceed as if the pledge of faith and credit had never been given . . . The constitutional prescription of a pledge of faith and credit is designed, among other things, to protect rights vulnerable in the event of difficult economic circumstances. Thus it is destructive of the constitutional purpose for the Legislature to enact a measure aimed at denying that very protection on the ground that government confronts the difficulties which, in the first instance, were envisioned."

cheerful disposition, good fortune in one's friends and family, physical beauty, or the capacity to recall perfectly all of Mozart's symphonies, then on what should the assessment be made?

Contributions and Physical Integrity The situation of persons with chronic kidney disease is indeed terrible. Without some replacement for the kidney function they are doomed to be poisoned by their own body wastes. Mechanical relief by hemodialysis is often only partially effective, dangerous, frequently more and more painful, and itself a cause of despondency because of the reliance on a cumbersome and dramatically external device. By contrast, a successful kidney donation restores function so that the patient may begin to feel whole again. On the other side, we do not need *two* kidneys; the second is—as it were—a spare. Now, if we are serious about the general proposition that no one is entitled to the benefit of unearned natural advantages, so that the more fortunate should contribute to the situation of the less fortunate, what could be a clearer obligation than to enter, say, a lottery, the "winners" of which would be compelled to donate just one of their kidneys? Let us consider what this might mean: would a sheriff levy execution upon a reluctant "winner's" kidney, or would an unwilling "winner" be jailed for contempt of a court order to donate—like a reluctant witness before a grand jury?

Recall the discussion of the importance of bodily integrity to a sense of personal worth and integrity; recall further that the decision to give the negative right to the victim in the hypothetical assault was based on the notion that only in this way do we assert that a person, being in possession of her own body, is in possession of herself. In this way the negative right furnishes part of the foundation for the moral personality of individuals, who then enter society as bargainers in the marketplace and as members of a justly cooperating community. But surely, if the victim's moral entitlement to her bodily integrity must be assumed *before* we undertake any inquiry into the fair distribution of income and wealth, it follows too that my right to my own "spare" kidney must stand on as solid a grounding of right. Nor does it have the least relevance that those who would intrude upon the unwilling kidney donor's body would be surgeons and anesthetists acting for the good purpose of vastly improving the life prospects of a desperately sick person. The gratification of the rapist in case III was excluded from consideration not on any puritanical grounds, but because he had no right to use another person's body to obtain that gratification. The donee's need may be more urgent than the rapist's (our moral feelings about it may be different), but that is not the point; he too is using another person's body against that person's will. Nor does it make any difference that in this case, the intrusion takes place pursuant to some fair scheme like a lottery. For imagine that V had been forced to submit to R after "winning" a lottery. No considerations of fair distribution can justify violating my right not to be assaulted—in order to obtain my kidney or for any other good or bad purpose. And so no such considerations can justify an official in directing another that he assault me. Though the remote official does not act directly, he is implicated in the wrong since he uses those who carry out the scheme as the instruments of his intention.*

Let us try another way of getting the kidney out of the donor. Might we not either pay a donor enough that he would consent to part with the kidney or tax him enough that he would rather part with it than pay the tax? If what is meant is that we hold our kidney lottery and then assess a special tax against an unwilling "winner," or that we compel the donation but pay some kind of compensation, then I think these proposals represent little advance over straight compulsion and violation of rights. Certainly the payment of compensation is better than violating the unwilling donor's rights and not paying compensation. Nevertheless, if it is a violation of right to take my kidney against my will, it is still a violation of right to take my kidney against my will and pay me for it. And, of course, the special tax (fine?) levied only upon losers of the lottery is still less justifiable.

The tax and compensation proposal might take a much more benign form. Kidney transplantation may be part of the services offered under the (national) health insurance scheme discussed in Chapter 5. The health providers would of course have to get their kidneys somewhere, and one of the ways they might get them is by buying them in the same way that they buy medicines, X-ray machines, hospital buildings, and the services of doctors, nurses, orderlies, bookkeepers, and so on. The cost of kidneys would then be like every other cost, and whether or not they

---

* Conscription in wartime or during emergencies might be urged as counter-examples. I have already argued why it is inappropriate to construct general arguments on the basis of the exceptional or catastrophic.

were provided would depend on how much health protection consumers would want to buy relative to all the other things they wanted to buy.

But should persons be selling their kidneys? Even though they may not be *compelled* to donate them, should they not be donating them freely? Do not all the arguments I have made against compelling donations—arguments about the priority of bodily integrity to tradable and distributable goods—do not all of these arguments compel the conclusion that there should not be a trade in body parts, perhaps for the same reason that there should not be a trade in sexual gratification (prostitution)? Certainly if what I have argued about the primacy of bodily integrity is correct, then anybody not acting under the compulsion of unjustly desperate circumstances would not want to engage in such commerce. We would not want anyone to sell his body because we would want all members of our society to share the moral convictions which underlie our conclusion that it would be wrong to compel anyone to yield his body for the use of another. I would hope that individuals who have a fair share of income in a just society and who have had a reasonable opportunity to insure themselves against misfortune would not want to sell their bodies in order to increase their income. But, of course, they would violate no one's rights if they did so. Nor will it violate the rights of the kidney-sellers if we tax their earnings just as we tax all other earnings, for it is they who choose to put a cash value on their bodies. After all, our distaste for prostitution does not imply that prostitutes' earnings should be exempt from income taxation.

Finally, selling one's body differs from selling one's talents or labor. In the latter case there is effort, choice, action, in the production of the commodity sold. True, choices too are intimate, personal, but when a man sells his body he does not sell what is his, he sells himself. What is disturbing, therefore, about selling human tissue is that the seller treats his body as a foreign object. *It* is sold—he is not. The man who sells his labor, his talent, even his willingness to take risks, however, offers the *product* of his effort, his freedom, his choices. The shame of selling one's body is just that one splits apart an entity one knows should not be so split. It is thus not the sale as such which is disturbing, but the treatment of the body as a separate, separable entity. For I assume that buying and selling as such are not shameful activities. On the contrary, in the context of just institutions, buying and selling—in other words, markets—are simply the organization and coordination on mutually beneficial and just terms of cooperative social endeavor. Buying and selling are preeminently human social activities, or rather the coordination and regulation of human social activities.*

We are thus brought quite naturally to the sale of one's talents and efforts, to the choice of leisure over effort, in short to the liberty to do what one wants, to live one's life as one wills.

Liberty: Talents, Effort, and Natural Advantages The constraints on the pursuit of positive rights derived from respect for personal integrity are real constraints, but they seem to apply only to rather farfetched cases. If all that negative rights do is to block compelled kidney donations and things of that sort, one could well say that the mountain has labored and brought forth a mouse—a mouse in the sense that I have produced arguments against doing things which nobody has much stomach for doing anyway. The impingements on individual rights in the name of communal goals which serious people have urged or implemented take other forms: taxes, regulations and restrictions, compelled service. And my previous arguments might seem to leave very wide scope for these things. Perhaps I cannot be strapped to a table and compelled to donate my kidney, but there are those who see taxation (particularly taxation to fund redistribution, which my theory of fair shares permits) as very like such a compelled exaction. Let us take it as given that society may not require from us our kidneys or blood; is it not as bad that society can require from us our talents and our efforts—

* So it comes to this: Society may not compel donations of kidneys, corneas or even blood; and though not wrong, it is somehow shameful—at least in a society with a decent distribution of income—for individuals to sell these things. But how are we to get blood and kidneys? The answer is obvious: voluntary donations. In a voluntary donation, I give up a part of myself not to satisfy some need or want, not to get anything, and thus I do not trade myself for anything, as if my person were an item of commerce. This is how I would solve the conundrum which Richard Titmuss raises in his book *The Gift Relationship* (New York: Pantheon, 1971). Titmuss holds that there is an obligation to give blood, and that therefore it should not be the subject of commerce. My conclusion is that it is personally bad (in a just society), though not in any sense wrong, to sell blood. It is certainly wrong to compel its donation. It is certainly good to give it freely: I have an excess and others badly need it. But if voluntary donations just are not forthcoming, if free citizens, not under economic duress, just don't want to give blood but are perfectly willing to sell it, then the commerce must go forward.

that the fruits of our labor can be required of us to provide benefits for others against our will? May I use my abilities as I wish, or not use them at all? If society determines that equality— or some other such distributive norm—is what distributive justice requires, does that mean that some more fortunate individuals will be actively prevented from enjoying more than their "fair share" even if they deprive no one else in their enjoyment? If we decide, for instance, that education is a peculiarly important positive right whose enjoyment must be equally distributed, would that mean that a teacher could be prevented from offering an advantage (perhaps not for money, though that would be the usual situation) to anybody, unless that advantage were available to everybody? Would it even mean that a man could be prevented from procuring educational benefits for himself by reading, talking, thinking, if he advanced himself beyond the norm? And, finally, what of the inequalities resulting from differential capacities for deriving satisfaction? In all of these instances we must consider the extent to which not physical or intellectual integrity but liberty to do and to become what we choose is the basis of rights—rights of individual inviolability in the face of the community's purpose to achieve fair distributive shares and to assure that the benefits of natural advantage are fairly enjoyed by all.

The most important issue relates to compelled contributions of talent, effort, and special ability. In order not to make the argument too easy, I shall not consider conscription by threats of force into providing needed talents (in return only for that compensation which our distributive norm characterizes as fair). Let us instead be more realistic and consider systems of taxation that would express the same judgment that natural advantages, talents and abilities are social property and that no one has a moral right to benefit unduly from their possession. The strongest example of a scheme built on this principle would be a tax measured by capacity to contribute—in other words, "From each according to his ability." To simplify the discussion, let us assume that earnings are determined by the market and that individuals spend all their earnings for consumption purposes.

Now imagine the situation of a number of individuals under such a regime. Surgeon (S), whose special and highly demanded skills command for him an exceptionally high income (two hundred thousand dollars); Veterinarian (V), who in fact possesses exactly the same skills but likes working with animals and earns an income one-tenth that of Surgeon; Basketweaver (B), who might have had these skills, but because of laziness, bad luck, drink, wenching, and so on, never developed them, and now is earning one-twentieth the income of Surgeon, doing about the only thing he is capable of doing; Commonman (C), who has about the average capacities and the average will to succeed and who is engaged in an average sort of job for an average sort of income—say, the same as Basketweaver's. Now, in the familiar schemes of fair contribution, whatever the formula of contribution, S would contribute on two hundred thousand, V on twenty thousand, and B and C on ten thousand. But if a person's *capacity* to contribute to the common good is to be the basis of assessment, then we would exact equal contributions from S and V. The assumption on which this would be done would be, after all, that Veterinarian either (a) is indeed withdrawing the equivalent of one hundred and eighty thousand dollars in resources from the economy in personal satisfaction (as the economists call it, "psychic income") or (b) is under some kind of obligation to the community to practice surgery, and though the community will not compel him directly to do so, yet it will not allow him to escape a charge he would have to pay were he doing his duty. The practical effect, of course, of assessing a twenty-thousand-dollar-a-year veterinarian as if he were a two-hundred-thousand-dollar-a-year surgeon would be to put considerable pressure upon him to move into surgery.*

If Veterinarian were assessed on the basis of his potential contribution, this would imply that the decision to exercise certain talents in a particular way is not his to make; this would imply that his talents to that extent are social property. For on what other basis can such an assessment be explained? Or, to put the point more pragmatically, an assessment on the basis of capacities will exert pressure toward the development of those capacities; but on what grounds can such pressure be justified other than on the argument that these capacities are somehow the community's to command? To be sure, the market also exerts pressure on all those subject to it—but there is a crucial difference: The differential in earnings of S and V cannot be seen as exacted *from* them by the market, but rather as determined by

---

* This would be like a property tax assessed on the income-producing potential of a parcel of land, quite apart from the use to which it is actually devoted.

what S and V are able to exact from others in return for their services.

Furthermore, a tax based on native capacity would be the same for B as for S, although S has twenty times B's income and consumption. And a capacity tax would fall on B twenty times as heavily as that assessed on Commonman, who has the same income as does B. The burden on B could be terrific. What would justify it? Unlike V, B cannot now switch to surgery even if he wanted to. Are we to say that that is his own fault, that if only he had worked harder as an adolescent, had been more serious, and so on, then at age thirty he would be able to switch to surgery if he wanted to? Not only is the inquiry which such an assessment authorizes ridiculously impractical, it is viciously intrusive. I have already argued that no man should be able to claim a greater distributive share of society's resources just because his subjective wants are greater, just because peacock's tongues and dancing girls by the dozens were the irreducible minimum below which he would sink into despair and ennui. To that hapless sybarite we said that his tastes were his own responsibility; we said that by *not* honoring his claim to subjective satisfaction we were respecting his integrity, his liberty to define his own tastes and passions. We must not then engage in exactly that same forbidden exercise and impose a tax on Basketweaver's exercise of self-determination in the formation of his tastes and capacities.

Could it be argued, however, that in the case of the sybarite, we were concerned with what it is fair to *give to* an individual, while now we are asking how much to *take from* him, what his fair contribution should be? This is a sufficient distinction only if we change the ground on which it was concluded that a man should be responsible for his own tastes and entitled to a fair share measured only by an objective (monetary) measure. We might say now that this objective measure is intended to put pressure on individuals to make their tastes as modest, as easily satisfiable as possible. Tastes would then be viewed as a public resource open to social manipulation. But that was not my analysis. I argued that a man is responsible for his own tastes because this responsibility is an expression of a certain conception of the relation of an individual to the collectivity. What a person is, what he wants, the determination of his life plan, of his concept of the good, are the most intimate expressions of self-determination, and by asserting a person's responsibility for the results of this self-determination we give substance to the concept of liberty. If we refuse to tax potential contributions, we respect that same liberty. For if we demand of a man that he contribute according to what he might have become, we are saying that this was a choice which was not his to make, while if we assess contributions only on the basis of what a man has chosen to be, we recognize that that choice was entirely his; we respect it. The contribution point does indeed mirror my earlier argument about tastes, but the question remains, how contributions to fair shares are to be measured. In sketching the main lines of an answer to this question, I hope to add more practical substance to the concept of rights—here, the negative right not to be coerced in respect to effort or to choice of an occupation and a way of life.

The Consumption Tax   We have a right to a fair share of the community's resources and so a corresponding duty to contribute, to do our part. This duty to contribute is consistent with a person's right of self-determination, a right to choose his own tastes and life plan so long as that person's contribution is required only by reference to the objective goods, the objective resources he withdraws from the common pool. On these premises the ideal tax is a consumption tax—measured in terms of the money value of goods and services consumed. (I set aside the question of the tax rate, which might be proportional, progressive, or whatever.) Such a consumption tax differs from a tax on the subjective satisfaction derived from what is consumed, including leisure, from a tax on what is earned, and from a tax on what an individual has the capacity to earn. A consumption tax is intended to express the idea that a man should contribute in relation (however the proportion is defined) to what he takes *out* of the pool of scarce social resources.*

---

* A difficulty is presented by the phenomenon of what the economists call public goods or collective goods. The classic examples are national defense, police, a court system, while other goods like public health or education have both public and private aspects. A public good has the characteristics that (1) the persons who enjoy it do not use it up in enjoying it (in which respect it is like a tunnel or painting in a museum), (2) they cannot practicably be excluded from that enjoyment and therefore they cannot practicably be charged a fee as a condition of their enjoyment, and so (3) no price mechanism can determine what a person's willingness to pay for collective goods might be. For these reasons it has seemed inevitable that the level

A consumption tax respects individual rights, because its incidence falls only on what a person chooses to do, not on what he
might do—as would a tax on capacities, talents, or dispositions.
Being measured, moreover, by the objective (money) value of
the consumption on which it falls, it asks no questions about and
imposes no charge on subjective differences of tastes and temperament. The man who loves his work and savors his every pleasure
pays no more on that account. These are familiar and obvious
points. The special feature of a consumption tax as a respecter of
liberty appears when we contrast it to the more usual mode of
exacting contributions, the income tax. The income tax is
troublesome because it requires a contribution in terms not of
the individual's withdrawals from the pool of social resources but
rather in terms of what he contributes to that pool, for a man's
income (in a well-functioning economy) should reflect the value
of his services, so that a person receiving a higher income is
making a more valuable (or valued) contribution. But why
should we tax a man on the worth of his contribution? If it is
thought that income is a surrogate for capacity to contribute,
then I have already argued that this capacity is an improper basis
for assessing taxes. And in any event, income is not at all a sure
measure of potential contribution, as the hypothetical cases of
Veterinarian and Basketweaver show. Undoubtedly people with
greater income have greater capacity in the sense just that they
have more money. Yet this can serve as the justification of an
income tax only on the assumption that how much we *can* get
out of a man is the proper measure of how much we *may* get out
of him, as if all possession were at the sufferance of the state.

The point is well illustrated by considering the objection that
both consumption and income taxes are unfair, as they fail to tax
leisure, giving an advantage to the person who chooses to take his
income in the form of leisure—working less than he might. Now,
one reason for not taxing leisure is that (problems of eligibility

---

of public goods expenditures, the choice of public goods, and the mode of
their funding must be determined politically and not by the market. But how
does the consumption of public goods enter into the determination of fair
shares? Are we to assume that in respect to some or all public goods the rich
enjoy a greater pro rata share—is it the case, for example, that the rich
derive a greater benefit from police protection because they have more to
protect and would probably be willing to pay more for the protection? If
the question is answered affirmatively, then in the case of a progressive fair-
share consumption tax, there would be double progressivity: the value of the
consumption by the rich would be assumed to rise progressively and so would
the proportion of tax on the consumption thus calculated.

for public assistance apart) no one is obliged to work and no one's capacity to work belongs to the state. By not working and not consuming, a man deprives no other person of anything to which that other is entitled. And if I am right about the non-working nonconsumer, then I should think the case against taxing the *working* nonconsumer is even stronger.

We should seek to have the incidence of a tax fall on that which justifies imposing a contribution, which is the fact that among the things a man enjoys are scarce resources, resources he cannot enjoy without depriving someone else of a chance for their enjoyment. It is enjoyment in scarcity which gives rise to the notion of fair shares—fair shares not of happiness, not of capacities, not of free goods like air and sunshine, but of scarce resources. By contrast, my happiness and my capacities are my own and my enjoyment of them does not deplete a stock which would otherwise be available to others. A consumption tax is a tax on what one withdraws from the pool of scarce resources. To measure contributions on the basis of that withdrawal is the fullest affirmation of the liberty of the individual to determine himself, for a man is free to determine how much he will consume. And if he chooses to consume very little, leaving that much more for others to satisfy their needs and wants, *that* should not give others a claim against him. True, under an income tax a man is also free to determine how much he shall earn. What could be more absurd, however, than to tax a man more heavily for the sole reason that he is making a greater contribution?* It is also true that if a person spends his entire income, a consumption and an income tax will come to the same thing—and it is a virtue of an income tax that it is easier administratively to vary

* The main problem with a consumption as opposed to an income tax would seem to be that those with very high incomes and low consumption will tend to accumulate considerable wealth in the form of savings. In itself this is not a problem or a basis for a claim of unfairness. The individual who is not consuming but saving is by hypothesis allowing productive resources to remain in the economy for such purposes as capital formation. True enough, he has a greater capacity to consume in the future from his accumulated savings, but the taxation would bite at that point. Another problem would be that such an individual, though he does not consume more than his fair share, may enjoy special satisfactions from the control of his (by hypothesis, productive) wealth. But that is a question not so much about fair shares as about fair measures of economic and political power, which can quite easily be disassociated from the present discussion. For instance, an extreme solution would require all such savings to be held in the form of claims upon the national treasury.

the rates with the level of income/consumption. This point of practical administration, equating income with consumption, may mean that reliance on the income tax to achieve fair shares is in fact based on a conception of rights similar to the one I offer here. If that is so, so much the better.

The discussion has focused on exactions of money through the tax system. If there is a violation of right in such monetary matters, it is less brutal, more remote, more impersonal than the violation of negative rights in compelled tissue donations or even than coerced choice of occupation. From this, some may conclude that therefore I really should be back in the realm of positive rights—and therefore once more in the realm of more or less, of balancing and weighing, rather than in the domain of moral absolutes, the domain of negative rights. But that is a mistake. Because the violation in an improperly conceived tax (such as a capacity tax) proceeds in an abstract and impersonal way does not mean that it is not felt as an assault on integrity, does not mean that it is not a violation of negative rights. My thesis is that there is a domain of negative rights that is to be understood as the domain of personal integrity, the domain that defines the foundation of moral personality, and that not only bodily integrity but integrity of mind (as in lying) and liberty are components of moral integrity. Therefore, just as respect for personal integrity generates the negative rights which forbid compelled organ donation, so respect for liberty limits the implementation of positive rights, the pursuit of fairness and even of sympathy. Liberty is a very general concept—too general. This discussion may give it some content, showing its connection with negative rights. The liberty protected by my proposed constraints on the assessment of contributions to the common good is an aspect of moral integrity: it is a liberty to choose how one will relate to, contribute to, and cooperate with one's fellow men, a liberty to define, develop and control what will give one satisfaction, a liberty to develop some and not other capacities, in short, the liberty to determine a life plan, to choose one's self.

FAMILY RIGHTS: A COMPLEX CASE

Certain moral phenomena are peculiarly elusive. On one hand we have powerful intuitions about them which we are reluctant to abandon, on the other hand they do not seem to fit our theories in any straightforward way, so that those intuitions are left without a sufficient foundation. The situation of the family raises a host of perplexities. Consider the conflict between family rights and the policy of providing fair opportunities for all members of society. Even if inheritance taxes remove what is thought to be unfair transmissions of wealth, and welfare measures provide access to free education and health care, still—as Rawls says—"the family will lead to unequal chances between individuals." Critics of the family are not only disturbed by the depressing effect of culturally or emotionally substandard homes; they deplore equally the persistent lines of elitism fostered by better-favored parents transmitting intellectually and attitudinally advantageous traits to their children. It is not just that some may be fated to be advantaged, but that family lines make the distribution of the advantage nonrandom. The ties between family members tend to cause excessive identification between lines of such unfairly advantaged persons. "Is the family to be abolished then?" asks Rawls in a forthright expression of perplexity.*

But why the anguish? If the family is such a nuisance, why not just abolish it? Critics of many persuasions have suggested just that. Obviously, something does not go down easily in such radical proposals, and the nature of the hesitation suggests the lurking presence of negative rights: here we have a laudable social end, an aspect indeed of implementing the positive right to fair shares, and yet we shrink from following that policy to the limit of its logic—just as was the case with organ donations or talents. But what is the negative right in question? Is it liberty, as in the case of self-improvement or occupational choice, or is it some kind of personal integrity? Both suggestions seem implausible. The liberty asserted by parents is not an aspect of self-determination, but rather a liberty to determine someone else. It is not even the associational liberty of friendship (to be discussed later), since the objects of the association start out as helpless, unreciprocating, wholly inchoate beings. Is there, then, just a negative right not to have one's family relations interfered with? This suggestion seems so ad hoc as to be hardly helpful. I propose the explanation that the family is in fact a complex moral object

* A perplexity which is quite reasonably mitigated by his belief that no serious inequalities or perturbations are very likely in the context of an otherwise just general structure. See *A Theory of Justice*, p. 511.

at the intersection of a number of negative rights (personal, political, and legal), a number of primary and secondary positive rights, and a congeries of simply adventitious circumstances. Negative rights are a crucial aspect of this complex moral object.

Consider some of the things that are *not* included under the notion of family rights. There is no right to harm your children, to abuse your spouse, to appropriate property which clearly belongs to the other. In addition, there is no right *not* to provide for one's children, not to assure they have proper schooling, and so on. At one time things may have stood differently in respect to the family, and family rights may have been like property rights, held by the father, to the person and service of family members, but that is not the present conception. And yet family rights do seem to include such things as discretion to direct the formation of the child's earliest and perhaps most basic value structures and to determine his education, so long as minimum standards are met. In the United States at least, if parents can show that their child is learning certain objective skills, then the parents' directives cannot be countermanded on the ground that community values would be better inculcated in a public school, and certainly not on the ground that the child is getting an unfair educational advantage.

The guiding conception, I suggest, is that the right to form one's child's values, one's child's life plan and the right to lavish attention on that child are extensions of the basic right not to be interfered with in doing these things for oneself. It is not sufficient to deduce these rights from the more general rights to associate with or even to teach willing adults, since children, unlike adults, are not presumed to be able to choose, accept, or reject such associations. In respect to associations between adults, we forbear to interfere, because we recognize the liberty of each to develop his own life plan. But a parent does not form his child by providing the child the occasions for making whatever choices the child deems best. The notion that the child is regarded as an extension of the self seems the better analogy, since, in determining one's own life plans, too, there is an identity between chooser and chosen-for—there is an inability to step completely aside and review the perspective from which the chooser chooses for the person for whom the choice is made.

But of course this is only an analogy, and the problem remains. For, given the power of whoever it is who forms the child, why should that power rest so wholly in persons who are by no means shown to be the most competent to exercise it? And if we could socialize that power, would we not also be able to assure fair distributive shares in the attention and advantages enjoyed at this crucial stage of childhood? Some of the arguments developed so far suggest a basis for the special right to determine and favor one's children. The main theme is the special bond between parent and child based on the facts of human reproduction.

What would it mean to hold that parents have no special title to determine—benignly, but according to their lights—their children's values? Surely such a view implies that the parents' reproductive functions are only adventitiously their own: they may, *perhaps*, be free to decide whether and with whom to reproduce, but they have no special relation to the product of that reproduction. Babies are born to their parents because they must be born to someone, but that is all. Now, such a view is reminiscent of the argument that I have already rejected about talents and other natural advantages: the notion that talents are only adventitiously the property of those who have them, that a talented person holds his talents strictly in trust for the collectivity since talents reside in him only because they have to reside somewhere. I rejected this argument because to sunder a person from his talents and dispositions is to sunder him from himself, to violate his basic integrity. And so it was with kidneys and blood also. But are babies like that? It seems to me they are, because of their tie to the bodies of their parents and to their parents' sexual functions in particular.

Consider again case III. The point might be made that rape is no violation of personal integrity and should really be analogized to cases I or II. After all, no physical injury, pain, or impairment is necessarily associated with rape. An act of rape does, however, necessarily entail the assailant's appropriation of a function, the sexual function, which is incontrovertibly bodily. This is a function whose connection with the sense of self, with personal integrity, can be explained and elaborated. Nor is it the case that these connections are merely contingent or cultural, though they certainly do vary from person to person and from culture to culture. The importance of the relation between sexuality and personality and between sexuality and relations to others is a psychological constant of human nature. It is, of course, imaginable that creatures might exist for whom sexuality would be a matter of indifference or who would have no deep involvement with it, but they would be very different from us.

Sexuality is implicated in two ways in the concept of self. First, the development of sexual identity is an important aspect of the development of identity overall. In acquiring a secure sense of oneself as an autonomous person, one advances by feeling progressively at home in one's body and progressively in possession of one's own faculties, progressively identified subjectively with the physical entity that makes up the person objectively. Now, sexual identity is an important aspect of this physical entity: it is implicated in the very form of the body, pervades its functionings, is related to neurological and temperamental structures, is related to reproduction, and so on. Second, for a fully formed, developed individual, sexuality provides resources for involvement with others and for gratification that are not available through other means. Compare this essentially physical capacity with that of locomotion, manipulation, defense: substitutions and aids for those are easily imaginable. Sexuality is less like them and more like sight and hearing, which determine not only the quantity but the quality of information received and which present gratifications without substitutes. (A blind person may develop other pleasures, but they will never be the same as the pleasures of sight.) Sexuality is part of one's basic equipment and resources as a person.

This argument shows we must be prepared to extend beyond physical harm the respect we owe to persons by virtue of their physical, bodily natures. It shows that the sense of possession of oneself, which negative rights protect, extends to possession of one's function. And this extends quite naturally to reproduction. But a baby is not, of course, just like the love or pleasure associated with sexual relations. It is an independent person (or will be one—I do not enter that debate) with rights of its own. This independent status is sufficiently recognized by obliging the parents to care for and educate the child in the child's best interests. The child's most intimate values and determinants, however, must come from somewhere. The child cannot choose them—rather, they choose the child. And society has no special right to choose them, since society, after all, is only the hypostasis of individual, choosing persons.

Consider the matter from the point of view of the mother. There is evidence that there are pervasive physiological changes of great subtlety associated with pregnancy and birth. Thus quite apart from the gross facts of parturition, motherhood is an experience which has persistent, biological roots and is not just a voluntary or customary social bond imposed upon the contingently prior fact of birth—it is not as if separating the breeding and the rearing functions could nevertheless yield an unaltered experience of parenthood. Rather, the physical facts are importantly implicated in the resulting social bond. The mother experiences the baby as peculiarly hers, and this affects her perspective. The child does not belong to the community, and in view of its helplessness, it does not even belong to itself, not yet at least. In this way the mother's (and by extension the father's) sense of autonomy is enlarged, enlarged to the point where by investing their autonomy in a growing, other person, their use of autonomy is the model for the deepest form of altruism. As has often been said, parenthood is the closest many of us come to overcoming the fact of mortality. Parenthood is a kind of physical continuity, a physical continuity which is also bound up with spiritual and moral continuity through our influence on our children. The family as an institution expresses these aspects of the parents' personality.

There are corresponding advantages to the child. Surely all my earlier arguments about the importance of our sense of ourselves as unique, particular beings imply the sense that our bodies and personal characteristics are uniquely our own (hence, perhaps, the unease about twins) . That sense would be undermined if, for instance, we were bred "to order" according to some plan. The random biological hazard of our parents' mating affirms that we belong to ourselves, for no one planned us. And our uniqueness is the sign of our individuality. Now, this conceptual advantage is carried forward by affirming that our parents not only conceived us but also transmitted through personal love our most primitive emotional formation. Belonging at first to our parents, whom we will replace, we have a chance of believing we belong to ourselves.

All this is a diversion intended to show how negative rights might serve as the kernel of further, quite complicated moral speculations.

UNINTENDED INVASIONS: A COMPLICATION

Recall case IV, an elderly pedestrian mowed down by a reckless motorist. Has there been a violation of Pedestrian's rights? Has the reckless motorist done anything wrong? These questions might be asked for several purposes. First, is Driver to be condemned morally? Did he do something which he ought not to have done? Second, should Pedestrian be compensated for his injuries, inconvenience, fear, pain? These are not equivalent questions. If we answer the first question affirmatively, it pretty well follows that Driver should pay for what he has done. As we have seen, the reverse is not true: we may require compensation for the infliction of harm without at all concluding that the compensator has acted badly.

It does seem natural to say that Driver has acted wrongly, that he should be condemned, and that he should pay compensation. One might even go further and argue that Pedestrian had a right to be where he was and that Driver violated his rights. As to Manufacturer (in case II), on the other hand, the most we would want to say is that it would be wrong for him *not* to pay compensation to Homeowner—that here is a case of a (secondary) positive right on H's part to compensation. But how do such intuitive judgments fare in my scheme? The gravest problem is that neither Driver nor Manufacturer intends the harm he does, in the sense of intention developed in Part I, as a means or an end. The harm is rather only a more or less certain concomitant of his conduct. We cannot condemn Driver categorically, since presumably his goal was at least permissible, and injury to Pedestrian was not his chosen means. He is not like the rapist in case III. Yet there is no great difficulty in accommodating my scheme to the intuitive thrust for condemnation. First of all, it is clear that acting for a permissible end by permissible means only lifts the burden of *categorical* wrongness; it did not dispense us from the requirement of weighing even unintended bad consequences. If the anticipated harm outweighs the value of our ends or if we have no right to ignore such harm, then here too it is wrong to proceed. Indeed, once the balance has been struck and comes out against the conduct, to proceed is just as wrong as if the harm *were* intended. One might say that the actor then intentionally violates his duty not to take this undue risk for the insufficient goal, or that the victim has an affirmative right to due care. The reckless motorist acts wrongly on this reasoning.

What remains to be done is to fit this set of judgments into the theory of rights. What Driver does is found to be wrong only as the conclusion of a process of weighing, in which (unlike the case of intentional wrong) the interests of *both* parties are entitled to consideration. But how is this process of weighing to go forward? Should we give Pedestrian's interests great weight on some a priori moral grounds? It does seem plausible to extend the argument for the value of bodily integrity to so fundamental a human capacity as getting about on one's own two legs.* And yet, where the incursion is unintentional, we cannot avoid striking a balance between the interests of the two parties. After all, the injuring party is also exercising a valued capacity and to condemn him is to restrict *his* moral liberty. On both sides of the equation, then, we have not rights and wrongs but the enjoyment of rights, the value of rights. But we have seen the *value* of rights is part of our fair share. The amount of physical security, the number of occasions to speak and be heard, how much ability to move about free from unintentional impingements we enjoy are all part of our fair share. Further, we have seen that the theory of fair shares is not concerned primarily with what particular things we get—it is up to each of us to choose for himself from the efficiently determined collection of goods. Efficiency is the province of economics, more specifically of the economic analysis of rights (EAR). Assuming Pedestrian and Driver enjoy a fair distribution of income and wealth, then in the absence of transaction costs, we may rest content with whatever arrange-

---

* The interest in moving about freely—which gives rise to a negative right not to be restrained in that movement—seems to me a primitive, bedrock interest related to the empirically universal relation between a person and his environment: the different objects of choice are spread out in space; it is an environment extended along spatial dimensions. Thus, freedom to act, to choose, entails freedom to move. Freedom and rationality rest on a secure sense of possession of one's body, and liberty of motion is an element of this sense of belonging to oneself. It would be bizarre to insist on the centrality of bodily integrity without at the same time considering the notion of integrity of function. It would be bizarre to say that integrity of one's arms and legs is crucial but the interest in moving them is not, that the interest in integrity of one's body attaches a particular significance to protecting a woman from rape but does not extend to the interest in her use of those same bodily capacities whose involuntary usurpation is prohibited. But there is no reason to limit this to a passive association—it is an association with one's body and the things it can do. To argue that this or that active bodily function or capacity is metaphysically contingent, that things might have been otherwise, that we might move ourselves by an operation which dissipates the atoms of our body at one place and reconstitutes them in another, and so forth, is in fact no different from arguing that we might not have had bodies of this form—they might have been circular, hard metal spheres, or they might even have existed connected with our brains only by radio waves, or spread out (our brains included) over large areas with no physical connection between parts. Some liberty of motion, then, is implied in the exercise of bodily functions and capacities and is therefore part of the notion of a free person.

ment regarding driving and walking they may conclude among themselves—certain streets designated for walking, others for driving only, or perhaps all cars to be equipped with spongy bumpers. And in the real world of substantial transaction costs, EAR tells us we should still fix the liability rule so as to attain efficiency, making lump-sum redistributions to offset any resulting distortion in fair shares thereafter. Thus EAR might tell us that Driver must compensate Pedestrian only if Driver was exceeding a certain speed or only if Pedestrian was on a designated walkway.

Now it might be argued that, though most cases of accidental loss must be submitted to a regime of efficiency, still certain interests are so important that the weight they carry in any balance of interests is fixed on moral, not on practical, grounds. For instance, that we must give substantial weight to the life of an innocent bystander, exposing him to mortal risk only for the gravest reason, seems a judgment whose power far exceeds anything like the reasoning of EAR. EAR holds that we forbid such risks just because most people would pay heavily not to have them imposed, or would exact a heavy price of anyone seeking to impose them. Fair shares are a moral imperative. And EAR also is a principle with moral force, as it tells us how to maximize the range of alternatives from which all may choose. EAR, as we have seen, respects a man's autonomy to choose his own values. Consequently if, in a world where fair shares are respected, it is efficient (that is, it accords with the maximal system of the coordinated preferences of all) that certain interests be protected to a determined degree, then that determination has moral force: the moral force of the principles of autonomy and distributive justice.

This economic account does *seem* to miss some of the moral force of the condemnation of culpable recklessness. To endanger another frivolously is just wrong; it is as much a manifestation of disrespect as making his misfortune a means or an end. This moral intuition is, however, substantially equivalent to what is asserted by EAR and the principle of fair distributive shares. EAR says—coolly and with an air of moral detachment—that the interest in personal integrity is very important, so important that people would pay heavily to assure it and would need to be paid heavily to give it up. The fair-share principle tells us that if shares are fairly distributed, then no one will be so destitute that he could not pay to keep reasonably safe or so destitute that he would readily accept payment to relinquish a condition of safety if it were his. Now, since fair shares are morally required and EAR tells us what rights emerge if the autonomy of all to choose their situations with their fair share is respected, then the resulting system is highly relevant to morality—autonomy and fair shares being moral notions. Someone violating a rule forbidding reckless driving does not then just act inefficiently; he grabs more than his fair share of a scarce resource, namely the moral space in which the members of the community go about their business while mutually imposing and accepting risks of various sorts. Thus, Driver in case IV is a kind of thief, and what he does is wrong. The violation of the rule is, via the notions of fair shares and efficiency, a violation of right. Though we come to this conclusion by a different route than in the case of intentional harm, we do come to it.

I have just concluded that Driver violates a right of Pedestrian just as surely as does the assailant in case III. But imagine that we have not a clear case of reckless driving, but rather this case:

> V. If there were proper sidewalks and guardrails, then those driving on the highway at 50 mph would pose no excessive threat to pedestrians. Let us assume that responsible legislators should have appropriated money for guardrails and sidewalks and highway administrators should have mandated their construction. Unfortunately, through a combination of neglect and venality, they did not do so, with the result that the side of the road is safe only if drivers travel at 30 mph. Motorist knows all this, chooses to travel at 50, and swerves and hits Walker, who is making his way home by the side of the road.

Now we have assumed that Walker has a right not to be subjected to more than a certain level of risk. Motorist certainly exposes him to a greater risk, but only by doing something which would have been perfectly proper had legislators and bureaucrats done their duties. Thus it is clear that if Motorist proceeds at 50 mph, Walker's rights are violated, and when Motorist hits Walker, Walker is injured as a result of that violation. But is it Motorist who violates his rights? My inclination is to say that Motorist must take whatever precaution is needed to bring the risk where it would have been had all the other remote actors done their jobs. In effect this deprives Motorist of *his* right to proceed quickly on his way. But the fact is that though the real culprits are the shadowy, bureaucratic actors behind the scenes, still it is Motorist who would hit Walker, and therefore it is Motorist who must take on at least some of the burden. Perhaps the correct speed is 35 mph—the reasonably safe speed in a situation where a community has determined not to spend money on guardrails and both drivers *and* walkers have to share some portion of that increased burden.*

Compare this case to an important feature of case III. Although there is no doubt about the wrongness of R's conduct, it should be noted that there are the same shadowy abstract characters in that case too. Police, the courts, prisons, the education system, highways, and so on will determine whether a person is assaulted, harmed, impeded in his motion, lied to. And, of course, when I mention government officials charged with determining budgets and programs for such matters, I am only using them as the clearest examples of remote actors with an influence on the ultimate enjoyment of rights; all of us are implicated if we belong to the same community as those whose rights will be violated and as those who will violate rights unless prevented. And yet none of these remote actors violates negative rights. The city council might corruptly siphon off money that should be spent for police protection, so that an incremental number of persons are assaulted, but it does not violate the rights of those persons not to be assaulted; the council members do not assault those peaceful citizens, only the assailants do that. The officials violate rights to fair shares and duties of honesty. They steal, but they do not rape. After all, the corrupt city councillors do not intend that the citizenry should be assaulted (if they did, then they would indeed violate the negative rights of exactly those citizens whose assault they intended); and if they act negligently, nevertheless it is not they who intentionally inflict the injury. Although such a distinction may seem quixotic and pointless, it is an expression of the principle of personal responsibility.

CONCLUSION: THE SYSTEM OF POSITIVE AND NEGATIVE RIGHTS

The system of rights I have offered should be contrasted to two familiar conceptions. First, there are teleological conceptions of

---

* This is a particular example of the general problem regarding the individual's duty to contribute to fair shares when institutional structures are not in place to provide such fair shares as a general matter.

various sorts—maximizing utilitarianism is only one example. The defining characteristics of such conceptions is that they propose a goal—for instance, the maximization of some material or abstract quantity like pleasure or excellence, or the attainment of equality or perhaps some weighted average of equality and a maximum social product*—and if this goal is reached, or at least aimed at, this will guarantee the rightness of the result. Second, there is the type of system which Robert Nozick has called historical. In such a system, the rightness of the result is also guaranteed but only so long as no one has actively harmed any other person. *Both* types of system aim at a kind of moral determinacy which I believe is neither possible nor even desirable. The consequentialist tells us we need only look to the end state reached or aimed at—how we get there is only of instrumental interest, a ladder we kick away once we reach our goal. Nozick says that rightness does not depend at all on where we are

* I do not include maximin among such end-state or pattern theories of right, at least as maximin appears in the context of Rawls's theory. Recall a puzzle about maximin: Rawls argues that justice should make persons' situations depend as little as possible on the morally irrelevant fact of unequal natural advantages, and thus the prima facie correct criterion of distribution of burdens and of benefits is equality. On the other hand, Rawls argues that, if to draw out the greater contribution of the more talented, differential rewards are necessary, those differential rewards are justified to the exact extent that the greater contribution improves the situation of the worst-off man over what it would be under a regime of equality. There appears at first sight to be an anomaly here. The more talented, it would seem, are not morally entitled to any greater enjoyment because of this natural advantage, so if they require differential rewards to contribute their greater talents, they are making a claim they are not morally entitled to press, a claim the recognition of which should not be sanctioned by the very principle of justice which purports to state what moral persons may fairly claim. (For a more elaborate statement of this problem, see my review of *A Theory of Justice* in *Harvard Law Review* 85 [1972]: 1691–97.) The answer to this dilemma lies in an appreciation of the richness of Rawls's argument. For Rawls the principles of distributive justice are secondary to the principles of personal and political liberty. Thus the pursuit of distributive justice must respect the claim of liberty, and a goal such as equality is consistent with liberty only if it is qualified as in Rawls's maximin principle. Finally, Rawls's principles apply only to institutional structures, so that whatever situation a person finds himself in as a result of the interplay of his own choices and those institutions is assumed to be just. Certainly Rawls does not argue for any readjustments of individual situations because that individual is worse off than he might be under some other arrangement. You make your own bed in the general institutional structure, and then you must lie in it.

going but only on our not getting in each other's way as we proceed. The system of positive and negative rights I have sketched here assumes that rightness depends on the pursuit *both* of fairness, compassion, and thus on a (loosely identified) end state, *and also* on respect for the absolute constraints of negative rights.

Some may object that there is nothing new here. What I have just described is the altogether familiar notion of a constrained maximum—the pursuit of the good, subject to the constraints of right. And, of course, in a very general sense, that is true. But the notion of "system" which I offer does have a rather special characteristic, one which is not generally associated with the familiar operation of constrained maximizing. The end result of pursuing positive rights subject to the constraint of negative rights is wholly indeterminate; the widest range of outcomes, patterns of distribution, and levels of welfare may obtain under this system. Two exactly similar states of the world might have widely different moral characteristics. Any attempt to discern an order in the array of situations arranged between the poles of right and wrong is doomed to failure if only the instantaneous situations are examined. So much is true, I think, also of Nozick's perspective. But there is this difference, that among the criteria for judging the rightness and wrongness of a situation will be included the striving to implement positive rights. One might say, therefore, that the "system" is less systematic even than Nozick's, just because among the criteria of right and wrong are included aspirations toward fairness, toward distributive justice. This indeterminacy is a function of the principle that wrong (and this includes the violation of rights) is personal; a person may not do wrong, even to prevent a greater wrong by others. This principle guarantees indeterminacy of result, and that indeterminacy is aggravated by the circumstance that among the rights I recognize are positive rights. It is wrong to fail to work for and respect the positive rights of others.

This indeterminacy appears as particularly acute if one considers the structure of goals and constraints appropriate to different actors following different roles in the society. Statesmen and bureaucrats may be obliged, because of their duty to implement positive rights, to pursue policies which unfortunately provide the occasion for wicked men to violate negative rights. Yet so long as the statesmen have not chosen such violations as their means to the attainment of positive rights, then the unfortunate fact of such violations does not necessarily condemn their policy. For example, the institution of a fair tax structure may create the occasion for bribery and cheating. Yet if the lawmaker does not intend that others bribe or cheat, he may disregard this side effect as outweighed by the good which he seeks to accomplish. On the other hand, in the pursuit of fairness, of positive right, lawmakers may not themselves violate negative rights, not even as a means to the end that others respect negative rights.

III

Roles

7

Rights and Roles

I T IS clear enough that after we have taken care to render
to others their fair share and have taken care also to avoid
doing wrong, there remains during the whole course of our
lives a large measure of discretion. In filling this discretionary
space we make a life which is characteristically our own. If no
judgments could be made about this intimate and discretionary
realm, then the superficial and specious charge that in liberal
moral theory values are subjective would be at least half right.
But we recognize a good man not only by his perfect justice
(avoiding wrong, rendering his fair share) but by the way he
lives his life. And yet there is a bafflement too, for there is a great
variety and indeterminacy in the forms a good man's life may
take. Some may seek to lead pleasant and interesting lives, sur-
rounded by friends and family. Some devote themselves to the
arts, to knowledge or science. Still others are not content to
provide for their families, to share with their friends or even the
chance stranger in need: they seek out the unfortunate and
devote their energies to them. What is to be said about this
variety; how to discern an order within it?

I find it helpful to think of the forms of life which good men
adopt as *roles*. The metaphor of role is not meant to have any
hidden significance—I do not mean to suggest, for instance, that
we are all actors in some drama or to subscribe to any pretentious
sociological theory. The term is intended rather to draw attention to two things: first, that the theory of right and wrong leaves
us discretion to determine how we shall live our lives; and
second, that our choices do fall into patterns, determined in part
by recurrent patterns in our circumstances (as in the case of
kinship) and in part by the system of positive and negative

167

rights. In this chapter I shall be concerned both with how a good man chooses the roles he assumes and with the content of these roles. Can a good man be a lawyer or physician or friend? And what is it that such roles authorize or require? Particularly, does a role authorize a more limited concern for humanity as a whole, and does it justify doing what would otherwise be a wrong? Thus friends may seem to display a degree of callousness to persons outside the relationship, and government officials are inclined to invoke their roles not only to limit the range of their concern but also to justify visiting harm on outsiders.

I identify roles with the discretionary space left by the categories of right and wrong, and yet some of our firmest categorical judgments are associated with these roles: one speaks of the obligations of friendship or of kinship, the iron requirement of loyalty of a doctor or lawyer to those in his charge, the obligations of public officials to those they serve. There is no mystery or paradox here, for it is the entry into the role which is free. Once one has assumed the role, it binds with the obligations of right and wrong. (And in general there are few worthwhile things we can do which do not end up committing us in one way or another.) The difficulty lies elsewhere. How are we justified in entering into roles and assuming obligations which constrain us to pursue goods more limited than the general good?

The dilemma is clarified in one respect by the system already proposed. No argument for a discretionary space can override negative rights, can justify doing wrong—intentionally harming innocent persons, lying, and so on. But since these wrongs require an intention to produce the forbidden result and mere knowledge or foresight that harm may (or even will) come about as an unintended side effect does not make the action categorically wrong, there is still considerable room for maneuver. Whatever else may be said about the lawyer who lawfully procures the acquittal of a guilty accused, there is no need to suppose that he intends (in my strong sense of intend) harm, that he intends, for instance, to endanger an innocent suspect who may be prosecuted instead or that he intends to let loose on society a vicious criminal. Those would indeed be forbidden intentions. And similarly a government official may not hide behind his agents if he intends wrongful harm, procuring the execution of that intention through others.

So much is clear, but the question remains whether it is justifiable, even without harming anyone, to lavish more time, substance, and energy on a friend, relative, or patient. The utilitarian standard, which I shall refer to as efficiency, and the standard of fairness both offer the same challenge to these ordinary conceptions of loyalty. One may ask why it is fair to distribute scarce resources (including human effort) according to the vagrant inclinations of friendship or the accidents of family ties. And an uncompromising utilitarian must raise an analogous objection about the obvious inefficiencies of such loyalty to role. So efficiency and fairness, though divergent principles for many purposes, cause the same problems for the role categories we examine here. I shall refer to the challenges from fairness and efficiency interchangeably.

In the case of harm, the moral man was said by the utilitarians to be obliged to minimize harm; the counterpart to this strict utilitarian position applied to benefit would be this: A moral man is obliged to deploy resources to accomplish, through his efforts, the greatest good for the greatest number. Now, just as I argued that it was at war with common moral intuitions to derive what we must *not* do from utilitarian premises, so also the affirmative obligation to maximize good conflicts with our ordinary moral sense. It conflicts with our sense that we may have a special care for the welfare of our friends and family; that our pursuit of worthy ends—the arts and sciences—need not always be demonstrated to be the best possible use of our talents; that we may indeed simply be moved by the need of the stranger at our door, though he may not be the neediest recipient of our beneficence; and finally that we may reserve for our own pleasure and satisfaction a measure of ourselves which nevertheless might perhaps have been better deployed in the service of mankind generally. This intuition that I am authorized to give a measure of preference to identified persons standing close to me over the abstract interests of humanity in general finds its sharpest expression in the sense that I am entitled to act with something less than impartiality towards that person who stands closest of all to me: myself. No reasonable morality asks us to look upon ourselves as merely plausible candidates for the distribution of the attention and resources which we command, candidates whose entitlement to our own concern is no greater in principle than that of any other human being. Such a doctrine, which holds that I am for myself no more than any other human being is for me, may seem edifying but in reality strikes us as merely fanatical.

There are, of course, a variety of utilitarian strategies for dealing with the intuitive preference for the concrete and immediate displayed in our moral lives. Mill and Sidgwick have argued that such a tendency is most efficient and leads to the greatest happiness after all, since we know more about and are better able to help those closest to us. Others have argued that such preferences, though not ideally optimific, should be encouraged since they represent about as much altruism as we can realistically hope to get out of people anyway. Finally, especially appropriate to the case of the professional loyalties of doctors and lawyers is the rule-utilitarian account. Rule-utilitarianism justifies the preferences of various roles and relations by pointing not to the good done in those relations in particular cases but to the good flowing from having such institutions in general. Now I shall review neither these familiar rule-utilitarian' arguments nor their familiar refutations. They are in any case parallel to the consequentialist arguments considered and rejected in relation to wrongs and rights. Rather, what is needed is an affirmative account of the intrinsic value of these relations of benefit.

The foundations of that account are implicit in the arguments of Part II. The system of positive and negative rights defines the inviolability of the individual by defining what he may expect from others, what he must contribute, and what may not be required of him. Thus (exceptional circumstances apart) we have seen that personal service may not be required, while a money contribution may be required in proportion (perhaps an increasing proportion) to the individual's consumption of scarce resources. This contribution goes to assure a fair measure of scarce resources to all. Now just as the contribution may only be levied on what might be called public consumption, not on leisure and not on satisfaction, so it would follow that this tax-exempt domain is also exempt as it is shared with others. If I may not be taxed for "consuming" leisure, so I may not be taxed for consuming my leisure in your company nor may you be taxed for receiving that consumption. If a person may not be taxed for the sexual pleasure he receives (consumes), so also he may not be taxed for the pleasure he gives. If parents must be free to care for and educate their children, so those children must be free to receive that care and education. In all these cases, we have seen, the community must respect the rights of the individual no matter how "unfair" or "inefficient" the resulting distribution of satisfactions may turn out to be.*

VIRTUE AND ROLES

Rights are to be used, and there are moral judgments to be made, judgments of good and bad, better or worse, regarding the enjoyment of these rights. The person who uses his leisure to study philosophy or music is indeed making a better use of it than one who uses it to read pornographic novels. Nothing which I have written suggests in any way that we are foreclosed from making that judgment of value. Rather, it has been my thesis that no one is entitled to *enforce* any judgment about the use of the discretion allowed us by rights. But that a judgment may not be enforced does not mean that one is epistemologically unable to make it. What needs to be considered, however, is whether we do not repeat within the realm of good and bad—within the realm of judgments that can only be made, but not enforced— the very utilitarian moves which I have sought to block within the realm of rights. Specifically, I would ask whether devotion to one's self-improvement, to friends, to relatives, perhaps even to the concrete stranger are good only insofar as they move in the

---

* Gifts of objective resources pose a more complex problem. On one hand it would seem to contradict the notion of a right to a fair share if we impose restrictions on how an individual may spend that fair share. The idea, after all, is that a certain income is *my* fair share, so why should I not be free to spend it how *and on whom* I wish? On the other hand, the ideal fair share tax is a tax on consumption, and so if I receive a money gift why should I not be taxed as I spend that money to command scarce resources? If the donee is taxed as he uses the gift for consumption, then, to the extent that our formula for fair shares tends towards equality of consumption, the gift will also tend to be canceled out. Gifts of objective resources remain possible to the extent that inequality is permitted in general—the donor voluntarily placing himself in a lower consumption bracket and the donee in a higher consumption bracket. Effective money gifts are also possible, however, even in a regime of strict equality if the donee's consumption is imputed to the donor. That is, if I give you dinner in my house as my guest, this counts against my consumption, not against yours. It would seem that a regime that views not satisfaction as such but control over the consumption of scarce resources as the subject of fair distribution would tend to allow gifts and tax the donor, not the donee. Thus when one man gives friendly advice to another, the donor is giving that which society may not treat as an objective resource at all. If he sells the advice, however, the income is taxable in an income tax scheme, and where there is a tax on consumption the adviser is taxed when he spends the fee and the advisee is taxed as a consumer of the advice.

direction of maximizing the welfare of humanity in general, and whether they fail in their goodness exactly to the extent that they fail to grasp to the fullest the opportunity to promote the greatest good of the greatest number. Put differently, one might ask whether what is done for particular persons, for instance in roles such as friendship, has a value which is intrinsic and immune from universalizing-maximizing judgments, or whether in fact what is good about it is derivative from such judgments.

It would violate the rights of individuals, therefore, to *enforce* notions of fairness or efficiency in respect to the deployment of what I have called a man's discretionary resources. But should we not at least recognize a *moral* duty to use these resources for the good of all mankind—fairly and efficiently? Yet if a man may not be compelled but may be blamed (and should blame himself) if he does not use his liberty to maximize the good of all mankind, then we have accomplished very little by affirming that negative rights establish the core of moral personality. For if total claims upon us, while not enforceable, are nevertheless morally valid, then moral personality is established on a foundation which makes it morally immune only from coercion but not from condemnation. But surely we would want moral personality to have a more secure foundation. It is not enough that a man cannot be forced to act like a utilitarian maximizer; it should also be the case that he cannot be morally condemned if he does not act that way. If my conclusion is sound, and yet there are moral judgments to be made about the use of discretionary values, then we must expect that these moral judgments will have a different form from the universalizing judgments in the domain of fairness.

The appropriate form of judgment for this discretionary realm has already been suggested. The arguments in Part I developed the concept of concrete personal responsibility for intentional harm. We saw how intention picks out the object of harm, creating between a wrongdoer and victim a concrete relation between particular persons. This engagement of one's individual efficacy makes for the special categorical wrongness of the harm. But the same is true, in reverse as it were, in relations of love, friendship and beneficence. For just as considerations of the greater abstract good do not justify intentional wrongs, so the good we do to a particular person for that person's sake is not completely accounted for by the universalizing duty to produce net maximum good. The best expression of this type of moral judgment is the New Testament parable of the good shepherd who leaves ninety-nine sheep to go out in search of one lost sheep. This is a parable which illustrates a form of judgment that is concerned with the particular act and the particular relation. Fairness and efficiency are simply irrelevant in this domain. Love may be seen as the perfection of the moral values within this discretionary sphere. It may well be that the good shepherd is not entitled (perhaps he is bound by a contract) to abandon the other ninety-nine sheep, and then indeed he must not do so. Similarly, it would be wrong for an individual to fail to pay his just taxes or meet his other obligations in order to bestow more on those whom he loves. But while the demands of justice are implacable within their proper domain, it is also inappropriate and unnecessary to extend them outside of that domain.

There is a variety of roles in which a person bestows his discretionary resources on other particular persons. Kinship is special in that children and siblings do not voluntarily assume all of the obligations of that relation. On the other hand, an act of mercy to a stranger is purely discretionary but discrete, without systematic entailment. There is no role involved. Friendship is the paradigm of a role freely assumed in which one chooses to benefit another. The special quality of friendship does not inhere in the benefits conferred, but in the relation: a friend chooses to make the good of another his own. Now, a person's good is part of the congeries of attributes (some chosen, others determined by birth and circumstance) which constitutes a particular person. Thus in saying that John makes Mary's good his own in friendship, we say that John chooses to define his personality, his conception of the good, in part by whatever needs and preferences make Mary the particular person she is. Moreover, John chooses to define himself, his good, in this way not because (or not solely because) of a virtue he recognizes in the good Mary has chosen but just because it is Mary's good. He values the particular good not for that good's sake but for Mary's sake. And in general, friends act for each other's sake.

Imagine what a utilitarian (or fairness) theory of friendship would look like. It would have to cover two things: the content of the relation and the choice of friends. Would there be room for the warmth and loyalty characteristic of friendship as we know it? For if fairness and efficiency dictate the content of the relation, how may we avoid the entailment that a friend may do no more (or no less, of course) for his friend than fairness and efficiency *to humanity as a whole* require? And how to avoid the entailment that the relation may not be continued beyond the time that efficiency or fairness requires? Yet if there is no loyalty in the relation beyond what the instantaneous application of justice and efficiency requires, there is in fact nothing to the relation beyond the fulfillment of the general obligations of justice. In such a view, all that would be left to friendship would be the fact that one makes his contribution personally, rather than indirectly, bureaucratically. A friend would be like a social worker, paid out of taxes to deliver services to particular "clients" as an agent of the social system, and the relationship of friendship would simply be the hypostasis of that social agency. Indeed, this is the utilitarian account of special relationships, according to which they exist only insofar as utility dictates that one individual have a special care for another. The addition of the fairness principles does not materially change this aspect of the argument—it provides no basis for ascribing intrinsic value to the relationship.

Now the answer might be made that friendship, with its attendant loyalty and warmth, is an indivisible good, and that as such it should be available for distribution no less than any other good. After all, there are other goods which are scarce and costly and not susceptible to indefinite subdivision: a play seen through to the end is just a different entity from random ten-second fragments, and if this good is to be distributed fairly some way must be found (a lottery for theater tickets) which does not destroy the very thing being distributed in the course of distributing it. But what would it mean to have regard for justice and efficiency in the allocation of friendship? That we befriend those who have no friends or who need our friendship? The suggestion is grotesque, but we must consider why. Surely the reason is that friendship must allow not only freedom to make allocations of personal energy, but freedom in the choice of the object of friendship as well. The love and affection implicit in friendship must be moved by inclination and temperament, not duty. Nor will it do to say that one will try to take inclination and temperament into account in order to distribute friends efficiently—just as talents and preferences are at least relevant to the assignment of soldiers to tasks in the military. The point is not that the choice of friends (or lovers) should take inclination into account, but that the choice be moved by inclination. And the choices of the good shepherd and the good Samaritan may be seen as moved by inclination, an inclination towards immediate, present needs.

Inclination, of course, is just an aspect of the particularity of concrete persons which a proper theory of rights and the good must recognize. An individual's investment of himself not only in friends but in art, science, knowledge, and nature may have the same discretionary quality. Justice and efficiency are not without bearing in this discretionary realm. We can lavish only such attention and resources on our friends as are ours to command. Society does not owe me more than my fair share of its resources, and if this does not suffice for me to choose the friends I want and to do for them what I will, I have no complaint. For it is the function of obligatory social principles—justice, duty—to determine the limits of our free choices. But these social principles must at the same time respect the freedom allowed within those limits. And so friendship and the other deployments of self must be concluded to be free, free at least in respect to any moral or legal compulsion under the principles of justice.

The moral right of an individual to determine these personal investments of himself according to inclination, chance, his own particular genius leads to apparent anomalies. I propose we embrace these anomalies, not seek to suppress them. Consider this anomaly. We would acknowledge that the man who loves his friends and does good to them is a good man (assuming that he fulfills all abstract obligations of justice), though he is not as admirable as the saint who gives his life for wretched persons he seeks out in their wretchedness. (And where on the spectrum of excellences shall we locate the devoted scientist or artist?) We make such judgments, we acknowledge such a hierarchy of perfection, and yet we eschew any title to condemn the just man who is merely a good friend. We do, however, stand ready to condemn—to exert compulsion against—the smallest declination from the obligations of justice. But surely the distance between the good friend and the saint is far greater than the distance between the friend and the minor chiseler. We must recognize a discontinuity: Between the merely just man and the chiseler comes the dividing line of right and wrong, while the whole distance between the saint and the merely just man occurs within the range of the morally good, and thus the categories of condemnation and compulsion are wholly inappropriate within that range. At most, what are in order are judgments of regret, but even those are questionable. The scale of judgment is marked, if at all, in degrees of praise only.

This leaves the positive aspect of the question very much up in the air. Inclination, imagination, and chance may propose first the goods and then the structures of their combination. There are, to be sure, indications, standards, even vague hierarchies. Goods pursued in concert with others present occasions for richness which solitary pursuits lack. Certain pursuits display and develop physical and intellectual capacities, so that the concept of excellence applies easily to them. The pursuit of knowledge widens the range of a man's grasp. And so on. Whatever may be said about such matters, the crucial point is that the statements are no longer within the domain of strict priorities. Rather, we are in a realm of freedom, the freedom of the self to make *of* and *for* itself what it chooses, a realm where standards guide and propose rather than oblige. This realm of freedom is also the realm of excellence, for excellence does not proceed by rules and admits of no rigid order and ranking. So the stuff of free choice, the choice of the self, is the stuff the self finds at hand: one's own inclinations, one's own qualities and particular circumstances. Out of this the person chooses his friends, his occupation, his conception of the good.

In order to make these generalities concrete, I proceed to consider a particular set of choices in practical and concrete circumstances: doctors and lawyers, how they choose their clients, and what they do for them.

Professional Roles: The Problem

The traditional conception of the doctor's or lawyer's role poses two sorts of problems. One problem is similar for both professions: Doctors and lawyers are said to owe a duty of loyalty to their clients, a loyalty which in its usual interpretation requires taking the medical or legal interests of that client more seriously than the interests of others in similar or greater need, more seriously, indeed, than formulas of either efficiency (utility, maximization) or fairness (equality?) would require or even permit. Viewing the doctor's or lawyer's time as a scarce resource, therefore, the conception of professional loyalty requires individual professionals to distribute this scarce resource in ways that may very well be incompatible with their fairest or most efficient use. The second problem is peculiar to the legal profession. Both doctors and lawyers have clients, but the clients of doctors are not ordinarily viewed as having adversaries—at most they may have competitors for medical resources. Lawyers, by contrast, often serve their clients by assisting them in defeating the claims and interests of other persons whose needs may be greater and whose causes may be more just.

The classic statement of the traditional conception of a lawyer's loyalty to his client was formulated by Lord Brougham:

> An advocate, in the discharge of his duty, knows but one person in all the world, and that person is his client. To save that client by all means and expedients, and at all hazards and costs to other persons, and, among them, to himself, is his first and only duty; and in performing this duty he must not regard the alarm, the torments, the destruction which he may bring upon others. Separating the duty of a patriot from that of an advocate, he must go on reckless of consequences, though it should be his unhappy fate to involve his country in confusion. (*The Trial of Queen Caroline,* ed. J. Nightingale [London: Albion Press, 1821], vol. 2, p. 8.)

Thus the lawyer's professional role may entail not only unduly favoring his client—an apparent violation of the principle of fair shares and of the positive rights of others—but also actually harming others, the client's adversaries, thus apparently violating these adversaries' negative rights.

The demands of fairness and efficiency would seem to be satisfied only if doctors and lawyers were obliged or felt obliged to function for the common good alone—that is, in an essentially bureaucratic mode, servicing the population in the same way that a maintenance crew services the capital equipment of an enterprise: seeking at all times to maximize output, minimize costs, repairing where efficient, amortizing, and allowing for replacement on the same grounds. The idea of loyalty to a client would be as inappropriate as loyalty on the part of a mechanic to the machines he services. The loyalty is to the enterprise and exactly so much care is devoted to a particular part as the whole demands.

An immediate objection to this conception is that the loyalty of the professional to his client seems to be part of the very good which is being provided, just as loyalty is part of the indivisible good of friendship. A patient may not expect that his doctor will minister to every whim, but he does expect that when he does come under the doctor's care the doctor will act in the patient's interest. (And this is as true in a state-financed system such as the British National Health Service as it is in the supposedly private system obtaining in the United States.) To be sure, a doctor cannot procure resources without limit, but a patient expects his doctor to do his best for him with what is available and not to omit or choose therapies on the grounds of what is best for society. It might be best for society if all nonproductive members expired quickly and costlessly, but it is not part of the doctor's role to procure that result.

It is even more difficult to conceive clearly what it would mean for a lawyer to govern his professional conduct not by the interests of his client but by the principles of distributive justice and social efficiency. The lawyer assists his client in respect to his legal position vis-à-vis the collectivity and others. There is by hypothesis a best arrangement of social interests, and the lawyer perhaps should seek to bring about that arrangement, irrespective of whether his efforts further his client's interests. This conception was expressed by the professors of the University of Havana law faculty: "The first job of a revolutionary lawyer is not to argue that his client is innocent, but rather to determine if his client is guilty and, if so, to seek the sanction which will best rehabilitate him" (Harold Berman, "The Cuban Popular Tribunals," *Columbia Law Review* 69 [1969]: 1341). The same conclusion was reached by a Bulgarian lawyer defending a client against a charge of treason: "In a Socialist state there is no division of duty between the judge, prosecutor and defense counsel . . . The defense must assist the prosecution to find the objective truth in the case" (John Kaplan, *Criminal Justice: Introductory Cases and the Materials* [New York: Foundation Press, 1973], pp. 264–265). In this view, then, a client coming to a lawyer is like a citizen making a request of a government agency: the bureaucrat owes him no special duty but must treat the client with impartiality and an eye solely to advancing the public interest.

Now I shall argue that the traditional conception of professional loyalty is sound and practical. It offers a form of life and work which a just society must permit and a morally sensitive person may confidently adopt. It is my thesis that if a lawyer *in a reasonably just society* gives good and faithful counsel, then he fulfills his role well and that role itself is a good one. Indeed, a good lawyer is a good man, and the fact that he chooses his clients among those who can pay the most or whose cases involve travel and excitement does not vitiate that conclusion. So too the doctor who serves his patients with skill and devotion is a good man, however he chooses those patients. To be sure those who devote their time to the unfortunate and downtrodden approach heroism or sainthood, but that is another matter.

THE ANALOGY TO FRIENDSHIP

The analogy of professional roles to the concept of friendship is striking. In both cases one person assumes the interests of another. To be sure, the range of interests (medical, legal) is much more sharply defined in the professional case, yet within that range there obtain similar notions of loyalty and personal care even in the face of the competing claims of the larger collectivity.* Indeed, we may even discern the same (inadequate) arguments—rule-utilitarianism being the most frequent example—brought into play to show that traditional professional loyalty is conducive to efficiency and fair distribution after all. I have argued that respect for individual personality requires that we recognize not only a legal but a moral privilege to confer some benefits on friends and relations just according to inclination, without regard to fairness or efficiency. What we do thus is, after all, good in itself and the resources we spend are ours to spend. I now suggest that the lawyer who assists a client in a lawsuit full of spite or a doctor who tends the hearts and entrails of the sedentary rich is a good man, just as the good friend is a good man, a man who has chosen a good and useful life.

Why not? Is it because the analogy to friendship is imperfect in a number of ways? Professional relations are one-sided in ways that friendship should not be, since the client owes no reciprocal loyalty to his doctor or lawyer. Further, the professional generally demands payment for his services, although the relation is understood to have the same contours whether undertaken from love of humanity, love of a cause, or plain greed. Finally, these are public professions and so it might seem that they may be socialized like other aspects of public economic life. Any yet,

---

* The professional relation is cooler, but this is only a function of its being focused on the particular interests in question. There can still be passion in respect to the interest. Moreover, it is important to the kind of "friendship" which a doctor or lawyer bears that he be able to abstract from the other, irrelevant aspects of his client's life plan, so that being indifferent to them, he is not responsible for them. That is why the doctor who cures a criminal is not implicated in his depredations any more than is the lawyer who procures the criminal's acquittal in a fair trial by legal means.

despite these differences, I believe the analogy to friendship is illuminating because, as in the case of friendship, an ultimate legal and moral discretion to enter into these relations and show loyalty within them must be allowed.

Consider the case of the doctor. Surely it would violate both negative rights and the notion of personal liberty in the bestowal of friendship to forbid a doctor from doing good to whomever he chose so long as he used his own time and resources. Now, there is a large problem about the resources (medicines, hospital beds, and so on), but the point is that all of the doctor's *time* is his own, because *everybody's* time is his own. But it will be objected that the doctor's time is valuable; there is so much good he might do if it were best used. Maybe, and yet I have argued that your right to your own time (to yourself, indeed) may not depend on how valuable you are to others. Nor can it be the case that you are less free because you choose to use your time helping people than if you had chosen to spend it playing cards. And finally, it is hard to see why your liberty in respect to your own time is lessened because you accept a fee for the good you do—provided you pay the taxes due on that fee. True, you might be doing so much more good elsewhere, but that, I have argued, may not be the basis of compulsion exercised upon the person of anyone, for no one owes his person or efforts to the common good—we all owe only a fair share of objective resources. If doctors may be drafted to serve the common good, why then not draft persons to *become* doctors (or hairdressers) if that is what efficiency requires? This is a path we should not even begin to travel.*

This is the case for recognizing a *right* to practice medicine on traditional lines of loyalty to one's patients and to choose those patients as one wills. But I have asserted that to cure the sick and to show loyalty and personal care is a *morally* good life, no matter who it is one cares for or how the patients are chosen. And why is it not a good life? One is doing good and by hypothesis is neither harming others nor depriving them of anything to which

---

* This argument should not be taken to prove too much. In particular, it does not at all show that the state may not choose to run a comprehensive system of free or subsidized health care. I express no view on socialist enterprise in general or socialized medicine in particular. I argue only that whether or not the state should own the means of production, a man's talents and labor are not social resources. They are his own. So the community is morally free to operate a health service and hire physicians. But it would violate rights to make such a state enterprise the only way in which persons may receive or confer medical benefits upon each other.

they are entitled. No doubt to seek out the neediest and most neglected is a nobler way of life still. But it is just my argument that to be a good man you do not have to be the best possible man you might be.

The case of the lawyer is somewhat different. I put aside for the moment the harm the lawyer may do as he assists his client against adversaries. Still, illness is a natural fact, while the legal difficulties in which the lawyer gives his aid are themselves the product of organized society. So why may not organized society control both the content of the lawyer-client relation and the basis on which clients are chosen? But it is a total nonsequitur to make the passage from the law's conventional nature to a social right to require that lawyers render legal service only when, how, and to whom it is efficient to do so. On the contrary, precisely because of the conventional nature of legal institutions, society is bound to permit legal advice to be given according to the traditional model: by lawyers who feel bound to serve loyally (within the law) the interests of their clients, clients chosen in any way the lawyer wishes.

The argument is a straightforward corollary of the general thesis about rights, that society is bound to respect individual rights even if it is socially inefficient to do so, even if fair distribution would be advanced by overriding rights. Now, a lawyer advises his client about what his rights are and assists him in exercising those rights (by bringing and defending lawsuits, drafting instruments, and so on). Moreover, among the rights that an individual has is the right not to be subjected to legal constraints except in accordance with duly enacted and applied rules of law—this is the principle of the rule of law. Thus in a reasonably just society it may be the case that distributive justice would be advanced if the tax laws were amended to tax capital gains as ordinary income or to forbid the deduction of interest on home mortgages, but until the law is so amended every citizen has the perfect right to use these tax advantages in determining his legal debt to society. And it would be an obvious violation of right to tax anyone *as if* the law had been amended just because it should be amended. Similarly, the right to freedom of speech includes the right to say many things it would be more efficient, more agreeable and decent not to say, but the right would be no right at all if society could restrict speech on that basis. But if society must allow. individuals to exercise their rights whether or not that exercise accords with efficiency or an ideal of fairness, then it follows that society must also allow individuals to learn what their rights are and to assert those rights. Moreover, since society may not restrict the assertion of rights on grounds of efficiency, it follows that it may not restrict access to those who would advise and assist in their assertion on such grounds. If society may not forbid the use of a legal tax deduction just because it is inefficient, it also may not forbid a client's finding out about the loophole or a lawyer's telling him about it. In short, it is as inadmissible to restrict, on grounds of social policy, seeking and giving help regarding the assertion of rights as it is to use social policy to restrict those rights themselves.

Nothing I have said argues, however, that society is also obliged to *furnish* legal assistance on the traditional model to all who desire it or that the traditional model should have the monopoly it now enjoys in providing legal services. As with medicine, citizens or the government acting on their behalf may find it cheaper and more efficient to provide legal services and hire lawyers whose loyalties are those of functionaries: they serve the efficient functioning of a larger abstract entity. Like military doctors, lawyers in such organizations would take only those cases deemed worth taking and pursue only those defenses worth pursuing on some organizational criteria. Provided the clients are not deceived, I see no objection to this. It would in all likelihood provide cheaper service and distribute it more fairly than the individualized mode which prevails at least in theory today. I argue only that neither lawyers nor clients may be *compelled* to operate within this bureaucratic model. If the bureaucratic model is cheaper and generally satisfactory, the traditional conception may all but die out. But recognizing this alternative is very different from restricting the right of lawyers and clients to operate in the traditional mode if they wish.

It may be an exercise of right, but is it good to advise rich clients about minimizing their taxes or to defend a vicious criminal? For I readily concede that a man who enjoys—even legally— more than his fair share is himself morally obliged to give to others, just as the criminal is morally obliged to accept, not resist, punishment. Now, while it may be morally wrong for the client to exercise his legal rights in such cases, the moral privilege of the lawyer to assist such clients derives from the theorem that it is morally right that people have legal rights. It is a morally good system of law which recognizes a privilege against self-incrimination, even though it may be morally wrong for an individual to invoke the privilege to prevent his own just punishment. In counseling the rich man or the criminal, the lawyer draws his moral justification not by reference to the ultimate exercise of autonomy which the client's right leaves the client (that exercise, I concede, may be bad) but from the good that inheres in the client's having the right, the autonomy, to make this choice. Once again, intention is crucial. The lawyer's activity is good because he intends to assist his client in exercising his rights; the lawyer does not intend the ultimate harm the client may do by exercising those rights. The lawyer's role is crucial. It insulates the lawyer from implication in that ultimate effect of the exercise of his client's rights. What the lawyer does intend, it is right to intend.*

Thus one who makes a life's work out of relieving the particular legal or medical needs of particular people and adopts as the regulative principle of his activity loyalty to the particular person before him acts not only justly but well. Nor does it matter that this activity provides a living as well as a way of life. For the relationship one assumes has the same quality, whatever the reason—pay, ambition, curiosity, excitement, pity, indignation— one may have had for assuming it. All this may seem just too pat and comfortable. It leaves out of account the individual's duty to the collectivity—whether he acts in a professional role or simply as a citizen. It leaves out of account his duty to help people who are not his friends, relations, or clients. And for the lawyer who helps his client to do moral wrong by asserting his legal rights, it leaves out of account the duty not to harm other people.

BUREAUCRATS AND FRIENDS

The friend, the doctor, the lawyer may only give what in justice is his to give. But what is that? Something, but how much? The professional case will permit a concrete development of my

---

* A difficult problem is presented when the lawyer's advice will be used not to exercise (perhaps in an undesirable way) legal rights, but to violate the law. A famous example is the lawyer who described the details of the defense of temporary insanity to his client—who had just admitted killing his wife—knowing (and perhaps intending) that the client would concoct a story to place himself within that defense. My argument does not cover such cases, since the lawyer is assisting his client in committing a fresh crime (perjury) and in defeating the legal system instead of assisting him to exercise legal rights. The client has no legal right to lie or to escape conviction by a perjured defense. The abuse of legal process to delay just claims by an opposing party falls by the same argument, as does the use of devices such as discovery or postponement of trial for purposes of delay.

general thesis, but before turning to that let me sketch out that thesis by reference to a less institutional example: aid to persons in an emergency. Imagine the case of miners trapped in a mine disaster or passengers in a shipping accident.* As I have been arguing, the inclination to do whatever is necessary, to do more than justice requires to assist such victims in their distress, is morally sound though not obligatory. What one can accomplish in the actual emergency, how much one can spend on relief, is to a significant extent determined, however, by what measures are available and *have been made available* for such an emergency. If rescue vessels have not been built, we cannot build them when the emergency arises; if an artificial heart has not been developed, we cannot use it when the particular need arises. And the decision to develop and deploy such emergency resources is obviously an abstract decision, governed by considerations of justice and efficiency. But there is only an apparent contradiction between the judgment that those charged with abstract decisions should make these decisions according to the principles of justice and efficiency and the judgment that those responding to particular emergencies may act on the principles of friendship and humanity.

In the case of a mine disaster there are two roles: there is the role of friend or immediate helper and then there is the role of planner or budget officer. The apparent anomaly is simply the working out of the different obligations implicit in the two roles. The budget officer is charged with working out appropriate schemes to benefit individuals who are abstract, anonymous for the purpose of the scheme. It is not known who may be the victim of a mine disaster, and the purpose of safety measures is simply to reduce the overall risk. The appropriate moral categories for the carrying out of such a role are efficiency, justice, and fairness. Any scheme, in other words, should accomplish the best result with whatever resources are devoted to it. The potential benefits should be justly distributed among all potential victims of mine disasters, and there should be open disclosure of what measures have actually been taken so that mine workers can

* There is what I now believe to be an unsatisfactory account of this case in my *An Anatomy of Values* (Cambridge, Mass.: Harvard University Press, 1970), Chapter 12. For an excellent criticism of my earlier views, see Bernard Williams, "Persons, Character and Morality," in Amelie O. Rorty, ed., *The Identities of Persons* (Berkeley: University of California Press, 1976).

decide what risks to run. The obligations of those who undertake rescue, by contrast, are governed by the principles of friendship. Those who undertake rescue assist not abstract, potential victims, but designated persons in actual distress. Thus rescuers may put themselves into a role which gives them the right to do that which greatly surpasses what might initially have been planned and budgeted for this kind of an operation. And sometimes the urgency of the particular distress is such that to fail to respond to it, while not unjust, would seem so insensitive as to be inhuman.

The inevitable result of this bifurcation of roles will be a radical indeterminancy of outcome. The budget officer will arrive at a "correct" figure for preventive measures, their costs, the proper valuation of injuries or lives lost in accidents, and so on, and yet if heroics are regularly engaged in, more money will have been spent and perhaps more lives saved than the budget officer had originally reckoned. But the "excess" of effort is of course just such effort as the budget officer was not entitled to prevent. The heroics were heroics engaged in by persons moved by the plight of concrete human beings, moved to do things which they did not have to do. Indeed, it would be wrong for the budget officer to calculate how much to spend on prevention by assuming that in case of an accident heroics would be engaged in. Moreover, the indeterminacy of result might mean that some victims were saved, while others were not. But none could complain: surely not those who were saved, and those who were not could also not complain since by hypothesis all proper measures had been taken for their safety (both preventive measures and such rescue efforts as justice and efficiency required). The rest was a risk they chose to run.*

The principal objection to the traditional conception of professional loyalty relates to its systematic social effects. Is the traditional conception really tolerable if it means that the poor or those living in rural areas are deprived of medical or legal services? Is it really tolerable if it means that those who already enjoy power can perpetuate their privileges by monopolizing the best legal talent? Is the individual practitioner absolved from

---

* This conception takes care of the argument that, after all, if the unit is small enough the potential victims of a disaster may all be personally known to the budget officer. The point is not whether they are or are not known, but on what principles one is acting toward them. One set of principles is derived from justice and another set (if they can be called principles at all) from the impulses of friendship or personal care.

caring about these implications of his choices? The case of the mine disaster suggests the resolution I have in mind. The availability of medical or legal services is indeed a matter of social concern, and therefore policy-makers, legislators, voters, and administrators must attend to that matter. They must decide what a fair distribution of medical or legal services would look like, and then they must seek to implement their conclusions, using whatever political, economic, or other incentives are available to them. That is their job. That is their obligation. The obligation of the individual providers of medical or legal services is, however, a different one. They are quite free in their choice of client, although once the client is chosen they are tied to the client by iron bonds of loyalty.

There is no anomaly here. Bureaucrats and government officials work to create a situation in which the correct distribution of medical care will come about as a result of the choices of doctors and their patients. If the criterion for the just distribution of benefits and burdens in the society is, say, equality, then the social system would have to put enough purchasing power in the hands of prospective patients and clients to attract the necessary number of persons into the profession. On the other hand, if the social system were wedded to a criterion not of equality but of a decent minimum, then once again redistribution would take place up to that point where the poorest sector of the society would be able to command decent medical and legal services along with other necessities of life. Individual doctors or individual lawyers would continue to choose their clients according to whatever inclinations move them. With reasonably free entry into the professions, the normal desire to make a useful, interesting living should deliver the requisite number of doctors and lawyers to the marketplace.

Now, in structuring a system of health or legal services, government officials must respect the constraints of right and wrong that were discussed in Part II. They may not make the system work by simply drafting doctors or lawyers and telling them what to do, to whom, and when—as, for instance, if they compelled the professionals to show less care for their individual clients or to breach duties of confidentiality or loyalty. On the other hand, a doctor can only use such external resources—medicines, hospital beds, appliances—as are available, and if these are socially rationed, it is no part of his loyalty to his patient to seek to circumvent the system by going into the black market or trying to jump the queue. Furthermore, although a just society must allow the traditionally conceived principles of professional loyalty to exist, it need not give them a monopoly on the delivery of legal and medical services. It may be that some individuals would prefer to spend their money on cheaper, more efficient, but less personally oriented delivery systems. That too should be their right.

It is said that the medical profession has a special responsibility for the health of society just as the legal profession does for justice. This has often been thought to entail a requirement that individual doctors and lawyers should give some of their time to care for the poor. In a just society this would not be a serious issue; for, as I have argued, it is the job of the society as a whole to assure that its citizens can afford a decent standard of living, and the task of providing the components of that standard should not fall specially on those who happen to provide necessities, whether they be doctors or grocers or plumbers. So this professional obligation must be understood differently, as a special obligation to work for these just social arrangements. It is quite clearly an entailment of my theory of positive rights that we all have a corresponding positive duty to work for the establishment of a regime in which people's right to their fair share will be accorded. This does not, however, mean that any individual must give up his property as if a general scheme existed when it does not. One is not obliged to emulate St. Francis by impoverishing himself in order to relieve a misery which he did not create and which all should share in alleviating. Similarly, it is not enough to emulate John D. Rockefeller, Sr., by giving out dimes to poor people, on the theory perhaps that this is all that any one person's share of a grossly excessive fortune would amount to. The obligation is a social obligation which is discharged by working socially—specifically, politically—for the establishment of just social institutions which will procure a fair share *from* and *to* everyone. This obligation to work for just institutions is the most particular devolution of the bureaucratic function. It is the sense in which we are all bureaucrats, the sense in which we are all responsible for realizing the abstract principles of justice.

The lawyer accordingly has a moral obligation to work for the establishment of just institutions generally, but entirely the wrong kinds of conclusions have been drawn from this proposition. Some more fervent critics of the profession have put forward a conception of the lawyer as a kind of anointed priest of justice—a high priest whose cleaving to the traditional conception of the lawyer's role opens him to the charge of apostasy. But this is wrong. In a democratic society, justice has no anointed priests. (It is a priesthood of all believers.) Every citizen has the same duty to work for the establishment of just institutions, and the lawyer has no special moral responsibilities in that regard. To be sure, the lawyer like any citizen, must use all his knowledge and talent to fulfill that general duty of citizenship, and this may mean that there are special perspectives and opportunities for him.*

There is a special difficulty when, in the context of a generally just social system, particular individuals fall through the cracks, as it were, of a well-designed system. Who is going to catch them? The bureaucrat, by hypothesis, cannot, since it is through the cracks of his well-devised system that the particular person has fallen. Does not the doctor or lawyer have an obligation at least in such a case to aid the anomalous person in need, while retaining his own general freedom? A good example of this is the unsavory criminal defendant whom nobody wants to represent.

---

* Regulations forbid qualified and financially responsible persons and bodies, such as banks, insurance companies, title companies, or real estate brokers, from supplying routine legal services which lawyers (or rather their secretaries and automatic typewriters) provide at high cost. There are also regulations prohibiting advertising by lawyers (recently declared unconstitutional) and limiting prepaid group legal services. All of these regulations are justified by the legal profession as necessary to protect the public and to maintain professional standards. In my view, such arguments are hypocritical or self-deluding rationalizations for what is essentially an anticompetitive conspiracy in restraint of trade. (The arguments are almost identical to those used by opticians, pharmacists, and funeral directors— with transparently self-serving motives.) It is no surprise that critics of the legal profession take it at its pompous word, and seek to fasten on it duties commensurate with its moralizing pretensions.

Unfortunately, many lawyers identify themselves with their clients' causes, rather than simply giving legal advice and performing legal services. To submit the most favorable legal argument on behalf of a client is one thing, to profess belief in it and to advocate it personally in extralegal contexts is quite another. Lawyers in the United States—unlike English barristers—too often consider it good business to identify personally and totally with their clients. Lawyers who represent unions will not represent management, and vice versa. There is a defendants' and a plaintiffs' antitrust, malpractice, and personal accident bar engaged in intense public relations and lobbying efforts. Lawyers for liquor companies feel they must drink and lawyers for tobacco companies feel they must smoke. In this sorry state of affairs—which is not justified by my argument—it is reasonable to judge the lawyer by the causes with which he chooses to identify himself. So here, too, the lack of discretion and of professional austerity makes lawyers fair game for the moralizing criticisms which I am seeking to refute.

There may be money for that person's defense, so that is not the problem. The legal profession has long affirmed a duty of individual lawyers to accept assignment to such cases—indeed, a duty to accept such cases without assignment if a particular lawyer knows that a person in great legal need may otherwise go unrepresented. I think we can accept such an individual obligation without compromising the two-tier system I have been developing. It is after all a special case of the duty of beneficence. By hypothesis the situations will be anomalous, so that the imposition of such an obligation will not compromise the general principle of the professional's right to choose his own client. Indeed, by recognizing such an obligation in rare instances, a certain independence of the lawyer might be affirmed, since it is thereby shown that the professional does not necessarily choose his case because of an unprofessional attachment to a client's cause.

Doing Harm in a Justifiable Role

I have left for last a special problem of lawyers. In fulfilling the obligation of their role, lawyers are often instrumental in bringing about harmful consequences to their client's adversaries. This is a serious problem, given the thrust of the first part of this book: that intentional harms of various sorts are not just bad, but wrong, in a special sense *absolutely* wrong. The lawyer's role, however, seems to require him to do things to others in his representative capacity that he would not do if acting for himself. How can this be compatible with the principle of personal responsibility I have presented: that whatever else one does, one should not be the instrument of wrong?

Now, I put aside at the outset any suggestion that the lawyer's duty of representation carries any privilege to break the law—to destroy evidence, bribe witnesses, and so on. The lawyer is the client's *legal* friend, and thus his duties and privileges arise out of the occasion and the institution that created the role. The lawyer furthers his client's interests within the law, and there is no reason to infer any privilege to step outside the law in so doing. To be sure, there are situations where the law grossly violates what morality defines as individual rights, and there have been lawyers who have stood ready to defy such laws in order to further their client's rights—the rights which the law should have recognized but did not. Whatever might be said about those cases, since the lawyer is no longer assisting his client in realizing his legal rights, the lawyer's conduct in those cases travels outside the bounds of legal friendship and becomes political agitation or friendship *tout court*.* Such cases apart, the moral claims which a client has on his lawyer are fully exhausted if that lawyer contains his advocacy strictly within the limits of the law. In a reasonably just system which properly commands the lawyer's loyalty, he must confine his advocacy to what the rules of advocacy permit. He may not counsel his client to commit a crime, or to destroy evidence, or to perjure himself. Of course, here as elsewhere there will be borderline problems. It may not be a crime to lie to the judge who has asked an improper and prejudicial question of the defense attorney, but the implicit or quasi-official rules defining the limits of the lawyer's advocacy may nonetheless forbid this. Nothing in my model should discourage the lawyer from observing such limits scrupulously.

There remains, however, perhaps the most difficult dilemma of the lawyer's role. It is illustrated by the lawyer who is asked to press the unfair claim, to humiliate a witness, to participate in a distasteful or dishonorable scheme. I assume that in none of these situations does the lawyer do anything illegal or in violation of the ethical canons of his profession, so that even if he acts in a way which seems to him personally dishonorable, there are no sanctions—legal or professional—which he need fear.

The right of the lawyer as friend to give extra weight and personal care to the interests of his client served to meet the criticism that principles of personal responsibility were unfair or inefficient. The only claims competing with those of the client were the abstract claims of the abstract collectivity. But now we confront a dilemma where there is a definable victim as well as a definable beneficiary, and the relation to the person whom we deceive or abuse is just as concrete and human, just as personal as to the friend whom we help. "But who is my neighbor?" is a

---

* Consider what should be done if the law imposes upon the lawyer an obligation first to seek and then to betray his client's trust, an obligation to do that which seems outrageous and unjust. I do not mean to say that the resolution of this dilemma would be easy, but my analysis at least clearly locates the area in which a resolution should be sought. For such laws, if they are to be opposed, ought to be opposed as are other unjust laws, and not because the lawyer is in general entitled to travel outside the constraints of law in protecting his client's interests. Maybe in such a dilemma a conscientious lawyer would keep his client's confidence as would a priest or a friend; but if conscientiousness requires this, it requires it as an act of disobedience and resistance to an unjust law, rather than as a necessary entailment of some general view of the lawyer's role.

legitimate question when affirmative aid is in question; however, it is quite out of order in respect to the injunction "Do not harm your neighbor." That is why I concluded that lying, stealing, degrading, intentionally inflicting pain or injury are personal relations too. If I claim respect for my own concrete particularity, I must accord that respect to others—my person is at stake both ways. Thus, what pinches here is the fact that the lawyer's personal engagement with the client urges him to do to his adversary something which the principles of personal engagement urge that he not do to anyone.

If personal integrity grounds the lawyer's right to serve his client as a friend and not as a bureaucrat implementing an efficient and just social plan for the greater good, then surely consideration for personal integrity—his own and others'—must limit what he can do in friendship. Consideration for personal integrity forbids me to lie, cheat, or humiliate, whether in my own interests or those of a friend, so surely they prohibit such conduct on behalf of a client, one's legal friend. This is the general truth, but it must be made more particular if it is to do service here, for there is a pull in the opposite direction. Remember, the lawyer's special kind of friendship is occasioned by the right of the client to exercise his full measure of autonomy within the law, and this suggests that one must not transfer uncritically the whole range of personal moral scruples into the arena of legal friendship. After all, not only would I not lie or steal for myself or my friends, I probably also would not pursue socially noxious schemes, foreclose the mortgages of widows or orphans, or assist in the avoidance of just punishment. So we must be careful lest the whole argument unravel on us at this point.

This dilemma is illuminated if we distinguish between kinds of moral scruples. Think of the lawyer as a soldier. If he is a citizen of a just state, where foreign policy decisions are made in a democratic way, he may accept an official judgment that the war he fights is a just war. He is personally bound, however, not to fire dumdum bullets, not to inflict intentional injury on civilians, not to abuse prisoners. These are personal wrongs, wrongs done by his person to the person of the victim. So also, the lawyer must distinguish between wrongs that a reasonably just legal system permits to be worked by its rules and wrongs which the lawyer commits himself. Now, I do not offer this as a rule that is tight enough to resolve automatically all questions of judgment at the border. Indeed, it is unreasonable to expect moral arguments to dispense wholly with the need for prudence and judgment.

Consider the difference between humiliating a witness or lying to the judge on the one hand, and on the other hand using the defense that a contract was not put in writing or that the suit was brought too late and so defeating what you know to be a just claim against your client. In the latter sort of case, if an injustice is worked, it is worked because the legal system not only permits it but specifies the very details by which the result is reached. Your conduct as a lawyer is efficacious only insofar as legal institutions have created the occasion for it. What you do is not personal; it is a formal, legally defined act. The moral quality of lying or abuse, on the other hand, obtains without and within the context of the law. A lawyer is morally entitled to act in this formal, representative way even if the result is an injustice, because the legal system which authorizes both the injustice (such as the plea of the statute of limitations) and the formal gesture for working it insulates him from personal moral responsibility. I distinguish, therefore, between the lawyer's own wrong and the wrong of the system on which the client chooses to rely.

The clearest case is a lawyer who calls to the attention of the court a controlling legal precedent or statute which establishes his client's position even though that position is an unjust one. (I assume throughout, however, that this unjust law is part of a generally just and decent system. I am not considering at all the moral dilemmas of a lawyer in Nazi Germany or Soviet Russia.) We should absolve the lawyer of personal moral responsibility for the result he accomplishes because the wrong is wholly institutional. It is a wrong which does not exist, has no meaning, outside the legal framework. And the only thing preventing the client from doing this for himself is his lack of knowledge or formal authority to operate the levers of the law in official proceedings. It is to supply that lack that the lawyer is authorized to act, and the levers he pulls are all legal levers.

Now contrast this to the lawyer who lies to an opposing party in a negotiation. Lying is wrong. It is an offense against the victim's integrity as a rational moral being, and thus the liar affirms a principle which denigrates his own moral status. Every lie is a betrayal. May a lawyer lie in his representative capacity, however? It is precisely my point that a man cannot lie *just* in his representative capacity; it is like stabbing someone in the back "just" in a representative capacity. The injury and betrayal are not worked by the legal process, but by an act which is generally harmful quite apart from the legal context in which it occurs. There may be cases in which it looks as if one lies in a representative capacity, but they merely show why the lawyer's own lie can never be justified. A lawyer might, for example, forward to the attention of the court a statement by another which he knows to be a lie, as when he puts a perjurious client-defendant on the stand. There is dispute as to whether and when the positive law of professional responsibility permits this, but clearly in such instances it is not the lawyer who lies, it is not the lawyer who asks that the lie be believed. He is like the letter carrier who delivers the falsehood, and whether he is free to do that is a matter more of legal than of personal ethics.

A more difficult case to locate in the moral landscape is abusive and demeaning cross-examination of a complaining witness. Presumably, positive law and the canons of ethics restrict this kind of thing, but enforcement may be lax, interpretation by a trial judge permissive, so the question arises, what is the lawyer morally free to do? There again I urge the distinction between exposing a witness to the skepticism and scrutiny the law envisages and the lawyer's engaging himself personally in an attack on the moral person of the witness. The latter is a harm which the lawyer happens to inflict in court, but it is a harm quite apart from the institutional legal context. It is perhaps just a matter of style or tone, but the crucial point is that the probing must not imply that the lawyer believes the witness is unworthy of respect.

The lawyer is not morally entitled, therefore, to engage his own person in doing personal harm to another, though he may work the system for his client even if the system then works injustice.*

CONCLUSION

Here we have the system of general ideas worked out in some quite particular contexts. Doctors, lawyers, and friends are good

* The situation of statesmen and military leaders whose choices visit consequences on foreigners raises different issues. The harm they do is not privileged—as is some of the harm done by lawyers—by the fact that both client and adversary participate in a common, presumably just, institutional structure. For a discussion of those special problems, with which I am largely in agreement, see Michael Walzer, *Just and Unjust Wars* (New York: Basic Books, 1977). See also Thomas Nagel, "Ruthlessness in Public Life" (forthcoming).

men and lead good lives if they fulfill their obligations of justice to society as a whole—obey the law, work for the furtherance of just institutions—and take wise and faithful care of their clients and friends. They are at liberty to construct their lives out of what personal scraps and shards of motivation their inclination and character suggest—idealism, greed, curiosity, love of luxury, love of adventure or knowledge—as long as they do indeed give wise and faithful counsel. There are those who may wish to give greater coherence to these elements of motivation and to live out their lives in closer connection with the general well-being of humanity. And we can recognize the perfection of such an attitude without at all denying the moral sufficiency of doing justice and doing such good as one chooses. That much freedom—moral and political—must be left us. It is the task of the social system as a whole to work for the general conditions under which everyone will benefit in fair measure from the true performance of doctors, lawyers, teachers, musicians, and friends. But I would not see the integrity of those roles or the sanctity of the self undermined in the name of the common good.

Those who argue for a different attitude, one in which we are all servants of the greatest good, like to remind us of the sacrifices and impersonality evoked by wartime, by catastrophes and famine. Now, I am willing to admit that emergencies create their own morality in which the rights and obligations of everyday life are loosened or altogether dispensed with. But it is a mistake to generalize from such contexts and to use them as the intellectual basis from which the total structure of our moral life is derived. On the contrary, the only thing that makes special principles tolerable for emergencies is just the fact that emergencies are extraordinary. It is when the general long-term situation of society is made to correspond to a continuing catastrophe that morality, civilization, and everything specially human are undermined. And there can be no doubt that my approach is less "efficient" than one in which each person acts or is forced to act as if he were responsible for the system as a whole. But such theoretically homogeneous systems would be sure to obliterate crucial aspects of a total, rich, human, moral life. We must resist even those idealists who would draft us only temporarily in order that their millennium may come sooner. After all, the millennium may never come, and then where would we be?

Notes

Index

Notes

Introduction

G. E. M. Anscombe's article "Modern Moral Philosophy," *Philosophy* 33 (1958) : 1, has suggested themes for an inquiry along the lines stated in this Introduction. The concept of integrity as introduced into philosophical moral speculation by Bernard Williams in his essay in J. J. C. Smart and B. Williams, *Utilitarianism—For and Against* (Cambridge: Cambridge University Press, 1973), is also crucial to the conception stated here.

A recent statement of the familiar problem about God's goodness and the problem of evil can be found in Gordon D. Kaufman, "God and Evil," in *God: The Problem* (Cambridge, Mass.: Harvard University Press, 1972). For the relation between various world views and corresponding moral and social doctrines, see John Passmore, *The Perfectibility of Man* (London: Duckworth, 1970).

A striking statement that the end justifies the means in Marxist terms is Maurice Merleau-Ponty, *Humanism and Terror* (Boston: Beacon Press, 1969). The relation between Marxist views and responsibility generally is examined in John Harris, "The Marxist Conception of Violence," *Philosophy and Public Affairs* 3 (1974) : 192.

Finally, recent strong statements of views different from those informing this work are Harris, "The Marxist Conception of Violence," and Peter Singer, "Famine, Affluence and Morality," *Philosophy and Public Affairs* 1 (1972) : 229.

1. Elements

RIGHT AND WRONG

The *locus classicus* for the distinction between the right and the good in modern philosophy is W. D. Ross, *The Right and the Good* (Oxford: Oxford University Press, 1930). The deontological conception of morals finds its first and deepest expression in the writings of Immanuel Kant. John Rawls's lectures on Kant, delivered at Harvard

197

in 1963 (see also his "A Kantian Conception of Equality," *Cambridge Review* 96 [February 1975]: 94), as well as his development of Kantian ideas in *A Theory of Justice* (Cambridge, Mass.: Harvard University Press, 1971) answer the shallow and unsympathetic interpretation—current at least since Hegel—that Kant's moral theory is merely formal, unconcerned with human happiness, and therefore unable to provide content, much less motivation for concrete choice. Though there is a great deal of rhetoric in Kant's work to feed this misconception, Rawls shows that the central conception is the priority of the right over the good. But that the right takes priority over the good, over human happiness, does not mean that it annihilates it. Indeed, Kant is explicit that human happiness has moral worth, but only as it is the happiness of moral beings. See, for example, *Tugendlehre* [386–387], translated by Mary Gregor (Philadelphia: University of Pennsylvania Press, 1964), pp. 46–47. Rawls expresses this idea by the lexical priority of the principles of justice and other aspects of the right over the satisfaction of the good of life plans. Rawls argues that this priority of the right over the good corresponds to the priority of a unified conception of the self over the particular goods which the self pursues (*A Theory of Justice*, §85).

Commentaries from which I have particularly learned are L. W. Beck, *A Commentary on Kant's Critique of Practical Reason* (Chicago: University of Chicago Press, 1960); H. J. Paton, *The Categorical Imperative* (Chicago: University of Chicago Press, 1948); and M. J. Gregor, *Laws of Freedom* (New York: Barnes and Noble, 1963). Two important recent works are Onora Nell, *Acting on Principle: An Essay on Kantian Ethics* (New York: Columbia University Press, 1975), Allen Wood, *Kant's Moral Religion* (Ithaca: Cornell University Press, 1970). Of particular interest is Nell's distinction between the "context of action" and the "context of assessment," which corresponds to the distinction I make between the category of right and wrong and the category of good and bad. Nicolai Hartmann, *Ethik,* 3d ed. (Berlin: W. de Gruyter, 1926), offers an interesting, suggestive, but to my mind rather confusing set of proposals regarding a variety of priorities and structural relations between types of norms. The norms which I call absolute, he notes, are at once more basic but less exalted than those directing our highest aspirations.

Consequentialism and the doctrine of priority of the good over the right find their clearest expression in utilitarianism, and the boldest, most unqualified statement of utilitarian consequential:sm is Jeremy Bentham, *An Introduction to the Principles of Morals and Legislation* (1789). John Austin, *The Province of Jurisprudence Determined* (1832), shows in Lectures 2, 4, and 5 how utilitarian methods can be adapted to express a version of traditional religious ethics. The most subtle and complete statement of utilitarianism is still Henry Sidgwick, *The Methods of Ethics.*

In recent years philosophers have distinguished several different kinds of utilitarianism, the most important of which have been act-utilitarianism and rule-utilitarianism. Act-utilitarianism is the theory that one should always perform acts which will result in at least as much good as will any alternative act. Rule-utilitarianism has been proposed in varying versions. One version holds that we should always perform acts which conform to a set of rules, general conformity to which would result in at least as much good as would conformity to any other set of rules. Some utilitarian theories hold that there are certain things that have instrinsic value apart from any pleasure they might bring. Utilitarian theories have also been characterized as "positive" if they aim to promote good or "negative" if they aim only to minimize evil. Some utilitarian theories ask us to maximize the total good, others only the average good to be enjoyed by each person affected. It should, however, be remembered that all forms of utilitarianism hold that it is only results or consequences (whether of individual acts, general practices or sorts of acts, or sets of rules) which count. An interesting version of rule-utilitarianism is offered by Richard Brandt, who argues that "an act is right if and only if it conforms with that learnable set of rules the recognition of which as morally binding—roughly at the time of the act—by everyone in the society of the agent . . . would maximize intrinsic value" ("Toward a Credible Form of Utilitarianism," in *Moral Rules and Particular Circumstances,* ed. Baruch A. Brody [Englewood Cliffs, N.J.: Prentice-Hall, 1970], pp. 145, 176) .

Rule-utilitarianism accepts and seeks to account for the stringency of judgments of right and wrong without yet abandoning consequentialist premises. Early versions of this position may be found in Hume's *Treatise* and in John Stuart Mill's *Utilitarianism.* An uncompromising modern act-utilitarian, J. J. C. Smart, has shown how this rule-utilitarianism cannot help but collapse into act-utilitarianism if it is to remain utilitarian and avoid "rule-worship." See "An Outline of a System of Utilitarian Ethics," in Smart and Williams, *Utilitarianism—For and Against,* and "Extreme and Restricted Utilitarianism," *Philosophical Quarterly* 6 (1956) : 344.

Other authors take up this same argument, but to urge the conclusion that therefore non-utilitarian elements must be admitted into our moral structures. See C. D. Broad, "On the Function of False Hypotheses in Ethics," *International Journal of Ethics* 26 (1918) : 377; David Lyons, *Forms and Limits of Utilitarianism* (Oxford: Oxford University Press, 1965) ; John Rawls, "Two Concepts of Rules," *Philosophical Review* 64 (1955) : 3.

RIGHT AND WRONG AS ABSOLUTE

Good discussions of the concept of a norm are Max Black, "The Analysis of Rules," in *Models and Metaphors* (Ithaca, N.Y.: Cornell

University Press, 1962); Hans Kelsen, *General Theory of Law and State* (New York: Russell & Russell, 1961); and G. H. von Wright, *Norm and Action* (London: Routledge & Kegan Paul, 1963). For discussions of Kant's concept of categorical norms, see the commentaries referred to in the notes to the preceding section.

The method of inclusion and exclusion which I claim is necessary for operating with systems of absolute norms is considered and compared to other methods in Max Weber, *Economy and Society* (New York: Bedminster Press, 1968), 2: 654–658, 784–838. This is the method ascribed by Bruce Ackerman to what he calls the "Ordinary Observer" in his *Private Property and the Constitution* (New Haven: Yale University Press, 1977). Although our concerns and perspectives are different, Ackerman and I appear to agree that this method is most appropriate to dealing with rights (or, I would say, the right), while a disaggregating, analytic maximizing method is proper to what we would both call the utilitarian (he says "scientific") policy-maker. I cannot tell, on the other hand, how the two methods, that of the right and that of the good, correlate with Ronald Dworkin's distinction between principles and policies. See his *Taking Rights Seriously* (Cambridge, Mass.: Harvard University Press, 1977), ch. 2, 3, and 4. It would seem that principles relate to the domain of the right, and yet the method Dworkin suggests for this domain is one of weighing and balancing. On the other hand, policies are explicitly stated to be utilitarian and therefore maximizing. Finally, Dworkin contrasts rules to principles, the former operating far more rigorously and absolutely than the latter, which, however, can override them. Rules, I suppose, may be used to embody both principles and policies.

The modern, formalized versions of utilitarian maximization are discussed in R. B. Braithwaite, *Theory of Games as a Tool for the Moral Philosopher* (Cambridge: Cambridge University Press, 1955); P. B. Heymann, "The Problem of Coordination: Bargaining and Rules," *Harvard Law Review* 866 (1973): 797; R. D. Luce and H. Raiffa, *Games and Decisions* (New York: John Wiley & Sons, 1957); Howard Raiffa, *Decision Analysis* (Reading, Mass.: Addison-Wesley, 1968); Donald Davidson, J. G. C. McKinsey, and Patrick Suppes, "Outlines of Formal Theory of Value," *Philosophy of Science* 22 (1955): 140. See also Robert Nozick "Moral Complications and Moral Structures," *Natural Law Forum* 12 (1968): 1; and on the absoluteness of utilitarianism, see Rawls, *A Theory of Justice,* §§ 83–84.

For the point that it is fallacious to generalize from emergencies and catastrophes, see William, in Smart and Williams, *Utilitarianism—For and Against,* and Charles Fried, "Rights and Health Care—Beyond Equity and Efficiency," *New England Journal of Medicine* 293 (1975): 241.

The Complexity of Deontological Systems

That absolute norms cannot be applied literally to consequences lest "nothing one could do would be morally permissible" is a point made by Thomas Nagel, "War and Massacre," *Philosophy and Public Affairs* 1 (1972) : 130. See also Williams in Smart and Williams, *Utilitarianism—For and Against,* to the same effect. This conclusion depends on a point noted by William Prosser, *Handbook of the Laws of Torts,* 4th ed. (St. Paul: West Publishing, 1971), p. 146: "Nearly all human acts, of course, carry some recognizable but remote possibility of harm to another. No man so much as rides a horse without some chance of a runaway, or drives a car without the risk of a broken steering gear or a heart attack."

A reasonable absolutism not only allows for a multiplicity of norms without leading to contradiction but also allows for a set of judgments discriminating between several permissible courses of action, thus leaving room for the concept of supererogation. Thus not only is something permissible, but more than one thing is, and indeed the best of these is not obligatory—that is, the best is not the solely permissible. On the problem of supererogation generally, see Roderick Chisholm, "Supererogation and Offence," *Ratio* 5 (1963) : 1; Joel Feinberg, "Supererogation and Rules," *International Journal of Ethics* 71 (1961) : 276; Joseph Raz, "Permissions and Supererogation," *American Philosophical Quarterly* 12 (April 1975) : 161 and J. O. Urmson, "Saints and Heroes," in *Essays in Moral Philosophy* (Seattle: Washington University Press, 1958) .

The complexity of absolute norms in Roman Catholic theology is explored with the aid of modern analytic philosophy by Bruno Schüller, "Direkte Tötung—Indirekte Tötung," *Theologie und Philosophie* 47 (1972) : 341; "Zu Problematik allgemein verbindlicher ethischer Grundsätze," *Theologie und Philosophie* 45 (1970) : 526. Finally, David Daube has suggested that rather than flee contradiction and paradox in moral systems we acknowledge their inevitability. See "Greek and Roman Definitions of Impossible Laws," *Natural Law Forum* 12 (1967) : 1.

For a strong attack on the view I offer here, see Jonathan Bennett, "An Argument Against Absolutes" (forthcoming) .

Causation and Negative Duties

Richard Epstein has recently argued that cause is the central concept for ascribing responsibility. That you "did it" is prima facie a sufficient reason to hold you responsible for "it." That you were unconscious or acting in self-defense, or that the victim did it too, comes in as a ground for overcoming that responsibility. See Richard A. Epstein, "A Theory of Strict Liability," *Journal of Legal Studies* 2 (1973) : 151; Epstein, "Defenses and Subsequent Pleas in a System of Strict Liability,"

Journal of Legal Studies 3 (1974) : 165; Epstein, "Intentional Harms," *Journal of Legal Studies* 4 (1975) : 391. Of course, any such theory is only as good as its conception of cause. Epstein relies heavily on that of H. L. A. Hart and A. J. Honoré, *Causation in the Law* (Oxford: Oxford University Press, 1959). Hart and Honoré propose as their central causal criterion that of the set of jointly sufficient conditions, which they believe overcomes the problems of "additional" (two bullets fired simultaneously through the same heart) and "alternative" causation (A poisons victim's canteen, B empties it, and C fills it with sand). Hart and Honoré also propose that the causal chain is broken by an unexpected and aberrational event or by the responsible intervention of another agent. A variation of Hart and Honoré's causal criterion has recently been proposed by J. L. Mackie, *The Cement of the Universe* (Oxford: Oxford University Press, 1974).

The distinction between positive and negative duties is made by Philippa Foot in "The Problem of Abortion and the Doctrine of the Double Effect," *Oxford Review* 5 (1967) : 5. It is also made by W. D. Ross in *The Right and the Good;* he agrees that negative duties tend to be more stringent. This distinction raises the difficult problem of acts and omissions and of responsibility for omissions. For a discussion of the law of omissions see my "Right and Wrong—Preliminary Considerations," *Journal of Legal Studies* 5 (1976) : especially pp. 174–5. A useful philosophical survey of this problem can be found in Eric D'Arcy, *Human Acts* (Oxford: Oxford University Press, 1963). But the act/omission distinction is merely a component of the larger theory of actions.

For further references, see notes to Chapter 2, under "Directness and Particularity: The Analogy to Benefit."

INTENTION: THE PERSON AS AGENT AND OBJECT

Intention Daube's discussion occurs in his *Collaboration with Tyranny in Rabbinic Law* (Oxford: Oxford University Press, 1965). An analogous principle in Roman Catholic moral theology holds that "formal cooperation includes consent to another's sin . . . material cooperation is in itself a good act which is abused by another through his own malice." Dominicus M. Prummer, *Handbook of Moral Theology* (Freiburg: Herder, 1957), pp. 103–104. This is but a particular case of the general law of double effect: "It is never lawful, even for the gravest reasons, to do evil that good may come of it—in other words, to intend directly something which of its very nature contradicts the moral order, and which must therefore be judged unworthy of man, even though the intention is to protect or promote the welfare of an individual, of a family, or of society in general." Encyclical letter of His Holiness Paul VI, "Humanae Vitae," *The Pope Speaks* 13 (1968) : 329, 337, § 14; see also New York *Times,* July 30, 1968, p. 20.

"A person may licitly perform an action that he knows will produce a good effect and a bad effect provided that four conditions are verified . . . (1) That the action itself from its very object be good or at least indifferent; (2) that the good effect and not the evil effect be intended; (3) that the good effect be not produced by means of the evil effect; (4) that there be a proportionally grave reason for permitting the evil effect." This is a standard formulation of the principle of double effect, here quoted from Joseph T. Mangan, "An Historical Analysis of the Principle of Double Effect," *Theological Studies* 10 (1949) : 41, 43. For a recent discussion of this problem as it relates to killing and self-defense, see Germain G. Grisez, "Toward a Consistent Natural Law Ethic of Killing," *American Journal of Jurisprudence* 15 (1970) : 64, 78: "The evil effect may not be the means to the good effect." Richard A. McCormick, *Ambiguity in Moral Choice* (Pere Marquette Theology Lecture, 1973), is a thorough critical review of recent writing on the law of double effect. For a useful review, see Anthony Kenny, *The Anatomy of the Soul* (Oxford: Basil Blackwell, 1973), Appendix: "The History of Intention in Ethics."

These distinctions are also drawn in the philosophical literature. G. E. M. Anscombe, for example, in "Modern Moral Philosophy," defends against utilitarianism the moral significance of the distinction between the doing of evil as an end in itself and bringing about the same evil as a foreseen but unintended result. And Bernard Williams argues for a distinction between doing evil oneself and allowing the same evil to be done by someone else *(Utilitarianism—For and Against)*. The most defensible because most modest statement of this proposition is Thomas Nagel's, in "War and Massacre."

Bentham, in *The Principles of Morals and Legislation*, ed. J. H. Burns and H. L. A. Hart (London: Athlone Press, 1970), recognizes a similar distinction. "A consequence, when it is intentional, may either be directly so, or only obliquely. It may be said to be directly or lineally intentional, when the prospect of producing it constituted one of the links in the chain of causes by which the person was determined to do the act. It may be said to be obliquely or collaterally intentional, when, although the consequence was in contemplation, and appeared likely to ensue in case of the act's being performed, yet the prospect of producing such consequence did not constitute a link in the aforesaid chain" (p. 84). But it should be noted that Bentham also argued that little should be made of the distinction between direct and oblique intention.

The most extensive modern discussion of the concept of intention is G. E. M. Anscombe, *Intention* (Oxford: Basil Blackwell, 1957).

Criticisms of the moral relevance of intention or of the means/ concomitant distinction may be found in Jonathan Bennett, "Whatever the Consequences," *Analysis* 26 (1966) : 83; Philippa Foot, "The Problem of Abortion and the Doctrine of Doubt Effect"; Judith Thomson, "Rights and Deaths," *Philosophy and Public Affairs* 2 (1973) : 146.

A balanced but critical treatment of intention in law and morals is H. L. A. Hart, "Intention and Punishment," in *Punishment and Responsibility* (Oxford: Oxford University Press, 1968), especially p. 119.

For the argument that legal consequences may turn on the means/concomitant distinction see my "Right and Wrong—Preliminary Considerations." In this regard, compare with the quotation from Prummer on formal cooperation, above, the following dictum by Learned Hand in *United States* v. *Falcone,* 109 F. 2d 579, 581 (2d Cir. 1940) : "There are indeed instances of criminal liability . . . where the law imposes punishment merely because the accused did not forbear to do that from which the wrong was likely to follow; but in prosecutions for conspiracy or abetting, his attitude towards the forbidden undertaking must be more positive. It is not enough that he does not forgo a normally lawful activity, of the fruits of which he knows that others will make an unlawful use; he must in some sense promote their venture himself, make it his own, have a stake in its outcome."

The conterfactual test for distinguishing a means from a concomitant is to be found in many places in the literature of this problem. See, for example, John Finnis, "The Rights and Wrongs of Abortion: A Reply to Judith Thomson," *Philosophy and Public Affairs* 2 (1973) : 117; Richard McCormick, *Ambiguity in Moral Choice,* and, indeed, the quotation from Bentham above may be thought to refer to this test by implication.

Problems about Intention My proposal that intention as efficacious desire is a primitive concept seems to me very close to an argument of Karl Rahner, "Some Thoughts on a Good Intention," *Theological Investigations,* vol. 3 (London: Darton Longman & Todd, 1967). See also Stuart Hampshire, *Thought and Action* (London: Chatto and Windus, 1959). My conception also relates to the problem of causal efficacy in general. See notes to Chapter 2, under "Directness and Particularity: Direct Harm."

My proposal gains plausibility from a consideration of what it means to say that we know our own intentions and how knowing our intentions differs from predicting our own future conduct. On this, see Stuart Hampshire and H. L. A. Hart, "Decision, Intention and Certainty," in *Freedom and Responsibility,* ed. Herbert Morris (Stanford: Stanford University Press, 1961). So also I suspect that the primitiveness of intention might be made out by considering the relation between the intention and the meaning of an utterance, given that speaking is a kind of acting. In that context I imagine we readily and naturally distinguish between a speaker's meaning (his intention) and what he appears to be saying—maybe even knowingly appears to be saying. See also the notes to Chapter 3.

Opposed to my thesis that intention is the primary object of moral judgment is Matt. 5: 27–28: "You have learned that they were told 'do not commit adultery.' But what I tell you is this: If a man looks on a woman with a lustful eye he has already committed adultery with her in his heart."

RESPECT FOR PERSONS

That there is a relation between right and wrong, intention, and respect for persons seems to me to be suggested by Nagel in "War and Massacre," especially pp. 134–136.

2. Harm

My definition of harming is narrower than that of battery in the law of torts. Battery is defined as a harmful or *offensive* touching, and this includes an offense to dignitary interests, akin to the interest in privacy. See, for example, *Harrigan* v. *Rosich,* 173 So. 28 880 (1966) (pushing with finger, saying, "Go home, old man"). My definition is more in accord with the Roman law, which groups spitting on somebody with other insulting conduct under the delict of *iniuria*. To be sure, the special offense in some touching may be the assertion of a right to make free with another's person, and such an *assertion* is threatening even though the particular touching is not. For a discussion of the normative elements in the concept of harm, see Philippa Foot, "Moral Beliefs," *Proceedings of the Aristotelian Society* 59 (1958–59) : 83.

DIRECTNESS AND PARTICULARITY

The Person and Disintegrating Universality The argument of this section is central to the conception of morality in this book. It represents a development from my earlier treatment of many similar problems in *An Anatomy of Values* (Cambridge, Mass.: Harvard University Press, 1970). For a criticism of that work, see Bernard Williams, "Persons, Character and Morality," in A. O. Rorty, ed., *The Identities of Persons* (Berkeley: University of California Press, 1976). I have been influenced in my view of the centrality of incorporation by P. F. Strawson, *Individuals: An Essay in Descriptive Metaphysics* (London: Methuen, 1959). For a collection of writings making the connection between the body and the moral entity which is the person, see Stuart Spicker, ed., *The Philosophy of the Body* (Chicago: Quadrangle Books, 1970). Of special importance are the excerpts from Jonas, Merleau-Ponty, Sartre, Scheler, and Williams.

That it is pleasure (or the good, however defined) and not respect for persons that is the organizing conception of utilitarian or other teleological systems is, of course, the central criticism made by Kant of such systems. His whole enterprise might be seen as an effort to give sense to the notion of the primacy of persons—especially in the face of the utilitarian counterthrusts that persons have all the primacy conceivable just insofar as it is the good of persons which is sought to be maximized. The Kantian conception receives the clearest and most elaborate statement in John Rawls, *A Theory of Justice* (Cambridge, Mass.: Harvard University Press, 1971) ; see especially pp. 26–27. Of course Rawls does not prove that his system is more consistent with the concept of respect for persons than utilitarianism. Rather, his system offers an interpretation of that concept.

Direct Harm   The anthropomorphic element in the concept of cause has been frequently noted. R. G. Collingwood has argued that because human agency is different from the agency of natural objects the notion of causation as applied to the natural world "is simply a relic of animism foisted upon a science to which it is irrelevant" ("On the So-Called Idea of Causation," in *Freedom and Responsibility,* ed. Herbert Morris [Stanford: Stanford University Press, 1961], pp. 303, 312) . Collingwood argues that the notion of causation derives "from our experience of occasions on which we have compelled others to act in certain ways" (ibid., p. 311) and that the notion was transferred to the natural world after the notion that God is the sole cause of natural events was abandoned for the view that things in nature themselves are causes. The transferral of the commonsense notion left scientists and philosophers with the task of explaining how natural events could compel or necessitate other natural events. Collingwood commends modern physics for eliminating the notion of cause altogether (ibid., p. 312). To Moritz Schlick, not only physics, but all "science does not speak of causes and effects, but of functional relations between measurable quantities" ("Causality in Everyday Life and in Recent Science," in *Freedom and Responsibility,* p. 297). Niels Bohr seems to take an intermediate position. While arguing that ordinary notions of time, space, and causality are wholly inappropriate to the realm of particle physics, he did not deny the applicability of these notions to all other realms of empirical knowledge. See also Strawson, *Individuals: An Essay in Descriptive Metaphysics.*

For the Roman law concept of *Damnum corpore corpori datum,* see *Corpus Juris Civile Digest,* title 1x.2 "Ad Legem Aquiliam," reprinted with a translation, commentary and reference in F. H. Lawson, *Negligence in the Civil Law* (Oxford: Oxford University Press, 1950) ; and Charles Fried, "The *Lex Aquilia* as a Source of Law," *American Journal of Legal History* 4 (1960) : 142.

For criticisms of the coherence and moral relevance of the concept of directness, see references to Bennett, Foot, and Thomson in the notes to Chapter 1, under "Intention: The Person as Agent and Object."

The Analogy to Benefit   The discussion in this section particularly, but in Chapter 1 and in my argument distinguishing positive from negative rights in Part II as well, enters the debate in the philosophical literature regarding the justification (if any) for a distinction between harming and not helping or between positive and negative duties. Gilbert Harman, using a point of departure certainly very different from my own, defends these distinctions as the plausible compromise between the rich and powerful on one hand and the weak and poor on the other: both parties are better off, but neither provides all the benefits at their own expense. See his *The Nature of Morality* (New York: Oxford University Press, 1977), pp. 110–111, and "Moral Relativism Defended," *Philosophical Review* 84 (1975): 3. Richard Trammell, "Saving Life and Taking Life," *Journal of Philosophy* 72 (1975): 131, argues for the distinction on the grounds that harming tends to lead to worse results than not helping. See also Trammell, "Tooley's Moral Symmetry Principle," *Philosophy and Public Affairs* 5 (1976): 305. Harman subjects Trammell's argument to withering analysis in "Relativistic Ethics: Morality as Politics," *Midwestern Studies in Philosophy* 3 (1978). See also Robert Coburn, "Relativism and the Basis of Morality," *Philosophy Review* 85 (1976): 87; John Harris, "The Marxist Conception of Violence," *Philosophy and Public Affairs* 3 (1974): 192; Harris, "The Survival Lottery," *Philosophy* 50 (1975): 81; Carolyn Morillo, "Doing, Refraining, and the Seriousness of Morality," *American Philosophical Quarterly* 14 (1977): 1; Bruce Russell, "On the Relative Structures of Negative and Positive Duties," ibid., p. 87. See also the references to Singer in the notes to the Introduction and to Foot and Bennett in the notes to Chapter 1. My own argument holds that harming is intrinsically wrong, while not helping may or may not be wrong depending on the circumstances and one's theory of positive rights. This debate connects also to the so-called problem of the Good Samaritan. For a recent review of that literature, see John Kleinig, "Good Samaritanism," *Philosophy and Public Affairs* 5 (1976): 382; Anthony D'Amato, "The Bad Samaritan Paradigm," *Northwestern University Law Review* 70 (1976): 798; Marc Franklin, "Vermont Requires Rescue: A Comment," *Stanford Law Review* 25 (1972): 51.

From Directness to Intention

For references see notes to Chapter 1, under "Intention: The Person as Agent and Object." See also Rachels, "Active and Passive Euthanasia," *New England Journal of Medicine* 292 (1975): 78. Since it is intention to harm and not act versus omission which I hold to be crucial, and since one can harm by an omission, I am not troubled by Rachels's argument.

Completing the Structure: Defense

The conception of justifiable self-defense as both intentional and relational is developed by Thomas Nagel, "War and Massacre," *Philosophy and Public Affairs* 1 (1972): 123. It is Thomas Aquinas who argued that killing in self-defense is justifiable because there is no intention to inflict harm. *Summa Theologica*, pt. II, q. 64, art. 7. See generally on this the excellent article by Germain G. Grisez, "Toward a Consistent Natural Law Ethic of Killing," *American Journal of Jurisprudence* 15 (1970) : 64. A very deep and thorough examination of problems of defense in the law may be found in Herbert Wechsler and Jerome Michael, "A Rationale of the Law of Homicide," *Columbia Law Review* 37 (1937) : 701, 1261. An excellent philosophical discussion is Judith Thomson, *Self-Defense and Rights* (Lindley Lecture for 1976, Lawrence: University of Kansas Press [forthcoming]). The problem of defense against a morally innocent aggressor is considered in George Fletcher, "Proportionality and the Psychotic Aggressor," *Israel Law Review* 8 (1973) : 367.

In law, where an agent does not intend harm but only risks it, the range of justifying purposes is infinite: any purpose whose importance outweighs the discounted probability of harm. Where the agent intends harm, however, he escapes liability only if he can show that he acted for one of a very few, specifically defined justifying purposes, such as self-defense. Due to the (I believe) mistaken equation in the law of torts of intended with foreseen, certain, but unintended consequences, the anomalous position ensues of making a very large difference as to the available range of justifications turn on very small differences of degree between "merely" risky conduct on one hand and conduct which is so risky as to be almost certain to produce an unintended harm. For a detailed discussion of this problem, see Fried, "Right and Wrong—Preliminary Considerations," *Journal of Legal Studies* 5 (1976) : 165. See also the text of Chapter 1 under "Causation and Negative Duties."

3. On Lying

Sissela Bok, *Lying: Moral Choice in Public and Private Life* (New York: Pantheon, 1978), is the most complete modern consideration of this subject. This book contains a survey of the literature and of many practical contexts of application, such as politics, medicine, and social science research. It also contains excerpts from many of the classic texts as an appendix.

The connection between intention (as in intending a result) and meaning (as in my meaning in saying something) is considered in the title essay of Stanley Cavell, *Must We Mean What We Say?* (New York: Scribner's, 1969), and in H. P. Grice, "Utterer's Meaning and Intention," *Philosophical Review* 78 (1969) : 147. David Lewis, in "Utilitarianism and Truthfulness," *Australian Journal of Philosophy* 50 (1972) : 17, offers a brief and pointed argument for a purely consequentialist account of the institution of truthfulness. For an argument that moral institutions in general find their source in conventions, see Gilbert Harman, *The Nature of Morality* (New York: Oxford University Press, 1977), ch. 9. Hume's discussion of convention is in

Bk. III, pt. II, sec. II of the *Treatise* and his discussion of promising in sec. V. Peter Singer defends a purely consequentialist, act-utilitarian account of the nature of truthfulness, in "Is Act-Utilitarianism Self-Defeating?" *Philosophical Review* 81 (1972) : 94.

Augustine's views on lying are found in *"De mendacio"* and *"Contra mendacium,"* in *Treatises on Various Subjects, Fathers of the Church,* vol. 16, ed. Ray J. DeFerreri (New York: Fathers of the Church, 1952). The latter of the two essays is a response to an overzealous Christian who offered to infiltrate the Priscillian sect, whose members pretended to be orthodox. Augustine is not impressed by the argument that after all the pretense of being a Priscillian was justified by that sect's own concealments. For Thomas Aquinas's very elaborate views on lying, see *Summa Theologica,* pts. I–II, q. 110.

4. Rights—The Economic Analysis

RIGHTS

The formal concept of rights I offer is based on a persistent theme in analytic philosophy that there are reasons or arguments or considerations which block appeals to consequences or to utilitarian considerations generally. An early statement is W. D. Ross, *The Right and the Good* (Oxford: Oxford University Press, 1930). John Rawls, in *A Theory of Justice* (Cambridge, Mass.: Harvard University Press, 1971), gives this conception of formal priority its sharpest focus in his argument for the lexical ordering of moral and political rights relative to economic equality and efficiency. His system shows how one can give a rich and reasonable meaning to the felt "absolute" quality of rights. H. L. A. Hart, "Are There Any Natural Rights?" *Philosophical Review* 64 (1955) : 165, reprinted in A. I. Melden, ed., *Human Rights* (Belmont, Cal.: Wadsworth, 1970) is an important precursor of Rawls's views and also contains a discussion of the concept of a right in legal discourse. The strongest recent statement of the concept of rights I offer here occurs at the beginning of Robert Nozick, *Anarchy, State and Utopia* (New York: Basic Books, 1974), p. ix: "Individuals have rights, and there are things no person or group may do to them (without violating their rights)." And certainly the most elegant statement of the priority of rights is that of "rights as trumps" offered by Ronald Dworkin, for it shows that not only do rights have priority over other elements in a moral argument but also that rights are held by individuals who may or may not choose to play them. Dworkin's views on the formal nature of rights are presented in *Taking Rights Seriously* (Cambridge, Mass.: Harvard University Press, 1977) especially pp. 82–123 and 188–192. Judith Thomson adumbrates a theory of the formal nature of rights, which is part of a major work in progress, in "The Right to Privacy," *Philosophy and Public Affairs* 4 (1975) : 295, and in "Some Ruminations on Rights," *Arizona Law Review* (Winter 1978 [forthcoming]).

The traditional analysis of rights in legal contexts is based on W. N. Hohfeld, "Some Fundamental Legal Conceptions as Applied in Judicial Reasoning," *Yale Law Journal* 23 (1913) : 16 and 26 (1917) : 710; and Arthur L. Corbin, "Legal Analysis and Terminology," *Yale Law Journal* 29 (1919) : 163.

THE ECONOMIC ANALYSIS OF RIGHTS

The economic analysis of rights has produced an enormous literature. Good bibliographies as well as useful selections can be found in Eirik Furubotn and Svetozar Pejovich, *The Economics of Property Rights* (Cambridge, Mass.: Ballinger Publishing Co., 1974) , Gene Wunderlich and W. L. Gibson, Jr., *Perspectives on Property* (College Park: Pennsylvania State University Press, 1972) , and A. Mitchell Polinsky, "Economic Analysis as a Potentially Defective Product: A Buyer's Guide to Posner's *Economic Analysis of Law*," *Harvard Law Review* 87 (1974) : 1655. Of the many writings in this area those which I have found particularly important are Ronald Coase, "The Problem of Social Cost," *Journal of Law and Economics* 3 (1960) : 1; Harold Demsetz, "Some Aspects of Property Rights," *Journal of Law and Economics* 9 (1966) : 61, Demsetz, "Toward a Theory of Property Rights," *American Economic Review: Papers and Proceedings* 57 (1967) : 347; Guido Calabresi, *The Costs of Accidents* (New Haven: Yale University Press, 1970) ; Calabresi, "Transaction Costs, Resource Allocation, and Liability Rules—A Comment," *Journal of Law and Economics* 11 (1969) : 67; Calabresi and A. Douglas Melamed, "Property Rules, Liability Rules, and Alienability: One View of the Cathedral," *Harvard Law Review* 85 (1972) : 1089; Polinsky, "Economic Analysis as a Potentially Defective Product"; Richard A. Posner, *Economic Analysis of Law* (Boston: Little, Brown, 1974) ; Frank I. Michelman, "Property, Utility, and Fairness: Comments on the Ethical Foundations of 'Just Compensation' Law," *Harvard Law Review* 80 (1967) : 1165; "Pollution as a Tort: A Non-Accidental Perspective on Calabresi's Costs," *Yale Law Journal* 80 (1971) : 647.

On the relation between the Coase Theorem and questions of distribution, see Harold Demsetz, "Wealth Distribution and the Ownership of Rights," *Journal of Legal Studies* 1 (1972) : 2; and "When Does the Rule of Liability Matter?" *Journal of Legal Studies* 1 (1972) : 13. Cf. Rawls, *A Theory of Justice*, §§ 46–47.

Harold Hochman and James Rogers developed their thesis in "Pareto Optimal Redistribution," *American Economic Review* 59 (1969) : 542. Ronald Dworkin argues correctly that preferences for oneself and preferences about distribution stand on different logical levels and must be judged differently. See *Taking Rights Seriously*, pp. 275–276. See also Kenneth J. Arrow, *Social Choice and Individual Values*, 2nd ed. (New York: John Wiley, 1963) , pp. 103–106.

BARGAINING AND MORAL FOUNDATIONS

In arguing for the necessity of some kind of normative point of departure for bargaining, I hope I am confounding the distinction made by Bruce Ackerman in *Private Property and the Constitution* (New Haven: Yale University Press, 1977) between the Scientific Policy Maker on one hand and the Ordinary Observer on the other. Ackerman's categories suggest that it is the latter who roots himself in intuitive judgments about our particular situation while the former submits all such judgments to total analysis (and annihilation) of either a Kantian or a utilitarian sort. I argue here, however, that useful as utilitarian-economic analysis might be, it requires a foundation in noneconomic judgments about the kinds of entities human beings are. Moreover, the view I am developing not only utilizes what I believe to be widely held intuitive judgments but purports to explain them.

For a criticism of the economic analysis of rights from a different perspective, see C. Edwin Baker, "The Ideology of the Economic Analysis of Law," *Philosophy and Public Affairs* 5 (1975) : 3. Also see Kenneth J. Arrow, *The Limits of Organization* (New York: W. W. Norton, 1974), especially ch. 1, for a discussion of the value of trust as a basis for economic organization.

CONCLUSION

On the economic analysis of crime, see Gary S. Becker and George Stigler, "Law Enforcement, Malfeasance, and Compensation of Offenders," *Journal of Legal Studies* 3 (1974): 1; Posner, *Economic Analysis of Law*.

A NOTE ON COMPENSATION

The thesis that fault may on occasion consist not in causing harm but in failing to make compensation is developed in Robert Keeton, "Conditional Fault in the Law of Torts," *Harvard Law Review* 72 (1959) : 401.

For additional references relating to this topic, see the works by Epstein cited in the notes to Chapter 1, under "Causation and Negative Duties."

5. Positive Rights

The extent to which Rawls offers a theory of rights which is focused primarily on guaranteeing participation in the political process on fair terms is discussed in my review of *A Theory of Justice, Harvard Law Review* 85 (1972) : 1691, 1697. Though I conclude that Rawls's menu of personal as opposed to political rights is remarkably meager, I do not believe that Rawls holds personal rights to be derivative from political rights solely. Certainly his strong argument for liberty of conscience goes beyond a concern for the integrity of the political process, as do his arguments against paternalism. See John Rawls, *A Theory of Justice* (Cambridge, Mass.: Harvard University Press, 1971), especially pp. 272–310 (freedom of association and free choice), 248 (paternalism), 331 (sexual relations). For a general discussion of liberty and rights in Rawls see Norman Daniels, ed., *Reading Rawls* (New York: Basic Books, 1975). Of particular interest to this thesis are the essays by Scanlon, H. L. A. Hart, and Daniels. For an excellent recent philosophical treatment of the right to free speech as a personal and political right, see Thomas Scanlon, "A Theory of Freedom of Expression," *Philosophy and Public Affairs* 1 (1972): 204. On the relation between moral rights and legal rights, see Ronald Dworkin, *Taking Rights Seriously* (Cambridge, Mass.: Harvard University Press, 1977), especially chs. 4 and 12.

Positive and Negative Rights

The distinction between positive and negative rights made in this section depends on the soundness of the distinction between harming and failing to help. This topic is dealt with in Chapter 1, in the section "Causation and Negative Duties," and Chapter 2, in the subsection "Directness and Particularity: The Analogy to Benefit." For references to the extensive recent philosophical literature on this topic, see the notes to Chapter 2, under "Directness and Particularity: The Analogy to Benefits." See also the references to the writings of Judith J. Thomson in the notes to Chapter 4, under "Rights."

The Sources of Positive Rights

For references to Rawls's views on the moral arbitrariness of differences arising out of natural advantage, see *A Theory of Justice*, index listing "Distribution of natural assets." For example: "The intuitive idea is that since everyone's well-being depends upon a scheme of cooperation without which no one could have a satisfactory life, the division of advantages should be such as to draw forth the willing cooperation of everyone taking part in it, including those less well situated . . . The two principles mentioned seem to be a fair agreement on the basis of which those better endowed, or more fortunate in their social position, neither of which we can be said to deserve, could expect the willing cooperation of others when some workable scheme is a necessary condition of the welfare of all. Once we decide to look for a conception of justice that nullifies the accidents of natural endowment and the contingencies of social circumstance as counters in quest for political and economic advantage, we are led to these principles. They express the results of leaving aside those aspects of the social world that seem arbitrary from a moral point of view" (p. 15). This passage makes clear two crucial aspects of Rawls's theory: that differences in natural advantage are morally arbitrary, and that it is the desire and necessity of all persons to join in schemes of social cooperation which account for the need to wash out the results of these morally arbitrary elements.

Rawls's theory of individual obligation is discussed in his ch. 6.

For a critical discussion of Nozick's work, see Thomas Nagel, "Libertarianism Without Foundations," *Yale Law Journal* 85 (1975) : 136. For further references to the argument that Rawls is *not* an end-state or pattern theorist, see the notes to Chapter 6, under "Conclusion: The System of Positive and Negative Rights."

The affirmative argument I make for a duty to contribute might be referred to Kant's speculative essay "A Renewed Attempt to Answer the Question: 'Is the Human Race Continually Improving?' " in *Kant's Political Writings,* ed. Hans Reiss (Cambridge: Cambridge University Press, 1971). This reference and its significance was pointed out to me by my colleague Roberto Unger, for whom it plays a great role in his *Knowledge and Politics* (New York: Free Press, 1975).

NEEDS AND WANTS

On distributive formulae, see Rawls, *A Theory of Justice,* pp. 34–40; and Amartya Sen, *Collective Choice and Social Welfare* (San Francisco: Holden-Day, 1970).

On the distinction between needs and wants, see Thomas Scanlon, "Preference and Urgency," *Journal of Philosophy* 72 (1975): 655; I. M. D. Little, *A Critique of Welfare Economics,* 2nd ed. (Oxford: Oxford University Press, 1957); Frank I. Michelman, "Constitutional Welfare Rights and 'A Theory of Justice,' " in *Reading Rawls,* pp. 319–347. Rawls's own treatment of this distinction is complex. In order to avoid the difficulties of interpersonal comparison of subjective utilities, he introduces the concept of the "primary goods," under which he classes rights and liberties, powers and opportunities, income, wealth, and self-respect. These are the general goods which every man wants, no matter what particular things he wants. But it is plain that Rawls's theory implies important priorities and structural relations between these primary goods. Income and wealth, for instance, would seem to be the subjects of the maximin principle of distribution. But the principles of equal liberty and open offices are both lexically prior to the maximin distributive principle. And certainly in Part III of his work Rawls makes clear that the conditions for a secure sense of self-respect are prior to income and wealth. Thus the theory of primary goods is more complex than the needs-wants dichotomy, of which it is an extension. The theory accords priority to various structural rights, personal and political, which form the starting point for the pursuit of the good. Finally, Rawls (p. 62) makes the distinction between natural primary goods (health, vigor, intelligence, imagination) and those primary goods which the social system not only influences but also distributes (rights, liberties, income, wealth). This distinction is important to my thesis in Chapter 6, but it is not clear what role it plays in Rawls's system. Certainly he holds that society is concerned with any inequalities in power or wealth that differences in the natural goods may produce. But what, then, are the limits of social concern for differences related to natural goods? My guess is that the limits may be just those I propose in Chapter 6.

My own earlier works which make more of the distinction between needs and wants than I am inclined to do now are "Difficulties in the Economic Analysis of Rights," in G. Dworkin, G. Bermant, and P. Brown, *Markets and Morals* (Washington, D.C.: Hemisphere Publishing Co., 1977), and *Medical Experimentation: Personal Integrity and Social Policy* (Amsterdam and New York: Elsevier Publishing Co., 1974), ch. 4. I signal my retreat from these views in "Equality and Rights in Medical Care," in *Implications of Guaranteeing Medical Care*, ed. J. Perpich (Washington, D.C.: National Academy of Sciences, 1976).

For discussions of the problems of applying economic analysis and conceptions of distributive justice to medical care, see Kenneth J. Arrow, "Uncertainty and Welfare Economics of Medical Care," *American Economic Review* 53 (1963): 941; Victor Fuchs, *Who Shall Live? Health Economics and Social Choice* (New York: Basic Books, 1974); Richard Zeckhauser, "Coverage for Catastrophic Illness," *Public Policy* (Spring 1973): 149. See also references in ch. 4 of Fried, *Medical Experimentation*.

Of special interest are the so-called "Maxwell effect," according to which the more money that is spent on medical care now the more will have to be spent in the future, and the "Roemer effect," according to which patient demand expands to fill existing hospital capacity. See Martin S. Feldstein, "Hospital Cost Inflation: A Study of Nonprofit Price Dynamics," *American Economic Review* 61 (1971): 853; Marc J. Roberts and Ted Bogue, "The American Health Care System: Where Have All the Dollars Gone?" *Harvard Journal on Legislation* 13 (1976): 635; John Morrow and Arch Edwards, "U.S. Health Manpower Policy: Will the Benefits Justify the Costs?" *Journal of Medical Education* 51 (1976): 795.

THE SYSTEM OF POSITIVE RIGHTS

The argument that we must all be provided with resources to develop and realize our own conception of the good, that the choice and implementation of that conception are a fundamental aspect of human personality, and that our tastes or wants are therefore our own responsibilities is an argument which derives from Rawls, *A Theory of Justice*, Part III. See also his "Fairness to Goodness," *Philosophical Review* 84 (1975): 536. The same argument is also made by Dworkin, *Taking Rights Seriously*, ch. 6, 10 and 11.

For Lionel Robbins's views on the moral significance of money, see his *Essays in the Nature and Significance of Economic Science* (New

York: St. Martin's, 1935). For dissenting views on the preferability of money over in-kind redistribution, see Arrow, "Uncertainty and Welfare Economics of Medical Care"; Herbert Gintis, "Welfare Economics and Individual Development," *Quarterly Journal of Economics* 86 (1972) : 572; Lester Thurow, "Government Expenditures: Cash or In-Kind Aid?" *Philosophy and Public Affairs* 5 (1976) : 361; see also Michelman, "Constitutional Welfare Rights and 'A Theory of Justice.' "

An argument against the insurance principle as it regards health care is suggested by Arrow, "Uncertainty and Welfare Economics of Medical Care," and others who point out the difficulties which an individual consumer would labor under in seeking to bargain intelligently and effectively for health care. But, of course, these objections assume that the bargaining would take place between individual consumers and providers. In reality, health care consumers are often represented by powerful groups such as labor unions, employer groups, and other units to which they belong. Moreover, the providers are not individual providers either, but rather various kinds of health plans. Consumer groups are very well situated to evaluate the costs and qualities associated with alternate health plans and, indeed, to wield a reasonable amount of influence in being able to determine the contents and costs of various plans. Thus it seems to me that we can indeed imagine something like a market operating in this area as well. The problems arise in respect to poor people and others who are not represented by labor unions, employers, or other groups. But if it is recognized that this is where the problem lies, special provisions can be made for such unrepresented consumers. They might, for instance, be represented by their states or municipalities.

The insurance principle might be seen as an expression of Rawls's point that a theory of justice should be primarily concerned not with distributions and results at a particular moment but with the long-term expectations of representative groups. The insurance principle also seems to me a way to begin to deal with the very difficult problems raised in Bernard Williams's classic article "The Idea of Equality," in his *Problems of the Self* (Cambridge: Cambridge University Press, 1973).

6. Negative Rights

NEGATIVE RIGHTS AND FAIR SHARES

The thesis that negative rights are a constraint upon the pursuit of fair shares is formally analogous to Rawls's thesis that the first principle of justice, the principle of equal liberty, is lexically prior to the maximin principle of fair distributive shares. The difference is one of content. I propose a more detailed and less institutional content for the lexically prior elements, while leaving unspecified a principle of fair shares. But this is not a disagreement, since Rawls does not purport to go into detail about the content of the principle of equal liberty, and the details I propose may well be consistent with that principle if elaborated. Moreover, it is quite clear that Rawls chooses maximim over, say, a principle of equal shares just because it can be accommodated to the priority of principles like that of liberty. The maximin principle holds that departures from equality are justified to the extent that they are necessary to improve the situation of the worst-off representative man, but these departures from equality are necessary in part at least precisely because we are bound to respect a number of principles which have priority over fair shares. If we could override (for Rawls) the equal liberty principle or (for Fried) negative rights, then departures from equality would be necessary much less frequently. Finally, the distinction Rawls makes between natural and social goods also suggests acceptance of constraints such as those I propose in this chapter. See the notes to Chapter 5, under "Needs and Wants."

The notion that interests and personal integrity, analogous to the negative right not to be harmed, might attach to some property rights, or at least to the right of privacy, might be made out on the basis of my argument for the value of privacy in *An Anatomy of Values* (Cambridge, Mass.: Harvard University Press, 1970), Chapter 9. That argument, however, speaks more of the value of privacy than of the right, and therefore it does not distinguish between intentional and unintentional violations of privacy. Judith Thomson's discussion is more sensitive to this point. See "The Right to Privacy," *Philosophy and Public Affairs* 4 (1975): 295. For the notion that property rights may to some extent be viewed as an extension of personality, see Bruce Ackerman, *Private Property and the Constitution* (New Haven: Yale University Press, 1977), ch. 5.

NEGATIVE RIGHTS AND FAIR CONTRIBUTIONS

Richard Titmuss, *The Gift Relationship* (London: George Allen and Unwin, 1971) is discussed critically by Kenneth J. Arrow, "Gifts and Exchanges," *Philosophy and Public Affairs* 1 (1972): 343, and defended by Peter Singer, "Altruism and Commerce," *Philosophy and Public Affairs* 2 (1973): 312.

My views on taxation and particularly on a consumption tax owe a large debt to William Andrews, "A Consumption-Type or Cash Flow Personal Income Tax," *Harvard Law Review* 87 (1974): 1113, and "Fairness and the Choice Between a Consumption-Type and Accretion-Type Personal Income Tax: A Reply to Professor Warren," *Harvard Law Review* 88 (1975); 947. See also John Rawls, *A Theory of Justice* (Cambridge, Mass: Harvard University Press, 1971), §43; Nicholas Kaldor, *An Expenditure Tax* (London: George Allen and Unwin, 1955).

John Harris in "The Survival Lottery," *Philosophy* 50 (1975): 81, argues that a kidney lottery of the sort discussed in the text would be proper, and that only the distinctions we are inclined to make between killing and letting die (quite properly, I contend) prevent us from equating refusal to go along with such a lottery with murder.

FAMILY RIGHTS: A COMPLEX CASE

The suggestions I make regarding the connection between personal and biological individuality are worked out in Fried, "Ethical Issues in Existing and Emerging Techniques for Improving Human Fertility," in *Law and Ethics of A.I.D. and Embryo Transfer,* Ciba Foundation Symposium 17 (new series) (Amsterdam and New York: Elsevier Publishing Co., 1973). This notion is developed with great power and subtlety by the science fiction writer Frank Herbert in *The Eyes of Heisenberg* (New York: Berkeley Publishing Co., 1973).

UNINTENDED INVASIONS: A COMPLICATION

For a further discussion of these problems, see Fried, *An Anatomy of Values,* ch. 11, and George Fletcher, "Fairness and Utility in Tort Theory," *Harvard Law Review* 85 (1972): 537. The connection between rights and liability rules for accidental injury is of course the subject of much of the literature of the economic analysis of rights, for which see references in the notes to Chapter 4, under "The Economic Analysis of Rights."

CONCLUSION: THE SYSTEM OF POSITIVE AND NEGATIVE RIGHTS

Ronald Dworkin, in *Taking Rights Seriously* (Cambridge, Mass.: Harvard University Press, 1977), offers a theory of rights and of the relation of rights to utility. For Dworkin the principal anti-utilitarian right is the right to treatment as an equal or the right to equal concern and respect. (See ch. 12.)

Dworkin sees this most fundamental of rights as the real foundation of Rawls's system (p. 180). Dworkin disagrees with the notion that we have any morally grounded right to liberty (p. 267) or to some menu of "basic" liberties (pp. 269–270). According to Dworkin, whatever particular moral and legal rights we may have are just the working out of this most basic right in concrete circumstances. Thus, for instance, freedom of speech and freedom to engage in non-standard sexual practices are rights to the extent that they may be derived from the principle of equal respect. For one person, or a substantial majority of society, to impose on others views about speech or personal life-styles is a violation of right because of the denial of equal respect implicit in one person's setting up his view of the good as superior to that other's (pp. 272–275). But if the principle of equal concern and respect is not violated, then Dworkin holds that the members of a society are free to pursue whatever social policies seem best to them, whatever utilitarian goals. Plainly, the structure of rights I offer here is more detailed and particular than that. I doubt whether

I could fit the system of negative rights and their priority under the general rubric of equal concern and respect. The subordinate principle of fair shares, of course, fits handily. Dworkin and I do agree that a right to liberty or to maximum liberty in general is hardly a helpful concept. He and I both are more interested in particular liberties. To the same effect, see Thomas Scanlon and H. L. A. Hart in *Reading Rawls*, pp. 184–185 and 233–239.

That Rawls's system is not simply an end-state or pattern system is suggested by his discussion of pure procedural justice. (*A Theory of Justice*, pp. 274f, 277, 303, 315, 545f, 564ff); by his distinction between liberty and the worth of liberty (ibid., pp. 204f, 224–227); by his discussion of personal liberties referred to in the notes to Chapter 5, above; by his statement that when the background principles of justice are satisfied, the actual distribution of income and advantages is just, whatever it may turn out to be (*A Theory of Justice*, §43); and by his insistence on the non-teleological character of his theory of right (ibid., §6 and §§83–85). See the discussion of this in Thomas Nagel's review article of Nozick's *Anarchy, State and Utopia*, *Yale Law Journal* 85 (1975): 136, 146 n.19.

Rights and Roles

VIRTUE AND ROLES

This argument depends on the distinction between obligation and supererogation (for references, see notes to Chapter 1, under "The Complexity of Deontological Systems") and the distinction between harming and failing to aid (see notes to Chapter 4). The concept of love and friendship I develop here I first set out in Fried, *An Anatomy of Values* (Cambridge, Mass.: Harvard University Press, 1970), ch. 5. The systematic significance of the parable of the good shepherd is developed by David Smith, "Paul Ramsey, Love and Killing," in *Love and Society: Essays in the Ethics of Paul Ramsey*, ed. James Johnson and David Smith (Missoula, Mont.: Scholars' Press, 1974).

PROFESSIONAL ROLES: THE PROBLEM

For references to the specifically legal literature of professional responsibility, see Fried, "The Lawyer as Friend: The Moral Foundations of the Lawyer-Client Relation," *Yale Law Journal* 85 (1976): 1060. General speculative articles of particular interests are Curtis, "The Ethics of Advocacy," *Stanford Law Review* 4 (1951): 3; Monroe Freedman, *Lawyer's Ethics in an Adversary System* (Indianapolis, Ind.: Bobbs-Merrill, 1975); John Noonan, "The Purposes of Advocacy and the Limits of Confidentiality," *Michigan Law Review* 64 (1966): 1495; J. F. Stephen, "The Morality of Advocacy," *Cornhill Magazine*, April 1861; and Richard Wasserstrom, "Lawyers as Professionals: Some Moral Issues," *Human Rights* 5 (1975): 1.

My colleagues Gary Bellow and Jeanne Kettleson have kindly shown me a draft of their paper, "The Mirror of Public Interest Ethics: Problems and Paradoxes," which is the most powerful and sympathetic case for a different, less adversary, less individualistic, more communitarian conception of the lawyer's role. This article will contain a wealth of concrete as well as speculative material and references.

My views on the nature of the doctor's role are set out in Fried, *Medical Experimentation: Personal Integrity and Social Policy* (Amsterdam and New York: Elsevier Publishing Co., 1974) : chs. 4 and 5. See also Elliot Freidson, *Profession of Medicine* (New York: Dodd, Mead, 1973).

The thesis of this section and indeed of this chapter might well be summed up by G. E. M. Anscombe's argument that if saving the life of one patient requires a massive dose of a drug that could be divided up and used to save five other people, not one of those five can claim that he has been wronged, that the smaller dose of the drug was owed to him, although "all can reproach me if I give it to none . . . but if it was used for someone, as much as he needed it to keep him alive, no one has any ground for accusing me of having wronged himself . . . I do not mean that 'because they are more' isn't a good reason for helping these and not that one, or these rather than those . . . but it doesn't follow that a man acts badly if he doesn't make it his reason" ("Who is Wronged?" *Oxford Review* 5 [1967]: 16–17) . This same argument is developed with great power and subtlety by John Taurek, "Should the Numbers Count?" *Philosophy and Public Affairs* 6 (1977) : 293.

Index